The King's Coffer

Cayagua/San Jorge
(Charles Town 1670)

YUCHI

CUSABO

Escamacu

ORISTA

Santa Elena
1566-87
(Parris Is.)

Tama

Guale (St. Catherines Is.)

Sapala (Sapelo Is.)

Asao (St. Simons Is.)

Gualquini (Jekyll Is.)

TACATACURU
San Pedro (Cumberland Is.)

Santa María (Amelia Is.)

San Juan del Puerto

San Mateo (Fort Caroline 1564)

St. Augustine 1565

Matanzas Inlet

JORORO

CHISCA

Río Dulce (Savannah)

Ocmulgee

Oconee

CHICHIMECO

Talaje (Altamaha)

(Chattahoochee)

APALACHICOLO

Pedernales

(Flint)

CHISCA

Apalachicola

CHACATO

(Ochlocknee)

Asile

Suwannee

Santa María

(St. Marys)

San Luis (Tallahassee)

Laguna

APALACHE

USTAQUA

San Marcos

Bahía de San Marcos

Guacara

San

UTINA

(Santa Fe)

Martín

San
Francisco

POTANO

la Chua

OCALE

Amajuro

(Withlacoochee)

ACUERA

MAYACA

TIMUCU

SATURIBA

Salamototo (St. Johns)

(Oklawaha)

SURRUQUE

Cabo de Cañaveral

GULF OF MEXICO

TOCOBAGA

AYS

*Bahía Juan
Ponce de Léon
(Tampa Bay)*

POHOY

Santa Lucía

Indian R.

*Ensenada de Carlos
(Charlotte Harbor)*

Carlos

*Maymi
(L. Okeechobee)*

CALUSA

JEAGA

TIQUESTA

BAHAMA CHANNEL

Los Mártires (The Keys)

‑‑‑‑‑‑‑‑‑ Spanish roads

miles

0   50   100   150

SPANISH FLORIDA
Composite of Tribal Territories and Place Names before 1702
(after Boyd, Chatelain, and Boniface)

The King's Coffer

Proprietors of the Spanish Florida Treasury
1565–1702

Amy Bushnell

A University of Florida Book
UNIVERSITY PRESSES OF FLORIDA
Gainesville 1981

University Presses of Florida is the central agency for scholarly publishing of the State of Florida's university system. Its offices are located at 15 NW 15th Street, Gainesville, FL 32603. Works published by University Presses of Florida are evaluated and selected for publication by a faculty editorial committee of any one of Florida's nine public universities: Florida A&M University (Tallahassee), Florida Atlantic University (Boca Raton), Florida International University (Miami), Florida State University (Tallahassee), University of Central Florida (Orlando), University of Florida (Gainesville), University of North Florida (Jacksonville), University of South Florida (Tampa), University of West Florida (Pensacola).

Library of Congress Cataloging in Publication Data

Bushnell, Amy.
   The king's coffer.

   "A University of Florida book."
   Bibliography: p.
   Includes index.
   1. Finance, Public—Spain—History.
   2. Finance, Public—Florida—History.   I. Title
   HJ1242.B87   354.460072'09   81–7403
   ISBN 0-8130-0690-2   AACR2

Contents

Preface ✍ vii

1. The Florida Provinces and Their Treasury ✍ 1

2. The Expenses of Position ✍ 15

3. Proprietary Office ✍ 30

4. Duties and Organization ✍ 50

5. The Situado ✍ 63

6. The Royal Revenues ✍ 75

7. Political Functions of the Royal Officials ✍ 101

8. Accounting and Accountability ✍ 118

Conclusion ✍ 137

Appendixes ✍ 141

Glossary ✍ 149

Notes ✍ 151

Bibliography ✍ 187

Index ✍ 192

v

To Catherine Turner
and
Clyde Bushnell

Preface

THE historiography of Spanish Florida has traditionally concentrated on Indians, friars, and soldiers, all dependent on the yearly *situado,* or crown subsidy. Other Floridians, poor and common, appear to have had no purpose beyond witless opposition to the royal governor. This was so unusual for a Spanish colony that I was sure the true situation must have been more complex. In the imperial bureaucracy, ecclesiastical, military, magisterial, fiscal, and judicial functions of government were customarily distributed among a number of officials and tribunals with conflicting jurisdictions. I believed that research would reveal an elite in Florida, encouraged by the crown as a counterweight to the governor, and that this elite was pursuing its own rational economic interests.

I began by studying a branch of the Menéndez clan, the Menéndez Marquez family, correlating their ranching activities to the determinants of economic expansion in Florida. Governors came and went, but the Menéndez Marquezes exercised power in the colony and held office in the treasury from 1565 to 1743. It became apparent that the way to identify and study a Florida elite was prosopographically, through the proprietors of the royal treasury. Such an investigation would serve a second purpose of wider interest and value: revealing how a part of the Spanish imperial bureaucracy operated on the local level. On the small scale of Florida, imperial organization and crown policies would leave the realm of the theoretical to become the problems of real people.

I do not present the results of my research as a quantitative economic or financial history. The audited accounts necessary to that type of history exist; those for the sixteenth century have been examined with profit by Paul Hoffman and Eugene Lyon, and scholars may eventually mine the exhaustive legajos for the seventeenth century. But my purpose has been different: to describe the administrators of one colonial treasury in action within their environment.

To keep the project manageable I have limited it chronologically to the Habsburg era, from the time St. Augustine was founded in 1565 to the change of ruling houses, which the city observed in 1702. My main source has been the preserved correspondence between the crown and its governors and treasury officials, whose overlapping responsibilities led to constant wrangling and countless reports, legal actions, and letters.

In a sense, every scholarly work is a collaboration between the researcher and his predecessors, yet one feels a special obligation to those who have given their assistance personally, offering insights, transcripts, and bibliographies with a generosity of mind that sees no knowledge as a private enclave. The foremost person on my list is L. N. McAlister, the director of my doctoral program. In the course of our long friendship, his standards of scholarship, writing, and teaching have become the models for my own. He and Michael V. Gannon, David L. Niddrie, Marvin L. Entner, Claude C. Sturgill, Cornelis Ch. Goslinga, Eugene Lyon, and Peter Lisca, reading and criticizing the manuscript for this book in various of its drafts, have delivered me from many a blunder. For the new ones I may have fallen into, they are not accountable.

Luis R. Arana, of the National Park Service at the Castillo de San Marcos, supplied me with interesting data on the Menéndez Marquez family. Overton Ganong, at the Historic Saint Augustine Preservation Board, permitted me to spend a week with the Saint Augustine Historical Society's unfinished transcript of the Cathedral Records of St. Augustine Parish. Ross Morrell of the Division of Archives, History, and Records Management of the Florida Department of State allowed me to see translations and summaries made under the division's auspices. Mark E. Fretwell, editor of the journal of the St. Augustine Historical Society, granted permission to reprint Chapter 2, which appeared as "The Expenses of *Hidalguía* in Seventeenth-Century St. Augustine," *El Escribano* 15 (1978):23–36. Paul E.

Hoffman, John J. TePaske, Charles Arnade, and Samuel Proctor gave me encouragement and advice. Elizabeth Alexander and her staff at the P. K. Yonge Library of Florida History, University of Florida, provided a research home. The care they take of that library's rich resources is something I never cease to appreciate.

For financial support I am indebted to the University of Florida, in particular to the Latin American Center, the Graduate School, and the Division of Sponsored Research. The United States government supplied three years of NDEA Title VI fellowships in Spanish and Portuguese, and the American Association of University Women awarded me the Meta Glass and Margaret Maltby fellowship.

My greatest acknowledgment is to the people I live with. My writer and scholar husband, Peter, has freed my time for writing without telling me how to do it. He, Catherine, and Colleen, listening with good grace to a hundred historical anecdotes, have helped me to believe that what I was doing mattered.

Amy Bushnell
Cluj-Napoca, Romania
July 6, 1980

1

The Florida Provinces and Their Treasury

THE Spanish Habsburgs liked their treasure tangible, in bars of gold, heavy silver coins, precious stones, chunks of jewel amber, and strings of pearls. By their command, each regional branch of the royal treasury of the Indies (*hacienda real de Indias*), a part of their patrimony, had a heavily guarded room containing a coffer of solid wood, reinforced at the edges, bottom, and corners with iron, strongly barred, and bearing three or four locks the keys to which were held by different persons. The keepers of the keys, who had to meet to open the coffer, were the king's personal servants, with antecedents in the customs houses of Aragon and the conquests of Castile. They were called the royal officials of the treasury.

In the Indies, individual treasuries grew out of the fiscal arrangements for expeditions of conquest. The crown, as intent on collecting its legitimate revenues as on the propagation of the faith, required every conquistador to take along officers of the exchequer. A factor guarded the king's investment, if any, in weapons and supplies and disposed of tribute in kind. An overseer of barter and trade (*veedor de rescates y contrataciones*) saw to commercial contacts with the natives and in case of war claimed the king's share of booty. An accountant (*contador*) recorded income and outgo and was the guardian and interpreter of royal instructions. A treasurer (*tesorero*) was entrusted with monies and made payments in the king's name. If the expedition resulted in a permanent settlement these officials continued their duties there, protecting the interests of the crown in a new colony.[1]*

*Notes begin on page 151.

1

There was a strongly commercial side to these earliest treasuries, supervised after 1503 by the House of Trade (*Casa de Contratación*) in Seville. The factor in particular served as the House's representative, watching the movement of merchandise and seeing that the masters of ships enforced the rules against unlicensed passengers and prohibited goods. He also engaged in active and resourceful trading, exchanging the royal tributes and taxes paid in kind for necessary supplies. In 1524 the newly created Council of the Indies (*Consejo de Indias*) assumed the supervision of overseas treasuries, a duty it retained throughout the Habsburg period except for the brief interval of 1557–62.

By 1565, founding date of the treasury under study, Spanish presence in the Indies was seventy-three years old. The experimental stage of government was past; institutions of administration had taken more or less permanent shape. A network of royal treasuries existed, some subordinate to viceroyalties or presidencies and others fairly independent. Principal treasuries with proprietary officials were located in the capital cities; subordinate treasuries staffed by lieutenants were at seaports, mining centers, or distant outposts. The factor had become a kind of business manager, administering tributes and native labor. The overseer's original functions were forgotten as the crown turned its attention from commerce and conquest to the dazzling wealth of mines. As a result of the overriding interest in precious metals, overseers were confined to duty at the mints; in places without a mint their office was subsumed under the factor's. And wherever there was little revenue from tribute the factorship was disappearing as well.

The treasury of Florida had its beginnings in a maritime enterprise. This was no haphazard private adventure, but the carefully organized joint action of a corporate family and the crown.[2] Pedro Menéndez de Avilés was a tough, corsairing Asturian sea captain known to hold the interests of his clan above the regulations of the House of Trade, but the king could not afford to be particular. In response to French settlement at Fort Caroline, Philip II made a three-year contract (*capitulación*) with Menéndez, naming him *Adelantado,* or contractual conqueror, of Florida. At his own cost, essentially, Menéndez was to drive out René de Laudonnière and every other interloper from the land between Terra Nova (Newfoundland) and the Ancones (St. Joseph's Bay) on the Gulf of

Mexico. Before three years were out he was to establish two or three fortified settlements and populate them.[3] He did all of this, but as the French crisis escalated, the king had to come to his support.[4] During the three years of the contract Menéndez and his supporters invested over 75,000 ducats; the crown, more than 208,000 ducats, counting Florida's share of the 1566 Sancho de Archiniega reinforcements of 1,500 men and seventeen ships.[5]

Despite the heavy royal interests, the new colony was governed like a patrimonial estate. The adelantado nominated his own men to treasury office: his kinsman Esteban de las Alas as treasurer, his nephew Pedro Menéndez Marquez as accountant, and a future son-in-law, Hernando de Miranda, as factor-overseer. This was open and honorable patronage, as Menéndez himself said: "Now, as never before, I have need that my kinfolk and friends follow me, trustworthy people who love me and respect me with all love and loyalty."[6] It was also an effort to settle the land, as he once explained:

> They are people of confidence and high standing who have served your Majesty many years in my company, and all are married to noblewomen. Out of covetousness for the offices [for which they are proposed], and out of love for me, it could be that they might bring their wives and households. Because of these and of others who would come with their wives, it is a fine beginning for the population of the provinces of Florida with persons of noble blood.[7]

Since there were as yet neither products of the land to tax nor royal revenues to administer, these nominal officials of the king's coffer continued about their business elsewhere: Las Alas governing the settlement of Santa Elena (on present-day Parris Island), Miranda making voyages of exploration, and Menéndez Marquez governing for his uncle in Cuba. With most of the rest of the clan they also served in the new Indies Fleet (*Armada Real de la Guardia de las Costas e Islas y Carrera de las Indias*) that Pedro Menéndez built in 1568, brought to the Caribbean, and commanded until 1573. From 1570 to 1574 the fiscal officers of that armada were the acting treasury officials for Florida, loosely supervising the substitutes who kept the supply records and muster lists for the various garrisons. They would not consent to live there.[8] Meanwhile, the king issued Miranda and

Menéndez Marquez their long-awaited titles. Las Alas, under investigation for withdrawing most of the garrison at Santa Elena and taking it to Spain, was passed over in favor of a young nephew of the adelantado's called variously Pedro Menéndez the Younger and the Cross-Eyed or One-Eyed (*El Tuerto*). Of the three royal appointees Pedro was the only one to take up residence.[9] The others continued to name substitutes.

Because it established claim by occupation to North America from the Chesapeake Bay southward, Florida was an outpost of empire to be maintained however unprofitable. Any one of its unexplored waterways might be the passage to the East. With this in mind, Philip II had renewed the Menéndez contract when it expired, letting the subsidy for the Indies fleet cover the wages for 150 men of the garrisons. Three years later, in 1570, the king changed this provision to give Florida a subsidy of its own.[10] Despite this underwriting of the colony the adelantado remained to all purposes its lord proprietor. When he died in 1574, acting governorship shifted from his son-in-law Diego de Velasco to the already-mentioned Hernando de Miranda, husband of Menéndez's one surviving legitimate heir. In 1576 the Cusabo Indian uprising resulted in the massacre of Pedro Menéndez the Younger and two other treasury officials. Governor Miranda abandoned the fort at Santa Elena and returned to Spain to face charges of desertion.[11] Once more the king came to the rescue, doubling the number of soldiers he would support.[12] Florida began the slow shift from a proprietary colony to a royal one.

The only person considered capable of holding the provinces against heretic and heathen alike was Admiral Pedro Menéndez Marquez, awaiting sentence for misdeeds as lieutenant-governor of Cuba. The Council granted him both a reprieve and the acting governorship of Florida, and he sailed for St. Augustine. Along with the three new appointees to the treasury, he had permission to pay himself half his salary from the yearly subsidy, or *situado*.[13] The provinces that he pacified did not remain quiet for long. In 1580 a French galleass entered the St. Johns estuary for trade and information. Menéndez Marquez took two frigates to the scene and defeated the Frenchmen in the naval battle of San Mateo. Four years later the Potano Indians of the interior staged an uprising and were driven from their homes.[14] Sir Francis Drake stopped by St. Augustine long enough to burn its two forts (the fifth and the just-finished sixth) and the town, which is why subsequent financial reports gave no figures earlier than 1586, "the year the books were burned." To consolidate their forces the Spanish again abandoned Santa Elena, and this time did not go back.[15] The twelve Franciscans who arrived in 1587 ready to commence their apostolic mission found Spanish settlement contracted to a single outpost.[16]

In these first uncertain years the *presidios* (garrison outposts) were little more than segments of an anchored armada, supported but not rigorously supervised by the crown. The sixteenth-century governors, who could be called the "Asturian Dynasty," filled the little colony with family intrigues and profiteering. All the officers, treasury officials included, were captains of sea and war who could build a fort, command a warship, smuggle a contraband cargo, or keep a double set of books with equal composure. Juan de Posada, for instance, was an expert navigator who sometimes doubled as lieutenant governor for his brother-in-law Pedro Menéndez Marquez. He once calculated for the crown that a good-sized galley, a 100-man fort, or four frigates would all cost the same per year: 16,000 ducats. Posada was bringing back a title of treasurer for himself in 1592 when his ship sank and he drowned off the Florida coast, which he had once called easy sailing.[17]

As the orders instituting the situado in 1570 explicitly stated that troops in Florida were to be paid and rationed the same as those in the Menéndez fleet or the Havana garrison, the first royal officials modeled themselves after their counterparts in the king's armadas and garrisons rather than his civilian exchequers.[18] Treasurer Juan de Cevadilla and Accountant Lázaro Sáez de Mercado, taking office in 1580, thought that this system allowed the governor undue power. It was not appropriate to transfer all the fiscal practices from the armadas, they said, when "the exchequer can be looked after better on land than on sea."[19] Auditor Pedro Redondo Villegas, who came in 1600, refused to accept any armada precedent without a *cédula* (written royal order) applying it to Florida.[20] Thereafter the officials compared their treasury with wholly land-based ones and demanded equal treatment with the bureaucrats of Peru, Yucatán, Honduras, and the Philippines. As payroll and supply officers for a garrison, however, they continued to envy the Havana presidio's royal slaves and the new stone fort built there between 1558 and 1578.[21]

During the course of the seventeenth century, the treasury at St.

Augustine built up precedents that achieved the practical force of law. Cédulas from the crown were respectfully received and recorded, but not necessarily implemented. In this the officials followed the ancient principle of "I obey but do not execute" ("*obedezco pero no cumplo*"), a form of particularism expounded for the adelantado in 1567 by his friend Francisco de Toral, Bishop of Mérida:

> For every day there will be new things and transactions which will bring necessity for new provisions and new remedies. For the General Laws of the Indies cannot cease having mild interpretations, the languages and lands being different, inasmuch as in one land and people they usually ignore things in conformity to the times. Thus it will be suitable for your lordship to do things there [in Florida] of which experience and the condition of those natives have given you understanding.[22]

The Florida creoles, born in the New World of Spanish parents, referred to long custom to justify their actions, and this argument was taken seriously.[23] The Franciscan commissary general for the Indies, writing the year after publication of the great *Recopilación de leyes de los Reynos de las Indias*, observed that some practices in the Indies were not amenable to change after so long a time.[24]

Perhaps it was only right that there should be flexibility in the application of laws. Florida was an exception to the usual colony. It had been founded for reasons of dynastic prestige, and for those reasons it was maintained, at a cost out of all proportion to benefits received. The colony did not mature beyond its initial status of captaincy general. It was a perennial military frontier that was never, under the Habsburgs, absorbed by another administrative unit. The governors were military men with permanent ranks of admiral, captain, sergeant major, or colonel, who took orders from the Council and the *Junta de Guerra* (Council of War) alone. It was a dubious distinction, for wartime coordination with New Spain or Havana depended upon mutual goodwill rather than any sense of obligation. The French, when not at war with the Spanish, made more reliable allies.[25]

In his civil role the governor answered neither to the *audiencia* (high court and governing body) in Santo Domingo nor the one in

Mexico City, and he took orders from no viceroy. In the seventeenth century the crown moved with majestic deliberation to establish the authority, first of the Audiencia of Santo Domingo, then that of Mexico City, over civil and criminal appeals; responsibility for treasury audits was handed back and forth between the Mexico City Tribunal of Accounts and the royal auditor in Havana. These measures did not affect the Florida governorship, which remained independent. As Governor Marques Cabrera explained more than once, no audiencia cared to be responsible for poor frontier provinces. Distances were great, navigation was perilous, and ministers were unwilling to make the journey.[26] If mines of silver had been found within its borders, New Spain would have annexed Florida without delay. Not everyone was satisfied with a separate status. The friars thought that prices would be lower if the governor were subject to some viceroy or audiencia (or were at least a Christian). And royal officials grumbled that there was little point in the king's having appointed them to a republic of poor soldiers, in which the governor disregarded his treasury officials and answered to no audiencia.[27]

For their own reasons, the accountant, treasurer, and factor often made the governor look more autocratic than he was. Florida may not have been a popular democracy, but neither was it a dictatorship. There were within the community carefully drawn class distinctions based on inequalities of status and income, and the officials of the treasury were gentlemen, expecting and receiving the honors due to their class. They were not mere quartermasters on the governor's staff. As proprietors of treasury office and judges of the exchequer they were his quasi-peers, and as titled councilmen of the one Spanish city in Florida they were his civil advisory council, just as the sergeant major and captains were his council of war and the priests and friars his ecclesiastical counselors. The governor who ignored the advice of these men of experience was spoken of disparagingly as "carried off by his own opinions."

The royal treasury of St. Augustine differed from the ones elsewhere mainly in that it had fewer revenues. For various reasons, the economy of Florida never approached that of a settled, populous, or productive region. European settlement there, however early by North American standards, had gotten a late start in Spanish terms. In the rest of the Indies, debate had been going on for years about Indian rationality, just wars and slavery, forced conversions, *en-*

comiendas (allotments of tribute or service), and the alienation of native lands—and while theologians and lawyers argued, soldiers and settlers exploited. By the time the Florida conquest began, these questions were more or less settled. Although not advanced enough to be subject to the Inquisition, the Indian had been determined a rational being. He could not be held in servitude or have his lands taken. It was forbidden to enter his territory with arms and banners or to resettle him anywhere against his will.[28] Florida was to be conquered through the Gospel—not the fastest way. As five Apalachicola chiefs once courteously told Governor Marques Cabrera, if God ever wished them and their vassals to become Christians they would let the governor know.[29]

Pacifying the natives by trade was not effective either, for the Spanish could maintain no monopoly. For over forty years the French continued to trade in Florida, and the Indians preferred them. In a single summer fifteen French ships were sighted off the coast of Guale, coming into the Savannah River for pelts and sassafras.[30] Dutch and English interlopers bartered with the adamantly independent Indians of Ais, Jeaga, and the Carlos confederacy to the south for amber and the salvaged goods of shipwrecks.[31] The Spanish crown no longer encouraged Indian trade in the late sixteenth century anyhow; it barely permitted it. St. Augustine was a coast guard station, a military base, and a mission center, not a commercial colony, and the government saw no reason to supply sailors, soldiers, and friars with trade goods. When Governor Méndez de Canzo made peace with the Guale Indians in 1600 the treasurer observed for the royal benefit that it was to be hoped the governor was acting out of a zeal for souls and His Majesty's service and was not influenced by the good price for sassafras in Seville.[32]

Pious disclaimers aside, Florida's colonists and governors did not agree with His Majesty's restrictions on Indian trade. The natives had many things that Spaniards wanted: sassafras, amber, deer and buffalo skins, nut oil, bear grease, tobacco, canoes, storage containers, and, most of all, food. And the Indians soon wanted what the Spanish had: weapons, construction and cultivation tools, nails, cloth, blankets, bells, glass beads, church ornaments, and rum. The problem was not to create a market but to supply it. When the amber-trading Indians demanded iron tools Governor Rebolledo made them from 60 quintals (6,000 pounds) of the presidio's pig iron, plus melted down cannons and arquebuses.[33] The 1,500-ducat fund that the king intended for gifts to allied chiefs, the governors sometimes diverted to buy trade goods. Soldiers, having little else, exchanged their firearms; the Cherokees living on the Upper Tennessee River in 1673 owned sixty Spanish flintlocks. Without royal approval, however, there was a limit to the amount of trading that could be done, and the crown favored the regular commerce of the fleets and New Spain. Throughout the Habsburg period Florida was licensed to send no more than two frigates a year to Seville or the Canaries, and a bare 2,000 to 3,000 ducats' worth of pelts.[34]

The English who colonized in North America suffered no such handicaps. As early as 1678, four ships at a time could be seen in the Charles Town harbor; at St. Augustine the colonists would have been happy to receive one a year from Spain.[35] Later on, when the English wanted in trade Hispanic Indian slaves or scalps, they had the wherewithal to pay for them. For a single scalp brought to the Carolina governor one warrior was supposedly given clothing piled to reach his shoulders, a flintlock with all the ammunition he wanted, and a barrel of rum.[36] The Indians of the Southeast shifted to the English side with alacrity. The bishop of Tricale reported in 1736 that natives who had been baptized Catholic put their hands to their heads saying, "Go away, water! I am no Christian."[37]

Protected Indians, limited exports, and a shortage of trade goods were only three of the factors hampering normal economic growth in Florida. Another was the continuing silver rush to New Spain and Peru. St. Augustine was not the place of choice for a Spanish immigrant. Soldiers and even friars assigned to Florida had to be guarded in the ports en route to keep them from jumping ship. In this sense the other North Atlantic colonies were again more fortunate. There were no better places for Englishmen, Scots, and Germans to go.

Ideally the presidio of St. Augustine should have been supplied through the free competition of merchants bringing their shiploads of goods to exchange for the money to be found in the king's coffer and the soldiers' wallets.[38] It did not work out this way for several reasons. Under the Habsburgs the situado for Florida soldiers and friars never rose above 51,000 ducats or 70,000 pesos a year, payable from 1592 to 1702 from the Mexico City treasury.[39] But supporting a presidio in Florida was not one of that treasury's priorities. The Mexico City officials paid the situado, irregularly and piecemeal. For a merchant, selling to the Florida presidio was equivalent to making a badly secured, long-term loan. The king, whose private interests might conflict with the national or general interest, once had all the Caribbean situados sequestered and carried to him in exchange for promissory notes.[40] Sometimes an entire situado would be mortgaged before it arrived, with creditors waiting on the Havana docks. In order to be supplied at all, St. Augustine was forced to take whatever its creditors would release: shoddy, unsuitable fabrics and moldy flour. The presidio was chronically in debt, and so was everyone dependent on it. Soldiers seldom saw money; Indians almost never used it.[41]

St. Augustine was a poor and isolated market with little to export. Its seaways were beset by corsairs in summer and storms in winter. No merchant could risk one of his ships on that dangerous journey without an advance contract guaranteeing the sale of his cargo at a profit of 100 to 200 percent.[42] Citizens sometimes tried to circumvent the high cost of imports by going in together to order a quantity of goods, making sure that anyone they entrusted with money had local ties to guarantee his return. But the price of bringing goods to Florida was still prohibitive. A single frigate trip to the San Juan de Ulúa harbor and back cost 400 ducats.[43] It was of little help to be located along the return route of the Fleet of the Indies. Once a year the heavily laden galleons sailed northward in convoy just out of sight of land, riding the Gulf Stream up the Bahama Channel to Cape Hatteras to catch the trade winds back to Spain, but the St. Augustine harbor, with its shallow bar which would pass only flat-bottomed or medium portage vessels, was not a place where these great 500- to 1,500-ton ships could anchor, nor would they have interrupted their progress to stop there. When the Floridians wished to make contact with a vessel in the fleet they had to send a boat to await it at Cape Canaveral, a haunt of pirates.[44]

By Spanish mercantilist rules nothing could be brought into a Spanish port except in a licensed ship with prior registration. At times the presidio was so short on military and naval supplies that the governor and officials waived the regulations and purchased artillery and ammunition, cables and canvas off a ship hailed on the open seas; or a foreign merchantman entered the harbor flying a signal of distress, news bearing, or prisoner exchange, and sold goods either openly or under cover.[45]

Except for trade goods, metals, and military accoutrements, which always had to be imported, St. Augustine with its hinterland was surprisingly self-sufficient.[46] The timber, stone, and mortar for construction were available in the vicinity; nails, hinges, and other hardware were forged in the town. Boats were built in the rivers and inlets. There was a gristmill, a tannery, and a slaughterhouse. Fruits, vegetables, and flowers grew in the gardens; pigs and chickens ran in the streets. Although it was a while before cattle ranching got started, by the late seventeenth century beef was cheap and plentiful.[47] The swamps and savannahs provided edible roots, wild fruit, and game; lakes and rivers were full of fish; oysters grew huge in the arms of the sea. Indians paddling canoes or carrying baskets brought their produce to the market on the plaza: twists of tobacco, pelts, painted wooden trays, packages of dried cassina tea leaves, rope and fishnets, earthenware and baskets, dried turkey meat, lard and salt pork, saddles and shoe leather, charcoal, and fresh fish and game; but especially they brought maize.

Maize, not wheat, was the staff of life in Florida. The poor, the slaves, the convicts and Indians all got their calories from it. When the maize crops were hurt, St. Augustine was hungry. But the problem was not so much supply as distribution. After the Indians were reduced to missions the friars had them plant an extra crop yearly as insurance against famine and for the support of the poor and beautification of the sanctuaries. The missionaries were highly incensed to have this surplus claimed for the use of the presidio, yet to guarantee an adequate supply the governor was ready to take desperate measures: raid the church granaries, even plant maize within musket range of the fort, providing cover to potential enemies. Each province presented its problems. The grain from Guale was brought down in presidio vessels. That from Timucua was carried 15 to 30 leagues on men's backs for lack of mules or packhorses, and it was easier to bring in relays of *repartimiento* (labor service) Indians and raise it near the city. The inhabitants of Apalache had a ready market for maize in Havana, and the governor had to station a deputy in San Luis, their capital, to collect it and transmit it 2,000 miles around the peninsula to St. Augustine.

To read the hundreds of letters bemoaning the tardiness or inadequacy of the situado, one would suppose that the presidio was always about to starve. This was largely rhetoric, an understandable effort by the governors and royal officials to persuade His Majesty to take the support of his soldiers seriously. Florida was not so much dependent upon the subsidy as independent because the subsidy was unreliable. Supply ships were sometimes years apart, and not even a hardened Spaniard could go for years without eating.[48] He might miss his olive oil, wheat flour, wine, sugar, and chocolate, but there was some sort of food to be had unless the town was suffering famine or siege and had exhausted its reserves. Such exigencies happened. After the attacks of buccaneers caused the partial abandonment of Guale Province in the 1680s, the maize source there dried up, while refugees increased the number of mouths in St. Augustine. Without provisions the militia and Indian auxiliaries could not be called out, nor repartimiento labor be brought in to work on the fortifications.[49] Food reserves were a military necessity, and the governor and *cabildo* (municipal council) had emergency powers to requisition hoards and freeze prices.[50]

To aggravate the economic problems, the colony was almost never at peace. The peninsula could not be properly explored; as late as 1599 there was uncertainty over whether or not it was an island. Throughout the Habsburg era there were two fluctuating frontiers with enemies on the other sides, for, converted or not, Florida Indians saw no reason to halt their seasonal warfare. From the south, Ais, Jeaga, Tocobaga, Pocoy, and Carlos warriors raided the Hispanicized Indians; Chisca, Chichimeco, Chacato, Tasquique, and Apalachicolo peoples were some of the enemies to the north and northwest. The coasts were no safer. In 1563, trading and raiding corsairs conducting an undeclared war were driven by Spanish patrols from the Antilles to the periphery of the Caribbean: the Main, the Isthmus, and Florida. The French crisis of 1565–68 was followed by the Anglo-Spanish War of 1585–1603 and the Dutch War of 1621–48.[51] Meanwhile, Floridians watched with foreboding the rival settlements of Virginia, Barbados, and, after 1655, Jamaica. When Charles Town was founded in 1670 they pleaded for help to drive off the colonists before there were too many, but the crown's hands were tied by a peace treaty, and its reaction—the building of a fort, the Castillo de San Marcos in St. Augustine—was essentially defensive.

During the sixteenth and seventeenth centuries Florida was afflicted by a severe demographic slump which reached nadir in 1706.

The first European slavers probably reached the peninsula with their pathogens and iron chains in the 1490s.[52] As there is little basis for estimating the population at contact, there is no way of knowing what the initial demographic loss may have been, nor its dislocating effects.[53] At the end of the sixteenth century Bartolomé de Argüelles, who had been in Florida twenty-four years and traversed it from Santa Elena to the Keys, said it was his impression that there were relatively few natives.[54]

The first epidemic reported among mission Indians was in 1570; the next, in 1591. The "pests and contagions," lasting from 1613 to 1617, to the best of the friars' knowledge killed half the Indians in Florida.[55] An incoming governor marveled in 1630 at the way "the Indians ... die here as elsewhere."[56] Six years later the friars reported that the natives between St. Augustine and Guale were almost totally gone. The Franciscans obtained gubernatorial consent to enter the province of Apalache partly because the depopulating of nearer provinces had depleted the Spanish food and labor supply. When Interim Governor Francisco Menéndez Marquez suppressed a rebellion of the Apalaches in 1647 and condemned loyal and rebel alike to the labor repartimiento, he explained that the other provinces of Christians were almost used up.[57]

The worst years were yet to come. Between 1649 and 1659 three epidemics descended on Florida: the first was either typhus or yellow fever, the second was smallpox, and the last, the measles. Governor Aranguíz y Cotes said that in the seven months after he took possession in February of 1659, 10,000 Indians died. These were also the years of famine and of the Great Rebellion of the Timucuans, which left their remnants scattered and starving.[58] From 1672 to 1674 an unidentified pestilence reduced the population even further. There were so few Indians in Central Florida that the Spanish gave land in Timucua Province to anyone who would introduce cattle. As native town structure broke down under the barrage of disasters, Indians began detaching themselves from their families and parishes to work as day labor in construction and contract labor on the ranches, or as independent suppliers of some commodity to the Spanish: charcoal, wild game, baskets, or pots. Efforts to make this migratory labor force return home to their family, church, and repartimiento responsibilities were largely ineffective. In 1675 a governor's census showed only 10,766 Indians under Spanish obedience in all Florida, and four-fifths of them were in Apalache, 200 miles from St. Augustine across a virtually empty peninsula.[59]

Some people were managing to profit by the situation. The Florencia family had led in the opening up and settling of Apalache Province and were the ones who had started trade from there to Havana. Descended from a Portuguese pilot who came to Florida in 1591, for three generations they supplied most of Apalache's deputy governors and many of its priests, treating the province as a private fief. A look at the names of provincial circuit judges and inspectors (*visitadores*) shows that these ingenious Floridians even cornered the market on investigating themselves.[60] Under their instigation, Apalache was considering breaking off administratively from the capital of Florida. The Florencias, the friars, and the Hispanic Indians all preferred to deal with Havana, only a week's sail from them and offering more opportunity.[61] Whether this would in time have happened, and what would then have become of St. Augustine, is a moot point. Colonel James Moore of Carolina and his Creek allies took advantage of the outbreak of Queen Anne's War in 1702 to mount slave raids against the Indians of Florida. By 1706 the raids had reduced the native provincial population to a miserable few hundred living beneath the guns of the fort.[62]

In the face of the many hindrances to the settlement and effective use of Florida—the crown's protective attitude toward natives, the obstacles to trade, the shortage of currency, the problems of food distribution, the slow Spanish increase in population and the rapid native decrease, and the exhausting wars—it was a remarkable achievement for the Spanish to have remained there at all. The way they did so, and the share of the royal officials of the treasury in the story, is a demonstration of human ingenuity and idealism, tenacity, and sheer greed.

2

The Expenses of Position

FLORIDA, with its frequent wars, small Spanish population, and relatively few exports, might not seem a likely place for the maintenance of a gentlemanly class, known to Spaniards as *hidalgos*. But wealth and position are relative, and people differentiate themselves wherever there are disparities of background or belongings to be envied or flaunted. In the small society of St. Augustine, where everyone's business was everyone else's concern, social presumptiveness was regarded severely.[1] One of the grievances against Governor Méndez de Canzo was that he had named one of his relatives, a common retail merchant, captain of a company and let him appoint as ensign a lad "of small fortune" who had been working in the tannery.[2] From the list of *vecinos* (householders) asked to respond with voluntary gifts for public works or defense construction we can identify the principal persons in town, for a voluntary gift was the hidalgo's substitute for personal taxation, to which he could not submit without marking himself a commoner. When Governor Hita Salazar needed to put the castillo into defensible order he gave the first 200 pesos himself, to put the others under obligation, and then collected 1,600 pesos from the royal officials of the treasury, the sergeant major, the captains, other officers and those receiving bonuses, and some private individuals who raised cattle.[3]

Whether transferred to Florida from the bureaucracy elsewhere or coming into office via inheritance, the royal official was presumed to be an hidalgo or he would never have been appointed. This meant, technically, that he was of legitimate birth, had never been a shop-keeper or tradesman, had not refused any challenge to his honor, and could demonstrate two generations of descent from *hijos de algo* ("sons of something") untainted by Moorish or Jewish blood and uncondemned by the Inquisition.

The advantages of being an hidalgo — someone addressed as *don* in a time when that title had significance — were unquestioned. There were, however, concomitant responsibilities and expenses. A gentleman was expected to "live decently," maintaining the dignity of his estate whether or not his means were adequate. Openhanded-ness and lavish display were not the idiosyncracies of individuals but the realities of class, the characteristics that kept everyone with pretensions to *hidalguía* searching for sources of income.

The personal quality that St. Augustine appreciated most earnestly in a gentleman was magnanimity. The character references written for a governor at the end of his term emphasized alms: the warm shawls given to widows, the delicacies to the sick, and the baskets of maize and meat distributed by the benefactor's slaves during a famine. They also stressed his vows fulfilled to the saints: silver diadems, fine altar cloths, and new shrines.[4] When local con-fraternities elected yearly officers, the governor and treasury officials were in demand, for they brought to the brotherhood gifts and favors besides the honor of their presence. The royal officials consistently turned over a third of their earnings from tavern inspections to the Confraternity of the Most Holy Sacrament, and the treasurer gave it his payroll perquisites.[5]

Alms and offerings were minor expenses compared to the cost of keeping up a household. The royal officials were admonished to be married; the crown wanted the Indies populated by citizens in good standing, not mannerless half-breeds, and a man with a family had given as it were hostages for his behavior.[6] Regular marriage to someone of one's own class was, however, expensive. According to one hard-pressed official, "The pay of a soldier will not do for the position of quality demanded of a treasurer." Another argued that he needed a raise because his wife was "someone of quality on account of her parents."[7]

A woman of quality in one's house had to be suitably gowned. In 1607 six yards of colored taffeta cost almost 9 ducats, the equivalent of 96 wage-days for a repartimiento Indian. A velvet gown would have cost 48 ducats.[8] A lady wore jewels: ornaments on her ears and fingers, and necklaces. In 1659 a single strand of pearls was valued at 130 pesos. Between wearings the jewelry was kept in a locked case inside the royal coffer, which served the community as a safety deposit.[9]

A lady had female companions near her own rank—usually dependent kinswomen, although Governor Menéndez Marquez introduced two young chieftainesses to be raised in his house and to attend his wife, doña María.[10] A gentlewoman maintained her own private charities; Catalina Menéndez Marquez, sister of one governor, niece of another, widow of two treasury officials and mother-in-law of a third, kept convalescent, indigent soldiers in her home.[11] The wives and daughters of hidalgos could become imperious: Juana Caterina of the important Florencia family, married to the deputy governor of Apalache Province, behaved more like a feudal chatelaine than the wife of a captain. She required one native to bring her a pitcher of milk daily, obliged the town of San Luis to furnish six women to grind maize at her husband's gristmill, and slapped a chief in the face one Friday when he neglected to bring her fish.[12]

A gentlewoman's dowry was not intended for household expenses but was supposed to be preserved and passed on to her children. Debts a husband had incurred before marriage could not be collected from his wife's property nor was he liable for debts inherited from her family. A gentlewoman kept her own name as a matter of course, and if her family was of better quality than her husband's it was her name that the children took.[13] Families were large: seven or eight persons, it was estimated around 1706.[14] The four generations of the Menéndez Marquez treasury officials are one example. In the first generation fourteen children were recorded in the Parish Register (all but two of them legitimate). In the second generation there were ten; in the third, nine; and the fourth generation numbered six. The number of recognized, baptized children in the direct line of this family averaged nearest to ten.[15]

All of the hidalgo's progeny, legitimate or illegitimate, had to be provided for. The daughters, called "the adornments of the house," had to have dowries if they were not to spend their lives as someone's servants. A common bequest was a sum of money so an impoverished gentlewoman could marry or take the veil. Pedro Menéndez de Avilés for this purpose endowed five of his and his wife's kinswomen with 200 to 300 ducats each.[16] The usual dowry in St. Augustine was a house for the bride, but it could also be a ranch, a soldier's *plaza* (man-space or man-pay) in the garrison, or even a royal office. Juan Menéndez Marquez became treasurer when he was betrothed to the daughter of the former treasurer. Nicolás Ponce de León II became sergeant major by marrying the illegitimate daughter of Sergeant Major Eugenio de Espinosa.[17] If a man died before all his daughters had been provided for, that duty fell upon their eldest brother, even if a friar. Girls were taught their prayers, manners, and accomplishments, and they learned homemaking at their mother's side; they seldom received formal schooling. When two young ladies from St. Augustine were sent to be educated at the convent of Santa Clara in Havana, the question of the habit they were to wear was so unprecedented that it was referred to the Franciscan commissary general for the Indies.[18]

The plan for the sons of the family was to make them self-supporting. Once a boy had finished the grammar school taught by one of the friars he had two main career options: the church or the garrison. To become a friar he entered a novitiate at the seminary in St. Augustine, if there was one in operation—otherwise, in Santiago de Cuba or Havana. He was then given his orders and joined the missionary friars in the Custody or Province of Santa Elena, embracing both Cuba and Florida.[19] If he was meant for a soldier his father purchased or earned for him a minor's plaza, held inactive from the time he got it at age nine or ten until he started guard duty around fifteen or regular service two years later. Whether as friar or as soldier the young man was paid a meager 115 ducats a year including rations—enough for him to live on modestly but not to support dependents. Even so, there were governors who felt that no one born in Florida should be on the government payroll, either as a religious or as a fighting man.[20]

Advancement cost money, whether in the church, the military, or the bureaucracy. A treasury official generally trained his eldest son to succeed him and bought a *futura* (right of succession) if he could.[21] The patronage of lesser offices was an important right and, if the family possessed any, every effort was made to keep them. When times were peaceful, markets favorable, and other conditions fell into line, an hidalgo might set up his son as a rancher or a merchant in the import-export business, but many sons of hidalgos found none of these careers open to them. Sometimes, they were deposited with relatives in New Spain or Cuba; they left Florida of their own accord to seek their fortunes; or they remained to form the shabby entourage of more fortunate kinsmen, serving as pages, overseers, skippers, or chaplains.[22]

Sixteenth-century property inventories studied by Lyon show that the contrast between social classes around 1580 appeared in costly furnishings and apparel rather than houses. It made sense, in a city subject to piracy and natural disasters, to keep one's wealth portable, in the form of personal, not real, property. The goods of an hidalgo included silver plate, carpets, tapestries and leather wall hangings, linens and bedding, rich clothing, and writing desks. The value of such belongings could be considerable. Governor Treviño Guillamas once borrowed 1,000 pesos against the silver service of his house.[23]

During the seventeenth century, houses gradually became a more important form of property. Construction costs were modest. Tools and nails, at five to the *real* (one-eighth of a peso), were often the single largest expenditure.[24] At mid-century it cost about 160 pesos to build a plain wattle-and-daub hut; a dwelling of rough planks and palmetto thatch rented for 3 pesos a month. Indian quarrymen, loggers, and carpenters were paid in set amounts of trade goods originally worth one real per day. When the price of these items went up toward the end of the seventeenth century, the cost of labor rose proportionately but was never high.[25] Regidores set the prices on lots and it is not certain whether these prices rose, fell, or remained stable. Shipmaster and Deputy Governor Claudio de Florencia's empty lot sold for 100 pesos after he and his wife were murdered in the Apalache rebellion. Captain Antonio de Argüelles was quoted a price of 40 pesos on what may have been a smaller lot sometime before 1680, when the lot on which the treasurer's official residence stood was subdivided.[26]

The value of better homes in St. Augustine rose faster than the cost of living during the seventeenth century, perhaps indicating houses of larger size or improved quality. In 1604 the finest house in town was appraised at 1,500 ducats and sold to the crown for 1,000 as the governor's residence.[27] The governor's mansion that the English destroyed in 1702 was afterward appraised at 8,000 pesos (5,818 ducats). In that siege all but twenty or thirty of the cheaper houses were damaged irreparably; 149 property owners reported losses totaling 62,570 pesos. The least valuable houses ran 50 to 100 pesos; the average ones, 200 to 500 pesos. Arnade mentions eight families owning property worth over 1,000 pesos, with the most valuable private house appraised at 6,000.[28]

Royal officials were entitled to live in the government houses, but in St. Augustine they did not always choose to. After the customs-counting house and the royal warehouse-treasury were complete, and even after the treasury officials obtained permission to build official residences at royal expense, they continued to have other houses. The Parish Register records one wedding at the home of Accountant Thomás Menéndez Marquez and another in the home of his wife. Their son Francisco, who inherited the position of accountant, owned a two-story shingled house which sold for 1,500 pesos after he died.[29]

In St. Augustine, houses were set some distance apart and had surrounding gardens. The grounds were walled to keep wandering animals away from the well, the clay outdoor oven, and the fruit trees, vines, and vegetables.[30] Near town on the commons, the hidalgo's family like all the rest was allocated land for growing maize, and after the six-month season his cows browsed with those of commoners on the dry stalks. In 1600 the eighty families in town were said to own from two to ten head of cattle apiece. Some distance out of town, maybe two leagues, was the hidalgo's farm, where he and his household might spend part of the year consuming the produce on the spot.[31]

A gentleman was surrounded by dependents. The female relatives who attended his wife had their male counterparts in the numerous down-at-the-heels nephews and cousins who accompanied his travels, lived in his house, and importuned him for a hand up the social ladder.[32] As if these were not enough, through the institution of *compadrazgo* he placed himself within a stratified network of ritual kin. On the lowest level this was a form of social structuring. Free blacks or mulattoes were supposed to be attached to a patron and not to wander about the district answering to no one. Indians, too, accepted the protection of an important Spaniard, taking his surname at baptism and accepting his gifts. The progress of conquest and conversion could conceivably be traced in the surnames of chiefs. Governor Ybarra once threatened to punish certain of them "with no intercession of godfathers."[33] The larger the group the hidalgo was responsible for, the greater his power base. He himself had his own more important patron. Between people of similar social background, compadrazgo was a sign of friendship, business partnership, and a certain amount of complicity, since it was not good form to testify against a *compadre*. Treasurer Juan Menéndez Marquez was connected to many important families in town, including that of the Portuguese merchant Juan Núñez de los Rios. Although it was illegal to relate oneself to gubernatorial or other fiscal authorities, Juan was also a compadre of Governor Méndez de Canzo and three successive factors.[34]

Servants filled the intermediate place in the hidalgo's household between poor relatives and slaves. Sometimes they had entered service in order to get transportation to America, which was why the gentleman coming from Spain could bring only a few. One manservant coming to Florida to the governor's house had to promise to remain there eight years.[35] The life of a servant was far from comfortable, sleeping wrapped in his cloak at the door of his master's room and thankful to get enough to fill his belly. Still, a nondischargeable servant had a degree of security, and though not a family member he could make himself a place by faithful service. The Parish Register shows how Francisco Pérez de Castañeda, who was sent from Xochimilco as a soldier, came to be overseer of the Menéndez Marquez ranch of La Chua and was married in the home of don Thomás.[36]

Slaves completed the household. Technically, these could be Indian or even Moorish, like the girl Isabel, who belonged to De Soto's wife Isabel de Bobadilla and was branded on her face.[37] In actuality, almost all the slaves in Florida were black. Moors were uncommon, and the crown categorically refused to allow the enslavement of Florida Indians, even those who were demonstrably treacherous. The native women whom Diego de Velasco had sold (one of them for 25 ducats), Visitor Castillo y Ahedo told through a translator that they were free, "and each one went away with the person of her choice."[38] Governor Méndez de Canzo was forced to liberate the Surruques and Guales whom he had handed out as the spoils of war. One of the few Indian slaves after his time was the

Campeche woman María, who was taken into the house of Governor Vega Castro y Pardo and subsequently bore a child "of father unknown."[39]

The names of slaves were significant. Those who had come directly from Africa were identified by origin, as Rita Ganga, María Angola, or Arara, Mandinga, or Conga. Those born in the house were identified with the family: María de Pedrosa was Antonia de Pedrosa's slave; Francisco Capitán belonged to Francisco Menéndez Marquez II, who in his youth had been Florida's first captain of cavalry. A good Catholic family saw that their slaves were Christian and the babies legitimate. In the Parish Register are recorded the occasions when slaves married, baptized an infant, or served as sponsors to other slaves, mixed-bloods, or Indians. The parish priest entered the owner's name and, starting in 1664, frequently noted the shade of the slave's skin color: *negro, moreno, mulato,* or *pardo.* One family of house slaves belonging to the Menéndez Marquez family are traceable in the registry for three generations.

Sometimes there was evident affection between the races, as the time the slave María Luisa was godmother to the baby daughter of a captain.[40] But on the whole, blacks were not trusted. Too many of them had run off and intermarried with the fierce Ais people of the coast.[41] The hundred slaves in St. Augustine in 1606 (who included around forty royal slaves) were expected to fight on the side of any invader who promised them freedom. Treasury officials objected strongly to the captains' practice of putting their slaves on the payroll as drummers, fifers, and flag bearers. In their opinion the king's money should not be used to pay "persons of their kind, who are the worst enemies we can have."[42]

The number of slaves belonging to any particular family is not easy to determine. The problem with counting them from the Parish Register is that they never appear all at once, and about all that can be known is that from one date to another a certain slave owner had at least x number of different slaves at one time or another. By this rather uncertain way of numbering them, Juan Menéndez Marquez owned seven slaves; his son Francisco, eleven (of whom three were infants buried nameless); Juan II had ten; and his brother Thomás, four besides those out at La Chua. When Francisco II died in penury he was still the owner of seven. Only three were of an age to be useful, the rest being either small children or pensioners rather like himself.[43] A conservative estimate of the number of adult slaves at one time in a gentleman's house might be about four.

The price of slaves remained fairly constant during the seventeenth century. In 1616 Captain Pastrana's drummer, whose pay he collected, was worth 300 ducats (412½ pesos). During the 1650s a thirty-year-old Angola ranch hand sold for 500 pesos and a mulatto overseer for 600; a mulatto woman with three small children brought 955 pesos, and two other women sold for 600 and 300. As Accountant Nicolás Ponce de León explained to the crown in 1674, an untrained slave cost 150 pesos in Havana, but after he had learned a trade in St. Augustine he was valued at 500 pesos or more.[44] The four trained adult slaves in the hypothetical household were worth some 2,000 pesos.

All of these dependents and slaves the hidalgo fed, clothed, dosed with medicines, supplied with weapons or tools, and provided with the services of the church in a manner befitting their station and connection with his house. There were other servants for whom he felt no comparable responsibility. Repartimiento Indians cleared the land and planted the communal and private maize fields with digging sticks and hoes, guarding the crop from crows and wild animals. Ordered up by the governor, selected by their chiefs, and administered by the royal officials, they lived in huts outside the town and were given a short ration of maize and now and then a small blanket or a knife for themselves and some axes and hoes. During the construction of the castillo as many as 300 Indians at a time were working in St. Augustine.[45] In an attempt to stop the escalation of building costs, their wages were fixed at so many blankets or tools per week, with ornaments for small change. Indians were not supposed to be used for personal service but they often were, especially if for some misdeed they had been sentenced to extra labor. Commissary General Juan Luengo declared that everyone of importance in Florida had his service Indians and so had all his kinsmen and friends.[46] If one of these natives sickened and died he could be replaced with another.

Native healers "curing in the heathen manner" had been discredited by their non-Christian origins and their inefficacy against European diseases, but there was no prejudice against the native medicinal herbs, and even the friars resorted to the women who dispensed them. Medical care of a European kind was not expensive for anyone connected with the garrison. A surgeon, apothecary, and barber were on the payroll, and the hospital association to which every soldier belonged provided hospitalization insurance for one real per month. When an additional real began to be assessed for apothecary's insurance, the soldiers by means of petitions got the charge revoked and what they had paid on it refunded.[47]

With housing, labor, and medical care relatively cheap, consumable supplies were the hidalgo's largest expense. There are two ways to estimate what it cost to feed and clothe an ordinary Spaniard in Florida: by the rations issued at the royal warehouses and by the prices of individual items. In the armadas, fighting seamen were issued a daily ration of one-and-a-half pounds hardtack, two pints wine, half a pound of meat or fish, oil, vinegar, and *legumbres*, which were probably dried legumes. During the period when the Florida garrisons were administered together with the Menéndez armada, this practice was altered to enable a soldier to draw up to two-and-a-half reales in supplies per day from the royal stores.[48] In spite of admonitions from governors and treasury officials that the cost of food was taking more and more of the soldiers' wages, the official allotment for rations was not changed, and any extra that the soldier drew was charged to his account. Gillaspie has figured that in the 1680s a soldier spent two-thirds of his regular pay on food, and it was probably more like 70 percent.[49] By the end of the seventeenth century a soldier's wages would barely maintain a bachelor.

A Franciscan, whose vow of poverty forbade him to touch money, received his stipend, tactfully called "alms," in two pounds of flour and one pint of wine a day, plus a few dishes and six blankets a year. He and his colleagues divided among themselves three *arrobas* (twenty-five-pound measures) of oil a year and the same of vinegar, six arrobas of salt, and some paper, needles, and thread. By 1640 the friars were finding their 115 ducats a year insufficient, in spite of the king's extra alms of clothing, religious books, wax, and the wine and flour with which to celebrate Mass. When they had their syndics sell the surplus from Indian fields to Havana, it was partly because they were 2,000 pesos in debt to the treasury.[50]

Commodity prices did not rise evenly throughout the period. According to the correspondence from St. Augustine, different necessities were affected at different times. From 1565 to 1602 the price of wine rose 40 percent and that of cotton prints from Rouen, 170 percent. The price of wheat flour seemed to rise fastest between

1598 and 1602.[51] From 1638 to the mid-1650s the primary problem was dependence upon moneylenders, compounded with the loss in purchasing power of the notes against unpaid situados and of the soldiers' certificates for back wages, both of which in the absence of currency were used for exchange. In 1654 the presidio managed to free itself from economic vassalage long enough to buy from suppliers other than those affiliated with the moneylenders. One *situador* (commissioned collector) said he was able to buy flour at one-sixth the price previous agents had been paying.[52] Between 1672 and 1689 there was rampant profiteering in the maize and trade goods used to feed and pay Indians working on the castillo. In 1687 the parish priest suddenly increased the costs on his entire schedule of obventions, from carrying the censer to conducting a memorial service.[53] Throughout the Habsburg period the expense of keeping a slave or servant continued its irregular rise, whereas the salary of a royal official remained constant.

Two undisputed facts of life were that imported items cost more in Florida than in either New Spain or Havana, and that any merchant able to fix a monopoly upon St. Augustine charged whatever the market would bear. Since prices of separate items were seldom reported except by individuals protesting such a monopoly, it is difficult to determine an ordinary price. Even in a ship's manifest the measurements may lack exactness for our purposes, if not theirs. How much cloth was there in a bundle or a chest? How many pints of wine in a bottle? Sometimes only a relative idea of the cost of things can be obtained. Wheat flour, which rose in 1598 from 58 to 175 ducats a pipe (126.6 gallons), at the new price cost two-and-a-half times as much by volume as wine or vinegar did in 1607. Nearly a hundred years later wheat was still so costly that the wages of the boy who swept the church for the sacristan were two loaves of bread a day, worth fifty pesos a year.[54]

In spite of the high Florida prices, an officer found it socially necessary to live differently from a soldier, who in turn made a distinction between himself and a common Indian. Indians supplemented a maize, beans, squash, fish, and game diet with acorns, palm berries, heart-of-palm, and koonti root—strange foods which the Spanish ate only during a famine.[55] An hidalgo's table was set with Mexican majolica rather than Guale pottery and seashells. It was supplied with "broken" sugar at 28 reales the arroba, and spices, kept in a locked chest in the dining room.[56] His drinking water came from a spring on Anastasia Island. Instead of the soldier's diet of salt meat, fish, and gruel or ash-cakes, the hidalgo dined on wheaten bread, pork, and chicken raised on shellfish. Instead of the native cassina tea he had Canary wines at 160 pesos a barrel and chocolate at 3 pesos for a thousand beans of cacao.[57] Pedro Menéndez Marquez, the governor, said he needed 1,000 ducats a year for food in Florida, although his wife and household were in Seville.[58]

An hidalgo's lady did not use harsh homemade soaps on her fine linens; she had the imported kind at three pesos a pound or nineteen pesos a box.[59] In the evening she lit lamps of nut oil or of olive oil at forty reales the arroba, instead of pine torches, smelly tallow candles, or a wick floating in lard or bear grease. There were wax candles for a special occasion such as the saint's day of someone in the family, but wax was dear: a peso per pound in Havana for the Campeche yellow and more for the white. When the whole parish church was lit with wax tapers on the Day of Corpus Christi the cost came to fifty pesos.[60] In St. Augustine, where the common folk used charcoal only for cooking, the hidalgo's living rooms were warmed with charcoal braziers. One governor was said to keep two men busy at government expense cutting the firewood for his house.[61]

Even after death there were class distinctions. The hidalgo was buried in a private crypt, either in the sixteen-ducat section or the ten-ducat. Other plots of consecrated earth were priced at three or four ducats. A slave's final resting place cost one ducat, and a pauper was laid away free. It cost three times as much to bury an attaché of Governor Quiroga y Losada's (thirty-six pesos) as an ordinary soldier (twelve pesos), on whom the priest declared there was no profit.[62]

Clothing was a primary expense and a serious matter. Unconverted Indians would readily kill parties of Spaniards for their clothes, or so it was believed. Blankets, cloth, and clothing served as currency. Tobacco, horses, and muskets were priced in terms of cloth or small blankets. Garrison debts to be paid by the deputy governor of Apalache in 1703 were not given a currency value at all but were expressed solely in yards of serge.[63]

Indians dressed in comfortable leather shirts and blankets. Rather than look like one of them a Spaniard would go in rags.[64] A manifest for the *Nuestra Señora del Rosario* out of Seville gives the prices asked in St. Augustine around 1607 for ready-made articles imported from Spain. Linen shirts with collar and cuffs of Holland lace cost forty-eight or sixty reales; doublets of heavy linen were twenty-nine, forty, and fifty-two reales; hose of worsted yarn cost twenty-eight reales the pair; a hat was thirty-four to forty-two reales. Breeches and other garments were made by local tailors and their native apprentices out of imported goods, with the cheapest and coarsest linen running six reales the yard, and Rouen cloth, ten and eighteen. Boots and shoes were made by a part-time cobbler from hides prepared at the tannery.[65] The cheapest suit of clothes must have run to twenty ducats (twenty-seven-and-a-half pesos). When Notary Juan Jiménez outfitted his son Alejandro as a soldier they ran up bills of seventy pesos to the shopkeeper, eleven pesos to the shoemaker, and unstated amounts to the armorer, tailor, and washerman.[66]

An hidalgo had to be better dressed in his everyday clothes than the common soldier in his finest, and his dress clothes were a serious matter. It was an age when state occasions could be postponed until the outfits of important participants were ready, and the official reports of ceremonies described costumes in detail. Governor Quiroga y Losada once wrote the king especially to say that he was having the royal officials wear cloaks on Sundays as it looked more dignified.[67] The hidalgo's cloak, breeches, and doublet were colored taffeta at sixteen reales the yard or velvet at eight ducats. His boots were of expensive cordovan; his hose were silk and cost four-and-a-half pesos; his shirt had the finest lace cuffs and collar, and detachable oversleeves that could cost twenty-four ducats. His dress sword cost eight ducats and his gold chain much more. When, to the professed shock of Father Leturiondo, Governor Torres y Ayala assumed the regal prerogative of a canopy during a religious procession, he may have been protecting his clothes.[68]

The elegant family and household, with sumptuous food and clothing—these were displays of wealth that anyone with a good income could ape. The crucial distinction of an hidalgo was his fighting capability, measured in his skill and courage, his weapons and horses, and the number of armed men who followed him. In Florida even the bureaucrats were men of war. Treasurer Juan Menéndez Marquez went on *visita* (circuit inspection) with Bishop Juan de las Cabezas Altamirano, as captain of his armed escort. His son, Treasurer Francisco, subdued rebellious Apalache Province almost singlehandedly, executing twelve ringleaders and condemning twenty-six others to labor on the fort. Francisco's son, Accountant Juan II, defended the city from pirates, and in 1671 led a flotilla to attack the English settlement of Charles Town.[69]

Treasury officials were ordered to leave their swords outside when they came to their councils, for in a society governed by the chivalric code, war was not the only excuse for combat. Any insult to one's honor must be answered by laying hand to sword, and the hidalgo who refused a formal challenge was disgraced. He could no longer aspire to a noble title; the commonest soldier held him in contempt.[70] In Florida, every free man and even some slaves bore arms. Soldiers, officers, officials, and Indian chiefs were issued weapons out of the armory and thereafter regarded them as private property. Prices of the regular issue of swords in 1607 and of flintlock muskets in 1702 were about the same: ten or eleven pesos. An arquebus, or matchlock musket, was worth half as much. Gunpowder for hand-held firearms was two-thirds peso per pound in 1702, twice as much as the coarser artillery powder.[71]

That other requirement of the knight-at-arms, his horse, was not as readily come by. A horse was expensive and few survived the rough trip to Florida. On shipboard they were immobilized in slings, and when these swung violently against the rigging in bad weather the animals had to be cut loose and thrown overboard. Until midcentury the most common pack animal in Florida was still an Indian.[72] Once horses had gotten a start, however, they did well, being easily trained, well favored, and about seven spans high. Imported Cuban horses were available in the 1650s at a cost of 100 to 200 pesos, with a bred mare worth double. In the 1680s and '90s, mares were selling for 30 pesos and horses for 25, about twice as much as a draft ox.[73] Horsemanship displays on the plaza had become a part of every holiday, with the ladies looking down in exquisite apprehension from second-story windows and balconies.[74] The Indian nobility raised and rode horses the same as Spanish hidalgos. The chiefs of Apalache were carrying on a lively horse trade with English-allied Indians in 1700, when the Spanish put a stop to it for reasons of military security.[75] By that time a gentleman without his horse felt hardly presentable. When the parish priest Leturiondo locked the church on Saint Mark's Day and left for the woods to dig roots for his sustenance, his mind was so agitated, he said, that he went on foot and took only one slave.[76]

The hidalgo of substance had an armed following of slaves or servants who were known as the people of his house, much as sailors and soldiers were called people of the sea or of war. Sometimes there were reasons of security for such a retinue. A friar feared to travel to his triennial chapter meeting without at least one bodyguard, and Bishop Díaz Vara Calderón, when he made his visit to Florida in 1674–75, hired three companies of soldiers to accompany his progress: one of Spanish infantry, one of Indian archers, and the other of Indian arquebusiers.[77] About town an entourage was for prestige or intimidation. The crown, trying to preserve order and prevent the formation of rival authority in faraway places, forbade treasury officials to bring their followers to councils or have themselves accompanied in public; it was also forbidden to arm Indians or slaves.[78] It was not merely the secular hidalgo who enjoyed his following. When Father Leturiondo went out by night bearing the Host to the dying, he summoned twelve soldiers from the guardhouse and had the church bell tolled for hours to make the faithful join the procession.[79]

With all the expensive demands on him (public and private charities, providing for children, keeping up a large household, living on a grand scale, and maintaining his standing as a knight-at-arms), the hidalgo was in constant need of money—more money, certainly, than any royal office could presumably provide. As Interim Treasurer Portal y Mauleón once observed through his lawyer, when one's parents were persons of quality it was not honor that one stood in need of, but a living.[80]

3

Proprietary Office

]$[$ N the provinces of Florida, as elsewhere in the empire of the
Spanish Habsburgs, a royal office was an item of property; the
person holding title to it was referred to as the "proprietor." He had
received something of value: the potential income not only of the
salary but of numerous perquisites, supplements and opportunities
for profit; and he had been recognized publicly as a gentleman whom
the king delighted to honor. Perhaps he had put in twenty years of
loyal drudgery on the books of the king's grants. Perhaps he had once
saved the plate fleet from pirates. Perhaps it was not his services that
were rewarded, but those of his ancestors or his wife's family. The
archives are studded with bold demands for honors, rewards and
specific positions, buttressed by generations of worthies. The petitioner himself might be deplorably unworthy, but such a possibility
did not deter a generous prince from encouraging a family tradition
of service.

Appendix 2 (pages 143–48) shows the proprietors of treasury
office, their substitutes and stewards, and the situadores. The date any
one of them took office may have been found by accident in the
correspondence or inferred from the Parish Register. In some cases a
proprietor went to New Spain before sailing to Florida, thus delaying
his arrival by at least half a year. Treasurer Juan de Cevadilla and
Accountant Lázaro Sáez de Mercado were shipwrecked twice along
their journey and reached St. Augustine two-and-a-half years after
they were appointed.[1] The scattering of forces among several forts

before 1587 called for multiple subsitutes and stewards. From 1567 to
1571 the fiscal officials assigned to Menéndez's armada for the defense
of the Indies doubled as garrison inspectors and auditors and possessed Florida treasury titles.

During the Habsburg era a process occurred which could be
called the "naturalization of the Florida coffer." To measure this
phenomenon one must distinguish between those royal officials
whose loyalty lay primarily with the Iberian peninsula and those who
were Floridians, born or made. The simple typology of peninsular
versus creole will not do, for many persons came to Florida and
settled permanently. Pedro Menéndez himself moved his household
there. Of the twenty-one royally appointed or confirmed treasury
officials who served in Florida, only eight had no known relatives
already there. Four of the eight (Lázaro Sáez de Mercado, Nicolás
Ponce de León, Juan de Arrazola, and Francisco Ramírez) joined the
Floridians by intermarriage; another (Juan de Cueva), by compadrazgo. One (Joseph de Prado) went on permanent leave, naming a
creole in his place. Only two of the king's officials seem to have
avoided entanglement in the Florida network: Santos de las Heras,
who spent most of his time in New Spain, and Juan Fernández de
Avila, who was attached to the household of the governor and died
after one year in office. From the time the king began issuing titles in
1571 until the Acclamation of Philip V in 1702 was a period of 131
years. The positions of treasurer and accountant were extant the
entire time, and that of factor-overseer until 1628, making the total
number of treasury office-years 319. The two royal officials who
remained pristinely peninsular served eight years between them,
deducting no time for communication lag, travel, or leaves. Floridians, whether born or naturalized, were in office at least 97 percent of
possible time.

One reason for the naturalization of the coffer was that the king
felt obligated to the descendants of conquerors, and his sense of
obligation could be capitalized on for appointments.[2] The Menéndez
Marquez family, descended on the one side from the adelantado's
sister, and on the other from a cousin of Governor Pedro Menéndez
Marquez, at one time or another held every office in the treasury, and
their efforts to keep them were clearly encouraged by the crown.
When in 1620 Treasurer Juan Menéndez Marquez was appointed
governor of Popayán in South America, he retained his Florida

proprietorship by means of his eighteen-year-old son Francisco. As the treasurer was aged and might not live to return, he requested a futura for the youth, assuring the Council that his son had been raised to the work of the office, had already served as an officer in the infantry, and was descended from the conquerors of the land. The official response was noncommittal: what was fitting would be provided.[3]

Francisco's position was ambiguous: neither interim treasurer nor proprietor. In 1627 word came to St. Augustine that the governor of Popayán was dead. When Francisco would not agree to go on half-salary and admit to being an interim appointee, Governor Rojas y Borja removed him from office and put in his own man, the former rations notary. The treasurer's son went to Spain to argue before the Council that "with his death the absence of Juan Menéndez Marquez was not ended that the use of his office should be." The young man pleaded that he was the sole support of his mother and ten brothers and sisters, and he bore down heavily on the merits of his ancestors. Philip IV's reaction was angry. If the king's lord and father (might he rest in glory) once saw fit to name Francisco Menéndez Marquez treasurer with full salary in the absence of his father, it was not up to a governor to remove him without new orders from the royal person. Rojas y Borja, personally, was commanded to restore Francisco's salary, retroactively. Since the governor's term was concluding, he had to sign a note for the amount before he could leave town. Even without a formal futura Francisco had found his right to succession supported by the crown.

Another way in which the coffer became naturalized was by purchase, with Floridians coming forward to buy. The sale of offices was not shocking to sixteenth- and seventeenth-century administrators, who regarded popular elections as disorderly, conducive to corruption, and apt to set risky precedents.[4] Many types of offices were sold or "provided." In 1687 one could acquire a blank patent of captaincy for Florida by enlisting 100 new soldiers in Spain.[5] To become the Florida governor, Salazar Vallecilla contracted to build a 500-ton galleon for the crown during his first year in office, and was suspended when the year passed and the galleon was not built.[6] It was also possible to buy a benefice. When Captain Antonio de Argüelles, old and going blind, wanted to provide handsomely for his Franciscan son Joseph, he asked friends with influence to persuade the king to give him the position of preacher or some other honor and proudly promised to pay "though it should cost like a mitre."[7]

By the second half of the sixteenth century most public offices in the Indies were venal, that is to say, salable by the crown.[8] In 1604 these offices also became renounceable: they could be sold to a second party for a payment of half their value to the coffer the first time, and one-third each time thereafter. Offices of the treasury, however, were not included. It was feared that candidates would use fraud to recover the purchase price or that incompetents would find their way into office, and it was the crown's sincere purpose to approve only the qualified.[9] This did not mean that no arrangement was possible. Juan Menéndez Marquez obtained the Florida treasurership in 1593 when he was betrothed to the twelve-year-old daughter of the former treasurer, Juan de Posada, and of Catalina Menéndez Marquez, the governor's sister. Francisco Ramírez received the accountancy in 1614 by agreeing to marry the former accountant's widow and support her eight children.[10] Not unnaturally, the members of the Council who made the proposals for treasury office regarded wealth as an evidence of sound judgment, and a candidate with means had ways to sweeten his selection. By the 1630s—halfway through the period we are studying—the king was desperate enough to extend to the treasury the sale of offices and also of renunciations, futuras, and retentions.

A governor in Florida might know nothing of the transaction until after the death of the incumbent, when the new proprietor presented himself with receipt and title; yet the only known opposition to the sale of treasury offices came from Governor Marques Cabrera and was part of his campaign against creoles in general. When Thomás Menéndez Marquez brought in the title to be accountant after the death of his brother Antonio, the governor refused to honor it, saying that Thomás was locally born and unfit. Marques Cabrera entreated the king to sell no more treasury offices to undeserving persons and to forbid the officials to marry locally—better yet, to transfer them away from Florida altogether. The Junta de Guerra responded with a history of the official transactions in the case. According to its records, Antonio Menéndez Marquez had paid 1,000 pesos cash to succeed his brother Juan II in 1673, when Juan was promoted from accountant in St. Augustine to factor in Havana. In 1682 Antonio (who was spending most of his time as situador in New

Spain) had bought a futura for their brother Thomás at a cost of 500 pesos. The Junta ordered the governor to install Thomás as accountant immediately with retroactive pay.[11] Three years later the *Cámara de Indias,* which was the executive committee of the Council, approved shipowner Diego de Florencia's request for a futura to the next treasury vacancy for his son Matheo Luis.[12] Floridians like Florencia were the ones who would know when offices were likely to fall vacant, and they may have been the only ones who wanted them.

Proprietary offices were politely attributed to royal favor and legitimized by royal titles, but the king had less and less to do with appointments. His rights of patronage were gradually alienated until all that remained as a royal prerogative was enforcing the contract. The complete contract between the king and his proprietor was contained in several documents: licenses, instructions, titles, and bond.

The appointee leaving for the Indies from Spain received a number of licenses, of which some served as passports. Ordinarily, one could take his immediate family, three slaves, and up to four servants to the New World. Because the crown was anxious to preserve the faith pure for the Indians, there could be no one in the household of suspect orthodoxy. To discourage adventurers, testimony might have to be presented that none of the servants was leaving a spouse in Spain, and the official might have to promise to keep them with him for a period of time. Other licenses served as shipping authorizations. A family was permitted to take, free of customs, 400 to 600 ducats' worth of jewels and plate and another 300 to 600 ducats' worth of household belongings. Sometimes the amount of baggage allowance was specified. Because of the crown policy of strict arms control, weapons were limited to the needs of a gentleman and his retinue. An official might be permitted six swords, six daggers, two arquebuses, and one corselet. At the option of the appointee the standard licenses could be supplemented by additional paperwork. Gutierre de Miranda carried instructions to the governor to grant him building lots and lands for planting and pasture as they had been given to others of his quality. Juan de Posada had a letter stipulating that situadores were to be chosen from the proprietary officials and were to receive an expense allowance.[13]

Instructions for treasury office in the Indies followed a set formula, with most of the space devoted to duties at smelteries and mints. An official's copy could be picked up at the House of Trade or in Santo Domingo, or it might be sent to his destination. If he was already in St. Augustine he would receive his instructions along with his titles.

Titles were equally standard in format. There were two of them: one to office in the treasury and the other as regidor of the cabildo. The treasury title addressed the appointee by name, calling him the king's accountant, treasurer, or factor-overseer of the provinces of Florida on account of the death of the former proprietor. After a brief description of the responsibilities of office the appointee was assured that in Florida "they shall give and do you all the honors, deferences, graces, exemptions, liberties, preeminences, prerogatives and immunities and each and every other attribute which by reason of the said office you should enjoy." The salary was stated: invariably 400,000 *maravedís* a year from the products of the land.[14] This was the only regular income the official was due, for municipal office in Florida was unsalaried. If the appointee was already in Florida, salaried time began the day he presented himself to be inducted into office; otherwise, on the day he set sail from San Lúcar de Barrameda or Cádiz. By the time the crown withdrew coverage for travel time in 1695, Florida treasury offices had long been creole-owned.[15] The one thing that never appeared in an official's titles was a time limit. His appointment, "at the king's pleasure," was understood to be for life. The governor, by contrast, had a term of five or six years. He could threaten, fine, suspend, even imprison a proprietor, but he could not remove him. And when the governor's term expired and his *residencia* (judicial inquiry) came up, every official in the treasury would be waiting to lodge charges.

The bond for treasury office, whether for the accountant, treasurer, or factor-overseer, and whether for the status of proprietor, interim official, or substitute, was 2,000 ducats. The appointee was permitted to furnish it in the place of his choice and present a receipt. Once such offices began to be held by natives the bond was raised by subscription. As many as thirty-eight soldiers and vecinos at a time agreed to stand good if the treasury suffered loss because of the said official's tenure. The effect of this communal backing was that if the treasury official was accused of malfeasance and his bond was in danger of being called in, as in the cases of Francisco Menéndez Marquez and Pedro Benedit Horruytiner, the whole town rose to his defense. Nicolás Ponce de León did not observe the formality of having his bond notarized. When the document was examined after his death, it was found that of his twenty-one backers, half had predeceased him, perhaps in the same epidemic, and only five of the others acknowledged their signatures.[16]

At the time of induction the treasury official bound himself by a solemn oath before God, the Evangels, and the True Cross to be honest and reliable. He presented his bond and his title. His belongings were inventoried, as they would again be at his death, transferral, or suspension. He was given a key to the coffer, and its contents also were inventoried. From that day forward he was meant never to take an independent fiscal action. Other officials at his treasury had access to the same books and locks on the same coffer. He would join them to sign receipts and drafts. Together they would open, read, and answer correspondence. In the same solidarity they would attend auctions, visit ships, and initiate debt proceedings.[17] Such cumbersome accounting by committee was intended to guarantee their probity, for the king had made his officials collegially responsible in order to watch each other. No single one of them could depart from rectitude without the collusion or inattention of his colleagues.

A Spanish monarch had elevated ideals for his treasury officials. By law no proprietor might be related by blood or marriage to any other important official in his district. In Florida this was impracticable. The creole families were intricately intermarried and quickly absorbed eligible bachelors. Juan de Cevadilla described his predicament:

> [When] Your Majesty made me the grant of being treasurer here eight years ago I decided to establish myself in this corner of the world, and not finding many suitable to my quality I married doña Petronila de Estrada Manrique, only daughter of Captain Rodrigo de Junco, factor of these provinces. If Your Majesty finds it inconvenient for father-in-law and son-in-law to be royal officials I shall gladly [accept a] transfer. But the limitations of the land are such that not only are the royal officials related by blood and marriage, but the governors as well.[18]

According to Spanish law, a proprietor was not to hold magisterial or political office or command troops.[19] In St. Augustine the treasury officials were royal judges of the exchequer until 1621. They held the only political offices there were: places on the city council. They were also inactive officers of the garrison, who returned to duty with the first ring of the alarum. In a place known for constant war, a man with self-respect did not decline to fight Indians or pirates.

During the early sixteenth century, royal officials were necessarily granted sources of income to support them until their treasuries should have regular revenues. Juan de Añasco and Luis Hernández de Biedma, De Soto's accountant and factor, had permission to engage in Indian trade as long as the residents of Florida paid no customs. They and the two other treasury officials were to receive twelve square leagues of land each and encomiendas of tribute-paying natives.[20] As the century wore on, such supplements to salaries were curtailed or forbidden. In most places treasury officials had already had their trading privileges withdrawn; they soon lost the right to operate productive enterprises such as ranches, sugar mills, or mines, for every time a royal official engaged in private business there was fresh proof of why he should not.[21] The laws of the Indies lay lightly on St. Augustine, where the proprietors were more apt to be governed by circumstance, and in 1580 the restriction on ranches and farms was removed. Accountant Thomás Menéndez Marquez owned the largest ranch in Florida, shipping hides, dried meat, and tallow out the Suwannee River to Havana, where he bought rum to exchange for furs with the Indians who traded in the province of Apalache. Pirates once held him for ransom for 150 head of his cattle.[22]

Encomiendas were another matter. The New Laws of 1542–43 phasing them out for others forbade them altogether for officials of the treasury, who could not even marry a woman with encomiendas unless she renounced them.[23] This created no hardship for the proprietors in St. Augustine. Although Pedro Menéndez's contract had contained tacit permission to grant encomiendas in accordance with the Populating Ordinances of 1563, they were out of the question in Florida—where the seasonally nomadic Indians long refused to settle themselves in towns for the Spanish convenience, and the chiefs expected to receive tribute, not pay it.[24] Eventually the natives consented to a token tribute, which in time was converted to a rotating labor service out of which the officials helped themselves—but there was never an encomienda.[25]

The expenses of a local treasury, including the salaries of its officers, were theoretically covered by its income. This was immediately declared impossible in Florida, where the coffer either had few revenues or its officials did not divulge them. The first treasurer, accountant, and factor-overseer occupied themselves in making their offices pay off at the expense of the crown and the soldiers. When instituting the situado, the king made no immediate provision for the payment of treasury officials. In 1577, however, when Florida was changed from a proprietary colony to a regular royal one, the crown was obliged to admit as a temporary expedient that half of the stated salaries might be collected from the situado. This concession was reluctantly repeated at two- to six-year intervals.[26] The widows of officials who had served prior to regular salaries were assisted by grants.[27]

The royal officials pointed out between 1595 and 1608 that the revenues which they and the governor were supposed to divide pro rata were not enough to cover the other half of their salaries. Fines were insignificant, as were confiscations; the Indians paid little in tribute, and the tithes had been assigned to build the parish church. They did not think the colony could bear the cost of import duties. The treasure tax on amber and sassafras was difficult to collect.[28] At last the crown resigned itself to the fact that the improvident treasury of the provinces of Florida would never pay its own way, much less support a garrison. The royal officials were allowed to collect the remainder of their salaries out of surpluses in the situado.[29]

In spite of an inflationary cost of living between 1565 and 1702, salaries, wages, and rations allowances did not rise in Florida. The king allowed his officials no payroll initiative. For a while the governor used the bonus fund of 1,500 ducats a year to reward merit and supplement the salaries of lower-echelon officers and soldiers on special assignment, but the crown gradually extended its control over that as well.[30]

Out of context, the figure of 400,000 maravedís, which was the annual salary of a proprietor, is meaningless.[31] Table 1 shows the salary plus rations of several positions paid from the situado. The date is that of the earliest known reference after 1565. For comparative purposes, all units of account have been converted to ducats. Rations worth 2½ reales a day were over and above salary for members of the garrison, among whom the treasury officials, the governor, and the secular priests counted themselves in this case.[32] By 1676 at least, a

TABLE 1

Yearly Salaries and Rations in St. Augustine in the Seventeenth Century

Year	Position	Salary as Stated	Salary without Rations (in ducats)	Value of Rations (in ducats)	Salary including Rations (in ducats)
1601	Governor	2,000 ducats/yr	2,000	83	2,083
1601	Treasury proprietor	400,000 maravedís/yr	1,067	83	1,150
1646	Sergeant major	515 ducats/yr	515	83	598
1655	Master of construction	500 ducats/yr	500	83	583
1594	Master of the forge	260 ducats/yr	260	83	343
1636	Parish priest	200 ducats/yr	200	83	283
1593	Carpenter	200 ducats/yr	200	83	283
1601	Company captain	200 ducats/yr	200	83	283
1636	Chaplain	150 ducats/yr	150	83	233
1593	Master pilot	12 ducats/mo	144	83	227
1603	Surgeon	10 ducats/mo	120	83	203
1601	Ensign	6 ducats/mo	72	83	155
1630	Overseer of the slaves	1,200 reales/yr and plaza	64	83	147
1693	Sacristan	200 pesos/yr	62	83	145
1601	Sergeant	4 ducats/mo	48	83	131
1601	Officer in charge (*cabo*)	4 ducats/mo	48	83	131
1641	Friar	115 ducats/yr	——	115	115[a]
1601	Infantryman	1,000 maravedís/mo	32	83	115
1676	Indian laborer	1 real/day in trade goods	33	50	83[b]
1693	Sacristan's sweeping boy	2 lbs. flour/day	——	36	36[c]

a. Beginning this year, stated supplies were given whose value increased with prices.

b. Approximate. Depended upon value of trade goods and maize.

c. Varied with the price of flour.

repartimiento Indian received almost exactly the same pay before rations as a soldier.[33] The soldier, of course, was often issued additional rations for his family, while the Indian got only two or two-and-a-half pounds of maize per day, worth perhaps 1½ reales—and he might have brought it with him on his back as part of the tribute from his village.[34] A Franciscan drew his entire 115-ducat stipend in goods and provisions. In 1641 the crown consented to let these items be constant in quantity regardless of price fluctuations.[35] It is ironic that natives and friars, both legendarily poor, were the only individuals in town besides the sacristan's sweeping boy whose incomes could rise with the cost of living.[36]

It was acceptable to hold multiple offices. Pedro Menéndez Mar-

quez's salary as governor of Florida began the day he resigned his title
of Admiral of the Indies Fleet—more important than his concurrent
one of Florida accountant.[37] Don Antonio Ponce de León usually
exercised several positions at once. In 1687 he was at the same time
chief sacristan of the church, notary of the ecclesiastical court, and
notary of the tribunal of the Holy Crusade. Periodically he was
appointed defense attorney for Indians. While visiting Havana,
probably in 1701, he was made ecclesiastical visitador for Florida and
church organist for St. Augustine. He returned home from Cuba on
one of the troopships sent to break the siege of Colonel Moore, and as
luck would have it, the day before he landed, the withdrawing
Carolinians and Indians burned the church with the organ in it. Don
Antonio presented his title as organist notwithstanding and was
added to the payroll in that capacity since, as the royal officials
pointed out, it was not his fault that there was no organ. By 1707 he
had taken over the chaplaincy of the fort as well.[38]

Members of the religious community had sources of income
other than the regular stipends. The parish priest was matter-of-fact
in his discussion of burial fees and other perquisites. If these ran short,
he could go to Havana, say a few masses, and buy a new silk soutane.
In St. Augustine the value of a mass was set at seven reales, and the
chaplain complained that the friars demanded cold cash for every one
they said for him when he was ill and unable to attend to his duties.[39]
Parishioners brought the Franciscans offerings of fish, game, and
produce in quantities sufficient to sell through their syndics. The
income was intended to beautify churches and provide for the needy,
but one friar kept out enough to dower his sister into a convent.[40]

In the garrison it was possible to collect the pay of a soldier
without being one. There were seldom as many soldiers fit for duty
as there were authorized plazas in the garrison, and the vacant spaces,
called "dead-pays" (*plazas muertas*), served as a fund for pensions and
allowances. A retired or incapacitated soldier held his plaza for the
length of his life. A minor's plaza (*plaza de menor* or *muchacho*) could
be purchased for or granted to someone's son to provide extra income, and if the lad developed no aptitude as a soldier the money did
not have to be paid back. Plazas were used variously as honoraria to
Indian chiefs, dowries, and salary supplements: a captain traditionally
named his own servants or slaves to posts in his company and pocketed their pay.[41]

Understrength in the garrison due to these practices was a perennial problem. Sometimes it was the governor who abused his power to assign plazas. The crown refused to endorse nineteen of them awarded by Interim Governor Horruytiner to the sons, servants, and slaves of his supporters. At other times the government in Spain was to blame. Governor Hita Salazar complained that every ship to arrive bore new royal grants of plazas for youngsters, pensioners, and widows. A few of these were outright gifts; on most, the crown collected both the half-annate and a fee for waiving its own rule against creoles in the garrison. Again and again governors protested that of the plazas on the payroll only half were filled by persons who would be of any use to defend the fort and the town.[42]

A soldier's plaza was not his sole source of income. On his days off guard duty he worked at his secondary trade, whether it was to burn charcoal, build boats, fish, cut firewood, make shoes, grind maize, round up cattle, tailor, or weave fishnets. A sawyer or logger could earn 6 or 7 reales extra a day. Every family man was also a part-time farmer, with his own patch of maize on the commons and cheap repartimiento labor to help him cultivate it.[43] The soldier had still other advantages. When traveling on the king's business he could live off the Indians, commandeer their canoes, order one of them to carry his bedroll, and cross on their ferries free.[44] His medicines cost nothing, although a single shipment of drugs for the whole presidio cost over 600 pesos. The same soldier's compulsory contribution to the hospital association of Santa Barbara, patroness of artillerymen, was limited to 1 real a month.[45] When he became too old to mount guard he would be kept on the payroll, and after he died his family would continue to receive rations. The weapons in his possession went to the woman he had been living with, and his back wages paid for his burial and the masses said for the good of his soul.[46]

An officer was entitled to these privileges and more. Not only might his slaves and servants bring in extra plazas, but he was in a position to sell noncommissioned offices, and excuses and leaves from guard duty.[47] It was possible for him to draw supplies from the royal storehouses almost indefinitely. With his higher salary he had readier cash and could order goods on the supply ship, purchase property at auction, or buy up quantities of maize for speculation.[48]

A treasury official possessed most of the advantages of an officer plus others of his own. When he served as a judge of the exchequer he was entitled to a portion after taxes, probably a sixth, of all confiscated merchandise. When he was collector of the situado he drew a per diem of thirty reales, which may have been why Juan de Cevadilla asked the crown to supplement his low salary as treasurer with the good salary of a situador.[49] As a manager of presidio supplies the treasury official favored his kinsmen and friends who were importers and cattle ranchers. In time of famine he drew more than his share of flour. As a payroll officer he credited himself with all the maravedís over a real, since there was no longer a maravedí coin in the currency. As a regidor the official took turns with his colleagues at tavern inspection. Each time a pipe was opened he collected one peso.[50] There must have been many similar ways to supplement a salary, some acknowledged and others only implied.

The duties of a royal official were not necessarily done by him personally. An official was often absent, traveling to New Spain or Havana, visiting the provinces, or looking after his property. He chose a substitute, the substitute posted bond, and they divided the salary. If the substitute found it necessary to hire a replacement of his own, the subject of payment was reduced to a private deal between the parties. When a proprietary office fell vacant, the governor enjoyed the right of appointing ad interim, unless the crown had sold a futura and the new proprietor was waiting. Interim officials were paid half of a regular salary, the same as substitutes.[51] The routine work of the Florida treasury may have been done more often by substitutes than proprietors, especially in the late seventeenth century, when officials serving as situadores were kept waiting in Mexico City for years. This raised questions of liability. Was the royal treasurer, Matheo Luis de Florencia, accountable for a deficit in the treasury when he had been in New Spain the entire five years since his installation? The crown referred the question to its auditors.[52]

The interim or substitute official was supposed to be someone familiar with the work of the treasury and possessed of steady character: rich, honorable, and married. It was unwise, though, to choose someone whose connections made him aspire to office himself. Alonso Sánchez Sáez came to Florida with his uncle Lázaro Sáez de Mercado, the accountant, and became a syndic for the friars. When Lázaro died the governor named Alonso ad interim on half-pay. At the next audit there was some question about his having been related to the former accountant, but the crown ruled that the governor could allow what was customary. Since at that time only a half of salaries was paid from the situado and the coffer had few revenues, the interim accountant's salary translated into 100,000 maravedís a year for a 400,000-maravedí position. His requests for a royal title and full salary were ignored, as were his complaints about his heavy duties. The next proprietor, Bartolomé de Argüelles, kept Alonso substituting in the counting house during his own lengthy absences.[53] The embittered nephew, who had inherited the work but not the salary or honor of his office, made a name for himself in St. Augustine by sequestering funds, giving false alarms, and being generally contentious. The governor forbade him to sit on the same bench during Holy Week with the other treasury officials. Alonso circulated a rumor that the governor was a defrocked friar. The interim accountant and his wife, whom he always called "a daughter of the first conquerors," were eventually expelled from town, carrying the governor's charges against them in a sealed envelope.[54]

In a place as precedent-conscious as St. Augustine, the cases defining what was to be done about leaves of absence were important. Factor Alonso de las Alas quarreled with Treasurer Juan Menéndez Marquez in 1595 over whose turn it was to go for the situado. Las Alas thought he had won, but when he got back from New Spain the treasurer and the governor indicted him for bringing part of the situado in clothing instead of cash. At their recommendation the Council suspended him for four years without salary.[55] After his reinstatement Las Alas requested a two-year leave to go to Spain. The treasurer had obtained a similar leave on half-salary the year before, but the crown felt no obligation to be consistent: Las Alas had to take his leave without pay.[56] The accountant, Bartolomé de Argüelles, also received a two-year leave to attend to personal business, and when it expired he did not return. Years later his widow, doña María de Quiñones, was still trying to collect his half-pay to use for the dowries of four daughters.[57]

An official who experimented with informal leaves of absence was Accountant Nicolás Ponce de León. He was a veteran of Indian wars in Santa Marta, a descendant of conquerors in Peru, and, most important, the son-in-law of a Council of the Indies porter. From the preserved slate of nominees, he was also the only one out of thirty-six candidates with no previous exchequer experience. When the governor of Florida died in 1631, shortly after his arrival, Nicolás found himself thrust into a co-interim governorship with the psychopathic Sergeant Major Eugenio de Espinosa.. In mortal fear of his partner, who had threatened to cut off his head, he took refuge in the Franciscan convent until the next governor should arrive. He assured the crown that this caused the treasury no inconvenience for he had named a reliable and competent person to do what work could not be brought to the convent.[58]

In 1637 this same Nicolás Ponce de León had Treasurer Francisco Menéndez Marquez imprisoned on charges of having spent situado funds in Mexico City on gambling and other things "which for modesty and decency cannot be mentioned." Perhaps the accountant decided that unmentionable sins deserved closer examination. In 1641 he went to Mexico City himself, where he got the viceroy to throw Martín de Cueva, a former situador, into prison and settled down for a leisurely lawsuit before the audiencia. After three years the governor of Florida sent word for Nicolás to return or have his powers of attorney revoked. Nicolás appealed the governor's order to the audiencia. In 1645 the next governor declared the accountant absent without leave and replaced his substitute, who had let the papers of the counting house fall into confusion. The king finally intervened in the case and ordered the viceroy of New Spain to send the recreant accountant of Florida, who had been amusing himself for the last five years in Mexico City, home to look after his duties. After an absence of seven years Nicolás returned to resume his office and family. His holiday does not seem to have been held against him.[59]

A case of purchased leave of absence was that of Treasurer Joseph de Prado. Prado did not buy his office: the position was given him when he was almost fifty, for his services to the crown. He did not distinguish himself in Florida. During the Robert Searles raid of 1668 he was the only grown man in town to be captured in his bed and carried out to the ships for ransom along with the women. A month later he was sold a license to spend ten years in Guadalajara for the sake of his health. In 1674 he left St. Augustine and thereafter replied to no letters. When the ten years were up Governor Marques Cabrera reported that no one knew whether Prado was dead or alive and asked that the office be refilled. An indifferent Junta de Guerra clerk replied that Prado had paid 600 pesos for the privilege of absenting himself for unlimited periods as he pleased.[60]

The "honors, deferences, graces, exemptions, liberties, preeminences, prerogatives and immunities" promised to the royal official in his title were as dear to him as his salary and substitutes and maybe more so, for they acknowledged his position as one of rank and privilege. He had precedence. He and his family were persons of consequence. Such perquisites of office were partly tangible and partly deferential.

Tangible symbols of office were the official's staff of office (*vara*), his key to the coffer, and his residence in a government house. In the seventeenth century it was a common sign of authority to carry a staff. The governor had his baton and so had Indian chiefs. Staves and banners even served as metonyms for office. Nicolás Ponce de León II said that "the banner of the militia company being vacant," his son Antonio was appointed company ensign. Governor Marques Cabrera, being rowed out to the waiting galley on the day he deserted, threw his baton into the sea, crying, "There's where you can go for your government in this filthy place!"[61] In his role of royal judge a treasury official bore one staff, and as a regidor he was entitled to another. When the choleric Sergeant Major Espinosa, enraged at Nicolás Ponce de León I, was restrained by companions from killing him, he called into the counting house to his adjutant to seize the accountant's symbol of authority and arrest him. The officer did so, breaking Ponce de León's staff to pieces.[62]

Keys were symbols of responsibility as staves were of authority. When the warden of the castillo made his oath of fealty to defend his post, he took charge of the keys of the fort and marched through its precincts with the public notary, locking and unlocking the gates.[63] A similar ceremony was observed with a new treasury official, who received his key to the treasure chest and immediately tried it. In legal documents this chest was sometimes called the "coffer of the four keys," from the days when there would have been four padlocks on it, one for each official. At important treasuries another key was frequently held by the viceroy, the archbishop, or an audiencia judge, who sent it with a representative when the chest was opened. The royal officials resented this practice as impugning their honor.[64]

It was the treasury officials' privilege and duty to reside in the houses of government (*casas reales*) where the coffer was kept. These buildings varied in number and location along with the relocations of the town. During the sixteenth century St. Augustine moved about with the sites of the fort. According to Alonso de las Alas, the first presidio, known to him as "Old St. Augustine," was built on an island facing the site of the town he lived in. St. Augustine was moved "across to this side" when the sea ate the island out from under it. In its new location on the bay front the town had a guardhouse, an arsenal under the same roof as the royal warehouse, and perhaps a customs-counting house at the dock.[65] There were no official residences. Three successive governors rented the same house on the seashore—Governor Ybarra thought it a most unhealthful location. This St. Augustine, and a new fort on the island of San Juan de Pinillo, were destroyed by Drake in 1586; a later St. Augustine, by fires and a hurricane in 1599.[66]

Disregarding Pedro Menéndez's idea to move the settlement to the site of an Indian village west of the San Sebastian inlet, Governor Méndez de Canzo rebuilt it a little to the south, where the landing was better protected and a curving inlet provided a natural moat. He laid a bridge across the nearby swamp, sold lots, and bought up lumber. In spite of the treasury officials' disapproval he began paying daily wages to repartimiento workers and put the soldiers to work clearing land. To finance his real development he exacted contributions from those with houses still standing, approved harbor taxes, cut down on bonuses and expense allowances, and diverted the funds sent for castillo construction. The king helped with four years of tithes, 276 ducats from salvage, and 500 ducats besides.[67] Following Philip II's 1573 ordinances for town planning, Méndez de Canzo laid out the plaza in back of the landing: 250 by 450 feet, large enough for a cavalry parade ground. Around the plaza he constructed a new guardhouse, a royal warehouse doubling as treasury, and a governor's mansion. He also built a gristmill and an arsenal and started a counting house onto which a customs house could be added.[68]

The royal officials might have the right to live in government houses, but they did not intend to move into quarters that were inadequate. In the time of Governor Salinas the crown finally approved construction of suitable residences to be financed from local revenues and, when these proved insufficient, from the castillo fund. The proprietors were satisfied. "In all places where Your Majesty has royal officials they are given dwelling houses," they had said, and now there were such houses in St. Augustine.[69] When the factor-overseer's position was suppressed a few years later, the vacated third residence was assigned by cédula to the sergeant major.[70]

All the buildings in town at this time seem to have been of wood, with the better ones tiled or shingled and the rest thatched with palm leaves. By 1666 the government houses, including the counting house and the arsenal, were ready to collapse. A hurricane and flood leveled half the town in 1674, but again rebuilding was done mostly in wood, although there was oyster shell lime and quarried coquina available on Anastasia Island for the stone masonry of the new castillo.[71] There seems to have been some subdividing of original lots. During the governorship of Hita Salazar, Sergeant Major Pedro de Aranda y Avellaneda bought a lot within the compound of the government houses close to the governor's mansion, although he had applied for a different one in the compound of the treasury and royal warehouse. The royal officials not only sold it to him but supplied him with the materials to build a house next to the governor's. The next governor, Marques Cabrera, managed to block Aranda's building there, but not on the lot beside the treasury. Displeased with what he called the deterioration of the neighborhood, the governor turned the gubernatorial mansion into a public inn and requisitioned for his residence the house of Ana Ruíz, a widow, two blocks away.[72]

The next governor, Quiroga y Losada, proposed to sell the government houses and put up a new stone building to contain the governor's residence, the counting house, and the guardhouse. The royal officials could move into his renovated old mansion and their houses be sold.[73] Six months later—suspiciously soon—the new government house was finished. Appraised at 6,000 pesos, it had been built for 500. Quiroga y Losada had not followed his own submitted plan, for the counting house, treasury, and royal officials were still housed as they had been, in buildings that he and the next governor repaired and remodeled in stone.[74] When Colonel Moore and his forces arrived to lay siege to the castillo in 1702, the treasury was on the point of being re-shingled. When they marched away, nothing was left of any of the government houses except blackened rubble.[75]

If the tangible symbols of office were staves, keys, and residences, the deferential symbols of office were precedence and form of address. Precedence was a serious matter. Disputes over who might walk through a door first, sit at the head of a table, or remain covered in the presence of someone else were not just childish willfulness but efforts to define the offices or estates that would take priority and those that would be subordinate.[76] When parish priest Alonso de Leturiondo locked the church on Saint Mark's Day because the governor had sent someone less important than the treasurer to invite him to the official celebration, it was not solely from offended pride. As he said, he must maintain the honor of his office.[77]

The order of procession at feast days and public ceremonies was strictly observed. Treasury officials, who embodied both fiscal and municipal dignities, took precedence over all exclusively religious or military authorities. The two first ministers of Florida at the local Acclamation of Philip V. were the interim accountant and the treasurer, "who by royal arrangement follow His Lordship in seat and signature." The accountant stood at the governor's left hand and the treasurer, serving as royal standard-bearer for the city, at his right, leading the hurrahs of *"Castilla Florida"* for the new monarch and throwing money into the crowd.[78]

In some treasuries precedence among the royal officials was determined by the higher salaries of some or by the fact that proprietors were regidores of the cabildo and substitutes were not. In St. Augustine, where these differences did not exist, the only bases for precedence were proprietorship and seniority. The one who first stepped forward to sign a document was the one who had been a proprietor in Florida the longest.[79]

The final right of a royal official was not to be mistreated verbally. The form of address for each level in society was as elaborately prescribed as the rest of protocol, and a lapse could only be regarded as intentional. The governor was referred to as *Su Señoría* (His Lordship) and addressed as *Vuestra Señoría* or *Vuestra Excelencia* (Your Excellency), abbreviated to *Vuselensia* or even *Vselensia* in the dispatches of semiliterate corporals.[80] Governor Ybarra implored the Franciscan guardian to keep the reckless Father Celaya confined in the convent, for "if he shows me disrespect [on the street] I shall have to put him into the fort ... for I must have honor to this office."[81] Friars were called *Vuestra Paternidad* (Your Fatherliness). A Spaniard of one's own rank was addressed as *Vuestra Merced* (Your Grace), shortened in usage to *Usarced, Usarcé,* or *Busted* (precursors of *Usted*).[82] Only the king could address officials in the familiar form, otherwise used for children, servants, and common Indians. After Governor Méndez de Canzo had addressed Treasurer Juan Menéndez

Marquez publicly as "*vos*," his epithets of "insolent" and "shameless one" were superfluous. The crown's reaction to such disrespect toward its treasury officials was to reprimand the offender and order him in future to "treat them in speech as is proper to the authority of their persons and the offices in which they serve us, and because it is right that in everything they be honored."[83]

As a proprietor of the exchequer the treasury official had the second highest salary in town, job tenure, free housing, and the opportunity to let substitutes do his work. In his connection with the garrison he could count on regular rations, supplies, and a career for his sons. Because he was regidor of the cabildo, the whole regional economy was laid before him to adjust to his advantage. And beyond all this were the prized "honors, deferences, graces, exemptions, liberties, preeminences, prerogatives and immunities." A proprietary official of the royal treasury was as secure financially and socially as any person could be who lived in that place and at that time.

4

Duties and Organization

THE work of the treasury was conducted mainly in the houses of government: the counting house, the customs house, the royal warehouse and arsenal, and the treasury. For all of this work the royal officials were collegially responsible, and much of it they did together; but each of them also had his own duties, his headquarters, and one or more assistants. The organization of the treasury is shown in Table 2, with the patron or patrons of each position. Those positions for which wages are known are in Table 3.

The title of accountant called for training in office procedures. Roving auditors might find errors and make improvements in the bookkeeping system, yet this could not take the place of careful routine. In the words of New Spain Auditor Irigoyen: "The accountant alone is the one who keeps a record of the branches of revenue and makes out the drafts for whatever is paid out, and any ignorance or carelessness he displays must be at the expense of Your Majesty's exchequer."[1] Unfortunately, not every hidalgo who was appointed accountant enjoyed working with figures. Some left everything in the hands of subordinates, signing whatever was put in front of them.

The accountant did not handle cash. He was a records specialist, the archivist who preserved royal cédulas, governors' decrees, and treasury resolutions. He indexed and researched them, had them copied, and was the authority on their interpretation. He kept the census of native tributaries—a count supplemented but not duplicated by the friars' Lenten count of communicants.[2] It was his business to maintain personnel files, entering the date when an individual went on or off payroll and recording leaves and suspensions. No one was paid without his certification. Sometimes the crown asked for a special report: the whereabouts of small firearms in the provinces, a list of Indian missions and attendant friars with the distances between them in leagues, a cost analysis of royal slave earnings and expenses, even an accounting of empty barrels. Instructions came addressed to

TABLE 2

Treasury Organization and Patronage in St. Augustine, 1591–1702

Positions and Dates Created	Patrons				
	King and Council	Governor	Royal Officials	Treasury Council	Other
Treasury Council					
Governor	x				
Accountant	x				
Factor–overseer	to 1628				
Treasurer	to 1628				
Treasurer-steward (1628)	x				
Interim officials		x			
Substitute officials		x[a]	x		
Public and govt. notary		to 1631			1631 on[b]
Commissioned Agents					
Situador				x[c]	
Procurador				x	
Supply ship masters				x	
Provincial tax collectors				x	
Expedition tax collectors				x	
Counting House					
Chief clerk (1593)			x		
Assistant clerk (1635)			x		
Lieutenant auditor (1666)					x[d]
Internal auditor		to 1666			
Customs House					
Customs constable (1603)		to 1636	1636 on		
Chief guard (1630)			x		
Guards (as needed)		x			
Warehouse and Arsenal					
Steward			x		
Rations and munitions notary		x			

a. With the governor's consent.

b. Auctioned.

c. Chosen by auditor and governor.

d. Most common practice; varied frequently.

TABLE 3

WAGES AT THE ST. AUGUSTINE TREASURY IN THE SEVENTEENTH CENTURY

Position	Salary without Rations	Per Diem or Daily Rations (in reales)	Bonus	Total (in ducats)
Proprietor	400,000 mrs/yr	2½		1,150
Proprietor as situador	400,000 mrs/yr	30		2,062
Captain as procurador	200 ducats/yr	15	20 ducats/mo	938
Interim or substitute official	200,000 mrs/yr	2½		618
Lieutenant auditor	500 pesos/yr	2½		444
Chief clerk	1,000 mrs/mo*	2½	200 pesos/yr	260
Chief guard	250 ducats/yr*			250
Steward	50,000 mrs/yr	2½		217
Customs constable	1,000 mrs/mo	2½	25,000 mrs/yr	182
Rations notary	5 ducats/mo	2½	400 reales/yr	179
Public and govt. notary	1,000 mrs/mo	2½	400 reales/yr	151
Assistant clerk	1,000 mrs/mo	2½	50 pesos/yr	151

*This figure may include rations.

all the royal officials and they all signed the prepared report, but the accountant and his staff did the work.[3]

The counting house was staffed by a number of clerks. Before their positions were made official the accountant sometimes hired an accounts notary (*escribano de cuentas*) out of his own salary.[4] In 1593 the crown approved a chief clerk of the counting house (*oficial mayor de la contaduría*) to be paid a regular plaza and 200 pesos from the bonus fund. When the accountant was away this clerk usually served as his substitute. The position of assistant clerk of the counting house (*oficial menor de la contaduría*) with a salary supplement of 50 pesos a year was approved in 1635. The assistant clerk was also known as the clerk of the half-annate (*oficial de la media anata*), although the half-annate was seldom collected.[5] If the work load at the office became heavy, temporary help might be hired, but the king did not want this charged to his treasury. When Accountant Ponce de León and his substitute allowed the books to get eight years behind, the other officials were told to deduct from salaries the cost of bringing them up to date.[6] In 1688, soon after a third infantry company was formed, Accountant Thomás Menéndez Marquez requested permission to hire a third clerk for the increased paperwork. Instead, he was ordered to reduce his staff from two clerks to one—an order that was neither rescinded nor, apparently, obeyed.[7] There was by that time another official at the counting house: a lieutenant auditor chosen by the royal auditor and the governor to replace the internal auditor who had been appointed periodically. These two positions are discussed in Chapter 8.

The treasury officials were a committee of harbor masters, registering the comings and goings of people as well as ships. It was their duty to see that no one entered the provinces without the correct papers, or left without the governor's consent and their own fiscal release. Impetuous young Pedro de Valdés, betrothed to Menéndez's daughter Ana, was probably the only person ever to stow away for Florida, but convicts, soldiers, and even friars tried to escape. The presidio's ships had to be manned by Indians and mixed-bloods who could be relied upon to return home.[8]

When the royal officials first began collecting harbor taxes, they recognized the need of a customs constable and inspector (*alguacil y fiel ejecutor de la aduana*) to record what was loaded and unloaded from ships. Otherwise they had to take turns at the customs house themselves, which Alonso Sánchez Sáez, at least, was unwilling to do.[9] The crown approved the new position in 1603, with a 25,000-maravedí bonus and no doubt a percentage of goods confiscated.[10] The governor appointed as first constable Lucas de Soto, a better sort of soldier sentenced to serve four years in Florida for trying to desert to New Spain from Cuba. By 1608 De Soto was in Spain with dispatches, receiving the salary of customs constable but not doing the work. In 1630 the crown approved a position of chief guard (*guardamayor*) for all ports, to be chosen by the treasury officials and to select his own assistants. In St. Augustine he was paid a respectable salary of 250 ducats. The royal officials soon objected that the governor appointed all the guards and was thus able to unload ships by night or however he pleased without paying taxes; the customs constable was no more than his servant and secretary. In response to their letter the officials were assigned patronage of the constable's post as well. Within ten years they too were letting him serve by proxy.[11]

It was a temptation to double up on offices and hire out the lesser one. In the early 1670s a Valencian named Juan de Pueyo came to St. Augustine and began to work his way up in the counting house, beginning as the clerk of the half-annate. According to the treasury officials, since counting house salaries were low they also gave him the post of constable, which carried its own assistant in the chief guard of the customs house. Pueyo knew the importance of family. He was promoted to chief clerk around the time his wife's sister married the accountant's son. As chief clerk of the counting house Pueyo supervised the assistant clerk, and as customs constable, the guards. By 1702 the Valencian, serving as interim accountant, stood at the governor's left hand during the Acclamation of Philip V as one of the provinces' first ministers. For someone who had started as an under-bookkeeper he had come a long way.[12]

As early as 1549 the offices of factor and overseer had begun to be combined in the Indies. Two years before St. Augustine was founded the crown determined that the smaller treasuries did not need the factor-overseer either, and that that official's duties could be divided between the accountant and the treasurer. A factor-overseer was named for Florida nevertheless, because Spanish occupation there began as an expedition of conquest: a factor was needed to guard the king's property, and an overseer to claim the royal share of booty and to supervise trade. The adelantado expected Florida to become an important, populous colony with port cities, which would need a manager of commerce.[13] Although the St. Augustine treasury turned out to be a small treasury indeed, it kept a factor-overseer for over sixty years. He was the business manager who received the royal revenues paid in kind and converted them to cash or usable supplies at auction, whether they were tithes of maize and cattle, the king's share of confiscated goods, tributes, or the slaves of an estate undergoing liquidation. Whatever was to be auctioned was cried about town for several days, for it was illegal for the treasury to conduct a sale without giving everyone a fair chance to buy. Cash was preferred, but the auctioneer sometimes accepted a signed note against unpaid wages.[14]

It was the factor in a presidio, as in an armada, who was accountable for the storage and distribution of the king's expendable properties: supplies, provisions, trade goods, and confiscated merchandise. For these duties he had an assistant called the steward of provisions and munitions (*tenedor de bastimientos y municiones*). The first steward for the enterprise of Florida, it happened, was appointed ahead of the first factor. Pedro Menéndez named his friend Juan de Junco to the position while they were still in Spain. In 1578 Juan's brother Rodrigo became factor-overseer and technically Juan's superior. Rodrigo suggested that stewards were needed at both St. Augustine and Santa Elena, and the crown agreed to consider it.[15]

The other officials saw the need of two stewards, but not of their colleague Rodrigo. Treasurer Juan de Cevadilla, shortly after he arrived, said that in the beginning a treasurer had been in charge of the armada provisions and supplies, assisted by a steward, who was paid 50 ducats a year above his plaza. If the same were done in Florida the factor's position could be abridged. Accountant Bartolomé de Argüelles tried to speed the cutback by saying that it looked as if Factor Rodrigo de Junco had nothing to do. The office of factor was meant for places with mines, he said. The work of an overseer—looking after musters, purchases, and fortifications—was done by the accountant in Havana, and Argüelles thought he could handle it in St. Augustine.[16] The Council might have been more impressed with his offer had he not gotten the duties of factor and overseer reversed.

In 1586 permission arrived for an extra 50,000 maravedís a year with which to pay two stewards. It was better to have persons with rewards and regular salaries in positions of responsibility, the authorizing official noted; a plain soldier could not raise bond, and losses would result.[17] Juan de Cevadilla, by now Rodrigo de Junco's son-in-law, had a brother Gil who became the second steward. This convenient arrangement lasted until Cevadilla died in New Spain in 1591. Junco was promoted to governor but, on his way to St. Augustine from Spain, was shipwrecked and drowned in the St. Johns estuary along with Treasurer-elect Juan de Posada. The king's choice for a new factor never made the trip to Florida. For the time being, Accountant Argüelles was the only royal official. With Santa Elena permanently abandoned there was need of only one steward. Argüelles persuaded the incoming governor to remove both Gil and Juan and install Gaspar Fernández de Perete instead, on the full 50,000 maravedís salary.[18]

The accountant's 1591 instructions to the new steward show the care with which royal supplies and provisions were supposed to be guarded.[19] Fernández de Perete must not open the arsenal save in the presence of the rations and munitions notary, a constable, and the governor. To guarantee this, it had three padlocks. He must keep the weapons, matchcord, gunpowder, and lead safe from fire. (There was little he could do about lightning. In 1592 a bolt struck the powder magazine and blew up 3,785 ducats' worth of munitions.) The steward must protect the provisions against theft and spoilage, storing the barrels of flour off the ground and away from the leaks in the roof; keeping the earthenware jars of oil, lard, and vinegar also off the ground and not touching each other, in a place where they would not get broken; examining the wine casks for leakage twice a day and tapping them occasionally to see whether the contents were turning to vinegar in the hot wooden buildings.[20] It was the steward's responsibility to keep a book with the values by category of everything kept in the warehouses, from ships' canvas to buttons. Once a year the royal officials would check this book against the items in inventory. Anything missing would be charged to the steward's account. On the first of every month they and the governor would make a quality inspection, in which anything found damaged due to the steward's negligence was weighed, thrown into the sea, and charged to him.[21]

Argüelles' opportunity to supervise the steward did not last. A new factor-overseer, Alonso de las Alas, quickly established his authority over the steward's position, which he had once held. When Las Alas' suspension was engineered a few years later, the governor replaced both him and the steward with Juan López de Avilés, a veteran of the Menéndez armada.[22] The harried interim official complained that of all the officials he was the busiest and most exposed to risk, answering for the laborers' wages, the royal ships, and the slaves, besides the rations and supplies.[23] After Factor Las Alas was reinstated and recovered control of the warehouses, he used them for storage of his own goods (flour, hardtack, wine, meat, salt, blankets), and, through a false door, the king's property found its way into his house. It was said that 100,000 pounds of flour went out through that door to be baked into bread and sold in one of the shops he and the treasurer owned in town—shops they secretly supplied with unregistered merchandise. Governor Fernández de Olivera suspended them both. His interim appointees to the treasury found Las Alas short 125 pipes of flour, 5,540 pints of wine, 1,285 pints of vinegar, and 94 jugs of oil—and this was only in the provisions.[24] On his way to defend himself before the Council, Las Alas was wounded by a pirate musketball and died owing the crown 5,400 ducats. Hoffman and Lyon, following his story, were surprised to discover three subsequent cédulas praising Las Alas' integrity and services during an attempted colonization of the Straits of Magellan to forestall Drake. An heir of the twice-suspended factor was granted 200,000 maravedís, the salary which had accumulated after Las Alas' death while his post was vacant.[25]

Although the king filled the factorship once more (or honored a commitment) with Juan de Cueva, this time was recognized to be the last. Governor Salinas suggested in 1620 that an accountant and a steward were all Florida really needed. The Council, considering his letter four years later, recommended that the royal will be to suppress the office of factor-overseer in Florida and combine the positions of treasurer and steward. A certain delay in implementing this will would be unavoidable, treasury offices being lifetime appointments, but Florida officials might be given first consideration for vacancies elsewhere. In 1624 Francisco Ramírez, the accountant, was offered a transfer to the treasury soon to be established at the mines of San Luis Potosí in New Spain; Factor Juan de Cueva was to become Florida accountant in his place. Ramírez declined to move. In 1628, the year Francisco Menéndez Marquez won his case to be recognized as Florida treasurer, Cueva began serving as accountant in place of Ramírez, who was semiretired. He may have continued his stewardship duties as well, but not with his old title of factor-overseer. After the king's new appointee arrived in 1631, Cueva left for San Luis himself, to be that treasury's accountant.[26]

The treasurer's individual functions were those of a cashier. He received the royal revenues paid in specie and disbursed the sums that he, the other officials, and the governor had approved. The coffer was his particular responsibility; he lived in the building where it was kept. Because little money got to Florida the duties of this office were light. The gossipy Accountant Argüelles said that once the yearly payroll had been met the treasurer had nothing to do.[27] Perhaps this was why in 1628, the year the factorship was suppressed, the duties of steward were given to the treasurer and the position treasurer-steward was created.[28] In vain Accountant Nicolás Ponce de León warned the king that letting Treasurer Francisco Menéndez Marquez have access to the supplies as well as the money would make him more powerful than the accountant and the governor together.[29] In 1754, after three sons and a grandson of Francisco had served their own proprietorships in the treasury, a Bourbon king took the further step of suppressing the accountancy and reducing the number of officials to one, the treasurer.[30] But that is outside the scope of this study.

Every day except Sundays and feast days the royal officials went to the work of the day directly after meeting at morning mass.[31] It might be the day for an auction, or for the monthly inspection of munitions and supplies. When a pilot came in from coastal patrol his declaration of salvage and barter had to be taken and his equipment and supplies checked in. A deputy governor in from the provinces would present his report of taxes collected, or a new census of tributaries. The masters of supply ships brought in their receipts and vouchers to find out what balance they owed to the treasury. If the ship had brought a situado, the time required would be magnified several times.

Once a week the treasury officials held a formal treasury council (*acuerdo de hacienda*) attended by the public and governmental notary (*escribano público y de gobernación*). Without this notary's presence there could be no legal gathering for government business, no public pronouncement, and no official action or message. Any letter not in his script was considered a rough draft; his signature verified a legal copy. The public and governmental notary was paid a plaza plus salary, which began at 100 ducats a year but around 1631 was reduced to 400 reales. Since no money or supplies passed through his hands he did not furnish bond.[32] Although in his public office a notary was supposed to be impartial and incorruptible, it was hard for him to oppose the governor, who had appointed him, could remove him, and might fine him besides.[33] Captain Hernando de Mestas, in a letter smuggled out of prison, said that the notary was his enemy and had refused him his office. "The former notary would not do what he was told," said Mestas, "so they took the office from him and gave it to the present one who does what they tell him, and he has a house and slaves, while I am poor."[34] In an effort to get the notaryship out of the governor's power, the royal officials suggested to the crown that the position be put up for public auction. The idea was quickly taken up, but the new system probably changed little. In a town both inbred and illiterate, notaries were not easy to find. When Alonso de Solana was suspended from that office by the king's command, and again when he died, the highest bid to replace him (and the one the royal officials accepted) was that of his son.[35] For these reasons of autocracy, patronage, and inbreeding, little reliance can be placed upon local testimony about a controversial topic. As the bishop of Tricale, visiting St. Augustine in the eighteenth century, explained: "Here there is a great facility to swear to whatever is wanted."[36]

At their treasury council the royal officials checked the contents of the treasure chest against the book of the coffer. Whatever had been collected since the last time the chest was open was produced; they all signed the receipt and saw the money deposited in the coffer and entered into the book of the coffer kept inside it. It was not unheard of for an official to keep out part of the royal revenues, so that they never entered the record at all. As long as the chest was open, those vecinos using it as a safe might drop by to make a deposit or to check on the contents of their own small locked cases, for the treasure chest was the nearest thing to a bank vault in town.

The treasury officials were not supposed to borrow the king's money or lend it to their friends, but from the number of deficits found by auditors, they must have done so regularly. When detected, they had to replace the money within three days or face suspension.[37] The treasury was not the only source of credit. Soldiers pledged their wages to provide bond for an officeholder or situador. Shipowners sold their vessels to the presidio on time. To ration the garrison Governor Hita Salazar borrowed produce stored up for sale by the Franciscans.[38] Even Indians operated on the deferred payment plan. The Christians of San Pedro sold cargoes of maize to the garrison on credit and so did the heathen on the far side of Apalache. The Guale women who peddled foodstuffs and tobacco required a pledge of clothing from Spanish soldiers, and it was complained that they returned the garments in bad condition.[39]

After the examination of the coffer the royal officials went on to important deliberations. Dispatches from the crown addressed to "my royal officials" were opened by all of them together. Their replies, limited to one subject per letter, were signed collegially except when one official in disagreement with the others wrote on his own. The notary wrote up a resumé of actions taken, which each official signed. If there had been disagreement each one signed after his own opinion (*parecer*), but the vote of the majority carried. The minutes of the meeting, in the book of resolutions (*libro de acuerdos*), had the force of a judicial action.[40]

The governor was entitled to attend the treasury council and vote in it, but not to put a lock of his own on the coffer. The royal officials considered it a hazard to the treasury for the governor to hold a key to it, and the crown agreed. No one should have access to the king's money, plate, and jewels without corresponding responsibility for them. Governors in Florida were forbidden to put a lock on the royal coffer by a 1579 restraining order that was repeated after further complaints in 1591 and 1634.[41] The governor's vote, although not decisive, had inordinate weight on the council, especially after the number of officials was reduced from three to two. The treasury officials were aware of what this meant. In 1646 they wrote:

> The governor who advised Your Majesty on this could have had no other motive than less opposition to his moneymaking, because three, Sire, are not as easy to trample on as just two; and besides, if one of them combines with the governor what can the other poor fellow do, in a place where a governor can do whatever he likes?[42]

The governor was most definite about this right when it was time to commission someone to collect the situado. Once a year the treasury council met to decide on the year's situador and what he should bring back from Mexico City, Vera Cruz, and Havana. Together they wrote out his instructions, signed his powers of attorney, and accepted his 2,000-ducat bond. Since it was not feasible for the agent to contact them after he left, they must choose someone of independent judgment and wide experience—one of themselves, thought the royal officials. It did not deter them to remember that a proprietor on per diem drew higher wages than the governor. Marques Cabrera, who was suspicious about most of what royal officials did, pointed out that the situador was supposed to answer to them and they could not fairly judge themselves. A governor usually proposed someone from his household. Nevertheless, of the twenty-one royally appointed officials from 1565 to 1702, seventeen are known to have been situador at least once, and many went several times.[43]

Another important commissioned agent was the *procurador,* or advocate, who represented the presidio on trips to Spain. As his primary duty was to bring back soldiers and military supplies, the procurador was usually either an officer with a patent from the crown or someone from the governor's house who had been appointed an officer ad interim. When he had time the procurador conducted business of his own, and for many this was their main object. The colony was allowed two ships-of-permission per year. Pelts worth 2,000 or (after Governor Salinas requested an increase) 3,000 ducats could be taken to Spain and cargoes brought back for resale, if anyone wanted to bother. Procurador Juan de Ayala y Escobar, whose career has been studied by Gillaspie, found the Spanish trade worth his while. His instinct for scenting profit in war and famine was something the crown overlooked in return for his keeping St. Augustine supplied.[44]

At the weekly treasury council, bills were presented. The treasury officials examined the authorization for each purchase, along with the affidavit verifying the price as normal, the bill of lading, and the factor's or steward's receipt for goods delivered. If everything was in order the bill was entered into the book of *libranzas* (drafts), which was a sort of accounts payable. Each entry carried full details of date, vendor, items, quantity, price, and delivery, as well as the signed certifications of the royal officials and the governor. Such entries had great juridical value. A libranza, which was acceptable legal tender, was no more than the notarized copy of an entry. Sánchez-Bella maintains that the libranzas, or drafts on the royal treasury, were the primary cause of friction between governors and royal officials in the Indies.[45] The governor of Florida had been ordered to make withdrawals in conjunction with the officials of the treasury, but many executives found this too restricting. When Governor Méndez de Canzo ordered payments against the officials' advice he did not want their objections recorded; Governor Treviño Guillamas told them flatly that it was his business to distribute the situado, not theirs; Governor Horruytiner presented them with drafts made out for them to sign.[46] The officials were not as helpless as they liked to sound. The governor endorsed the libranzas, but they had the keys to the coffer.[47]

Governors tried several methods of managing the royal officials. One was by appointment and control of their notary. Another was interference with the mails. Francisco de la Rocha and Salvador de Cigarroa complained that few of the cédulas they were supposed to index ever reached them. Another set of officials, going through the desk of Governor Martínez de Avendaño after his death, found many of their letters to the crown, unsent. Interim Governor Gutierre de Miranda stopped the passage of all mail, confiscating one packet smuggled aboard a dispatch boat in a jar of salt.[48] Other governors operated by the threat of fines. If Argüelles did not finish a report on the slaves and the castillo within six days—500 ducats; if Sánchez Sáez did not remain on duty at the customs house—500 ducats; if Cuevas, Menéndez Marquez, and Ramírez did not sign the libranza to pay the governor's nephew ahead of everyone else—500 ducats each, and 200 ducats from the notary.[49] A truly intransigent official could be suspended or imprisoned in his house—a punishment that carried little onus. Governor Ybarra confined Sánchez Sáez three times. Governors Fernández de Olivera and Torres y Ayala both arrived in St. Augustine to find the officials of the treasury all under arrest.[50]

While the governor could attend an ordinary treasury council and exercise a vote equal to a royal official's, he could also summon a general treasury council (*acuerdo general de hacienda*) with an agenda of his own. The crown insisted at length that there be no expense to the exchequer without prior approval, yet it was grudgingly conceded that in wartime, at a distance of 3,000 miles, emergencies could arise. At a general treasury council the governor authorized extraordinary expenditures personally and had the royal officials explain later. On the pretext that the counting house needed repairs, Governor Marques Cabrera had all treasury councils meet at his house and, using the excuse of seasonal piracy and Indian raids, spent as he pleased.[51]

Their reports could be depended on to get such a headstrong executive into trouble, but the treasury officials did not wholly rely on the slow workings of royal justice. St. Augustine had its own ways to bedevil a governor and to make him write, as Marques Cabrera did to the king: "Next to my salvation there is nothing I long for more than to have the good fortune of leaving this place to wherever God may help me—anywhere, as long as I shall find myself across the bar of this harbor!"[52]

5

The Situado

HE Florida coffer had two sources of income: locally generated
royal taxes and revenues, which will be treated in the next
chapter, and the situado, basically a transfer between treasuries.
Although the connections between principal treasuries were tenuous
and debts against one were not collectible at another, a more affluent
treasury could have charged upon it the upkeep of defense outposts
along its essential trade routes. The shifting fortunes of the West
Indies can be traced in the various treasuries' obligations. At first the
House of Trade and Santo Domingo did most of the defense spending; then it was the ports of the circum-Caribbean. By the 1590s the
viceregal capitals and presidencies had assumed the burden: Lima
provided the situado for Chile; Cartagena, the subsidies of Santa
Marta and Rio de la Hacha; Mexico City, those for the rest of the
Caribbean.[1]

In Pedro Menéndez's contract with the king (as rewritten following news of a French settlement in Florida) the adelantado was
promised certain trade concessions, the wages for 300 soldiers, and
15,000 ducats. This was the first stage of the Florida subsidy, lasting
three years. When the contract was renewed, along with its trading
privileges, only 150 men were provided for, and their wages were to
be taken from Menéndez's new armada's subsidy, which was funded
equally by the Tierra Firme and New Spain treasuries. In 1570 the
Florida subsidy was separated from that of the Indies Fleet, though
Florida support remained a charge on Tierra Firme, along with a new

subsidy for Havana.[2] When the Tierra Firme treasury was divided in 1573 into one at Nombre de Dios and one at Panamá, Philip II moved responsibility for Florida's subsidy to the New Spain coffer of Vera Cruz, which had financed the luckless Tristán de Luna expedition to the Pensacola area in 1559. In 1592 the obligation was transferred to the royal treasury in Mexico City, where it remained for the rest of the Habsburg period.[3]

The situado was not a single subsidy but a cluster of them, mostly based on the number of authorized plazas in the garrison. The 23,436-ducat total that the officials of Tierra Firme were told to supply yearly beginning in 1571 consisted of 18,336 ducats to ration 150 men and 1,800 ducats to pay them (at the rate of 1 ducat a month as in the fleet of Menéndez), 1,800 ducats for powder and ammunition, and 1,500 ducats for "troop commodities."[4] When Pedro Menéndez Marquez went to Florida with reinforcements to restore a fort at Santa Elena, the crown doubled the size of the garrison but increased the subsidy by only four million maravedís, or 10,668 ducats. This was corrected in 1579 when the situado was raised to 47,770 ducats. Soon afterward, the crown accepted the new royal officials' plan for collecting the situado themselves, by turn, and administering the supplies.[5]

The total did not change substantially for the next ninety years. An inflationary rise in the cost of provisions was absorbed by the soldiers, whose plazas were converted to a flat 1,000 maravedís per month (115 ducats a year) to cover both rations and wages. In an effort to economize, and at the recommendation of Governor Méndez de Canzo, the crown attempted to return the garrison size to 150 men; it succeeded only in making his successor, Governor Ybarra, unpopular.[6] Active strength was diminished more gradually and effectively by increasing the number of "useless persons" (*inútiles*) holding the plazas of soldiers. Perhaps most of these were friars. In 1646 a ceiling was set of 43 Franciscans to be paid out of the subsidy and the additional ones became supernumerary, covered by a separate situado for friars which their lay treasurer, or syndic, was permitted to collect directly. Later in the seventeenth century the same threat from the north that stimulated the construction of Castillo de San Marcos brought an increase in the size of the garrison. Fifty plazas were added in 1669, and in 1673 the 43 friars became supernumerary along with their colleagues. This gave the presidio an authorized strength of 350 soldiers, which in 1687 the crown increased to 355.[7] The situado was not equivalently raised by 55 plazas of 115 ducats. Its yearly total in 1701 was only some 70,000 pesos, or about 51,000 ducats.[8] Within that slowly rising total the nonplaza subsidies had varied considerably since 1571. New funds had been created, while old ones had been reduced in amount, changed in purpose, or eliminated.

A governor appointed to Florida usually left Spain on a presidio frigate loaded with troops for the garrison and also with armor, gunpowder, and ammunition. The money for these essential military supplies was sometimes advanced by order of the crown from one of the funds at the House of Trade, the amount being deducted from the next situado by a coffer transfer. In wartime, a presidio-appointed procurador made extra trips to Spain for matériel. The funds for these large, irregularly spaced expenditures accumulated in a munitions reserve.

The 1,500 ducats for "troop commodities" was a bonus (*ventajas*) fund used for increasing the base pay of officers and of soldiers on special assignment, such as working in the counting house or singing in the choir. It doubled with the size of the garrison in the 1570s, but after the temporary reduction during the governorship of Ybarra the second 1,500 ducats was not restored. Periodically the crown asked for a list of bonus recipients, and any change was supposed to receive its approval.[9] In time, bonuses were used like plazas, to reward or to pension petitioners. As was to be expected, the crown was more generous in allocation than in fulfillment, and recipients waited years for "first vacancies" and futuras of bonuses in Florida, as grantees waited elsewhere in the Indies for encomienda revenues.[10] Toward the end of the seventeenth century the bonus fund was liquidated. As the holders of bonuses transferred or died, their portions were applied toward officers' salaries in the third infantry company, formed in 1687.[11]

In 1577 a new fund was added to the situado when Governor Menéndez Marquez and the treasury officials were given permission to collect half their salaries out of it. The governor's half-salary was 1,000 ducats. When there were three proprietary officials in the treasury, each one getting 200,000 maravedís (533 ducats) in cash, the figure for administrative salaries came to 2,600 ducats a year. Menéndez Marquez soon got permission to draw his entire salary from the situado—for a limited period, he was cautioned; but the privilege was extended to succeeding governors, raising the budget for salaries by 1,000 ducats. This was reduced by one royal official's half-salary when the position of factor-overseer was suppressed. Only when an auditor was residing in St. Augustine did the salaries fund rise above 3,067 ducats.[12]

In 1593 the crown authorized an unspecified fund for making gifts to Indians: the *gasto de indios*. Perhaps it was meant to take the place of the allowance for munitions, for Philip II was serious about his pacification policy. Those on the scene never achieved unanimity over whether to accomplish the conquest by kindness or by force. The friars once asserted that the cost of everything given to the natives up to their time, 1612, would not have bought the matchcord to make war on them. Anyway, since they moved about like deer, without property, there was no way to defeat them. Juan Menéndez Marquez, an old Indian fighter, had a contrary view. He observed that since the time of his cousin not one governor had extended a conquest or made a discovery: all had gone about gratifying the Indians at the expense of His Majesty. This was not totally true, but it should not have been surprising. It must have been more pleasant to sail up the Inland Waterway, as Governor Ybarra did in 1604, distributing blankets, felt hats, mirrors, beads, and knives, than to burn houses and trample crops.[13]

In 1615 the Indian allowance was set at 1,500 ducats, but little effort was made to stay within it. Governor Rojas y Borja made 3,400 ducats' worth of gifts in a single year to the Indians, who called it tribute. Governor Salazar Vallecilla and the royal officials who substituted for him distributed an average of 3,896 ducats' worth, and in one year, 6,744.[14] Unquestionably, part of this was used for trade, but when the Indian allowance was reduced or withheld, the chiefs attached to the Spanish by that means became surly. Eventually, the fund was used for purposes far from its original intention. Two hundred ducats and two rations of flour were assigned in 1698 from the "chiefs' fund" to the organist of the parish church and two altar boys respectively.[15]

The base figure of the situado was not necessarily the amount of money supplied. Superimposed upon it were the yearly variations. Occasionally funds were allocated for some special purpose: 26,000 pesos to rebuild the town after the 1702 siege of Colonel James

Moore; a full year's situado to replace the one stolen by Piet Heyn, and one lost in a shipwreck; 1,600 pesos to pay the Charles Town planters for runaway slaves the king wished to free.[16] Additional money was sometimes sent for fortifications: commonly 10,000 ducats or pesos, delivered in installments.[17] It was characteristic of these special grants that they were seldom used for the intended purpose. A greater emergency would intervene; the governor and royal officials would divert the fund to that, explain their reasons, and demand replacement.[18] When it was possible the crown obliged.

In the sixteenth century the officials of the supporting treasury were supposed to ask for a muster of the garrison and deduct the amount for vacant plazas from the situado. During the seventeenth century it was more common to use the surplus (*sobras*) from inactive plazas as a separate fund.[19] In 1600, encouraged by the presence of a royal auditor, the officials volunteered that funds were accumulating in the treasury from the reserve for munitions, the freight on presidio vessels, and royal office vacancies. The surplus amounted to around 60,000 pesos by 1602—almost a whole year's situado. They suggested that as it was difficult to find the revenues locally to cover the unpaid half of their salaries, they could draw on these reserves.[20] The king's financial advisors, greatly interested, told the officials of the Mexico City treasury to send the next Florida situado to Spain and to reduce future situados to reflect effective rather than authorized strength. From the Florida royal officials they asked an accounting of all unused monies to date. Much later, other officials received permission to collect the rest of their salaries from reserves, but the reserves no longer existed.[21]

The crown had its own opinions on likely surpluses and what to do with them. The soldiers evacuated from Santa Elena in 1587 were reimbursed for their lost property by 1,391 ducats from the surpluses of the situado. In 1655, the year the English took Jamaica, the treasury officials were ordered to use the unpaid wages of deserters and the deceased to improve the presidio's defenses. Accountant Santos de las Heras objected that deserters forfeited their wages, the back wages of the deceased without heirs went to purchase masses for their souls, and, with situados three years behind, nobody was being paid anyway. The king's advisors replied that the accountant was to pay the living first and let the dead wait. Twenty years later a royal order arrived to use the unclaimed wages of deserters and deceased to provide plazas to crippled noncombatants.[22] Not long afterward the royal officials were told to report on the funds from vacant plazas. It was the governor's prerogative to allocate the surplus, not theirs, the crown pointed out—a moot point, since a separate cédula of the same date instructed the governor to use the money on the castillo. At the end of the Habsburg period the viceroy of New Spain was instructed to send the surplus of the 1694 subsidy to Spain. It amounted to a third of the sum earmarked for plazas.[23]

There were many problems with the situado, part due to unavoidable shortages and part to venality and graft. From the beginning there was a scarcity of currency. Both the Vera Cruz and the Mexico City officials were instructed to deliver the situado to its commissioned collectors in reales, since that was the coin in which to pay soldiers. Yet in spite of repeated injunctions to pay in coined reales (*reales acuñados*) the officials preferred to keep their specie at home. Instead they supplied silver in crudely shaped and stamped chunks called *planchas* or even in assayed ingots (*plata ensayada*) which the soldiers chopped into pieces. In 1601 Accountant Juan Menéndez Marquez acting as situador could collect only 37 percent of the total in coin.[24]

Throughout the Habsburg period hard specie continued to be scarce in the provinces. In 1655 Auditor Santa Cruz estimated that in twenty years not 20,000 pesos in currency had entered the presidio. In place of money the creoles used such expediencies as yards of cloth or fractions of an ounce of amber.[25] Wages were paid either in imported goods at high prices, in obsolete or inappropriate things the governor wanted to be rid of, or in libranzas or wage certificates that declined drastically in value and were bought up by speculators with inside knowledge.[26] Although two resourceful Apalaches were caught passing homemade coins of tin, Indians ordinarily used no money, but bartered in beads, blankets, weapons, twists of tobacco, baskets, horses and other livestock, chickens, pelts and skins, and cloth. Great piles of belongings were gambled by the players and spectators at the native ball games. The Spanish governors begged for some kind of specie to be sent for small transactions and suggested 7,000 or 8,000 ducats in coins of silver and copper alloy (*vellón*) to circulate in the Florida provinces. Where there was no money, they explained, people were put to inconvenience.[27]

The quality of silver was another problem. In 1612 the Florida officials sent over 1,000 reales' worth of miscellaneous pieces to the House of Trade for the receptor of the Council to buy them presidio weapons. The silver from Florida turned out to be of such low fineness that no one would accept it at more than 43 reales the mark. The crown demanded to be told the source of such degraded bullion and specie. In reply, the royal officials admitted that part of the consignment was in adulterated silver and clipped coins, but they had sent it as it had been received in fines, which the crown, in order to retire what was debased, allowed to be paid in any silver bearing the royal mark. They protested, however, that most of the offending silver had come from New Spain and could not be used in Florida, where the soldiers were supposed to be paid in reales. Certainly the base alloy had not been added to the silver while it was at their treasury.[28]

Over the seventeenth century the viceroy and royal officials of the Mexico City treasury allowed the situados to fall seriously behind. By 1642 the drafts against unpaid situados amounted to 250,000 pesos, four times the yearly subsidy. Four years later the situador was forced to ask for a cédula ordering the Mexico City officials to turn over the current situado to him instead of to Florida's creditors. In 1666 the situados were seven years behind, or some 461,000 pesos. In 1703 they were again 457,000 pesos in arrears.[29] Although something was applied to these arrearages from time to time, the case seemed hopeless to the unpaid soldiers and to the local men and women who made their shoes and did their laundry. The crown set guidelines for paying back salaries in a fair manner, then circumvented its own instructions by giving out personal cédulas for some individuals to collect their wages ahead of the rest.[30] The officials at St. Augustine treated payments toward back situados as a totally fresh and unexpected revenue. They inquired in writing whether such money might not be used to build a stone fort or to found Spanish towns.[31]

The practice of letting some subsidies fall into arrears created new expenses to consume the other ones. Some of these expenses were for servicing the presidio's loans. A loan was taken out at the Mexico City treasury as early as 1595. Governor Salinas, in an effort to consolidate the treasury's debts, asked in 1621 for another loan of 30,000 or 40,000 pesos to be paid off in installments of 2,000 pesos from every situado. The crown was unhelpful about retiring this debt. A representative of the Council, making a grant of 150 ducats in

1627 to Florida's sergeant major, observed that the money was to come from the situado surpluses as soon as there were any, "which will not be for many years because it is so far in debt now."[32] In 1637 Governor Horruytiner inquired about yet another loan to pay the soldiers, who had had no wages in six or seven years.[33] The Franciscans, dependent like the garrison on the situado, did their borrowing separately. In 1638 they were given permission to take out a travel loan from a fund at the House of Trade. Twenty years later they took out another, and in 1678 they were again forced to borrow, probably against their subsidy, paying 8 percent on a loan for 3,567 pesos.[34] When the cost of credit was built into a bill of exchange to circumvent usury restrictions, the price could be steep. The spice merchants (*mercaderes en drogas*) who exchanged the notes against unpaid situados discounted them 18 to 75 percent. Soldiers trying to spend their certificates for back wages were obliged to pay higher prices and accept inferior goods.[35]

Collection charges were nothing new. In 1580, when the subsidy came in care of the governor of Cuba, he kept out 530 ducats for himself, and the collectors charged an exorbitant 1,000 ducats. In the new system initiated by the proprietors who took office that year, one of them went for the situado, receiving an expense allowance of 1,000 maravedís (rounded to 30 reales) a day, double the per diem for a procurador or envoy to Spain. In the six or seven months that a situado trip was supposed to last, the per diem came to 500 or 600 ducats. The largest collection expense was probably for the bribes in the viceregal capital. Accountant-Situador Santos de las Heras said ruefully that to get anything accomplished there cost "a good pair of gloves."[36]

Transportation costs varied according to whether the ships were chartered or presidio-owned. In 1577 it cost 2,000 ducats to bring a year's worth of supplies from New Spain in two hired frigates; the governor said that owning the ships would have saved three-fourths of it. Yet in 1600, Juan Menéndez Marquez as situador had to charter three boats in San Juan de Ulúa and a fourth in Havana.[37]

Auditor Santa Cruz, who wanted the Florida situado to pass through his hands, declared that the governor of Florida once had seven different situadores in Mexico City simultaneously, suing one another over who was to make which collections and receiving 30, 40, or 50 reales a day apiece while their boat and crew expenses mounted in Vera Cruz. A single trip cost the treasury nearly 30,000 pesos, he said, out of a subsidy of 65,000. Ten years later the auditor added that the bribes at the Mexico City treasury came to 20,000 pesos, of which 18,000 went to the greater officials and 2,000 to the lesser. Any situador could make a profit of 26,000 pesos, Santa Cruz insisted, by borrowing money to buy up Florida wage certificates and libranzas at a third to a half of their face value, then redeeming them at face value with situado funds. The rest of the money he could invest in clothing to be resold to the soldiers at high prices.[38] Parish priest Leturiondo's accusations were vehement on a smaller and perhaps more accurate scale. The situador discounted 15 or 16 percent collection expenses from the priest's small stipend, he said, and took up to two years to deliver the items ordered.[39]

Partly because of the shortage of currency and the inadequate harbor—but also because Florida's east coast had little to export, once the sassafras boom ended—St. Augustine was not a regular port of call. This meant that whoever was chosen collector of the situado must double as garrison purchasing agent. Wine and flour produced in New Spain and sold in Havana cost over twice as much there, in 1577, as the same provisions in Spain. Governor Menéndez Marquez found it necessary to exchange situado silver for gold at a loss and send it to Spain by a light, fast frigate, to buy meat and olive oil. In 1580 the presidio obtained permission to send two frigates a year to the mother country or the Canaries, but as prices and taxes rose there, flour and other foodstuffs had to be found increasingly in the colonies.[40]

The rare accounts written by situadores en route describe the difficulties of collection, purchasing, and transportation from their point of view. After giving bond and receiving his instructions and power of attorney, the situador was issued a boat and crew. He left them in the harbor of San Juan de Ulúa and journeyed up the road past Puebla de los Angeles to Mexico City. There he paid the appropriate bribes and waited for his report on presidio strength to be checked, his supply ship's tonnage approved, and the situado delivered. All of this took time. The situador executed private commissions, saw friends, and enjoyed a taste of big-city life. Perhaps he put a portion of the king's money out at interest or made other imaginative use of it. By the early seventeenth century, household items, coarse fabrics, and Indian trade goods were available at the workhouses of

Mexico City and Puebla. In Vera Cruz there was flour of questionable quality. The paperwork for this large-scale shopping took more time, for local fiscal judges had to supply affidavits that Florida was not being charged an inflated price. Loading at San Juan de Ulúa proceeded relatively undisturbed by port authorities: presidio supplies were exempt by royal order from either sales tax or customs. With his ship loaded, the situador waited with his counterparts from other Caribbean presidios for a warship to escort them and carry their registered money as far as Havana.[41] Floridians preferred to avoid this stop if they could, for creditors lay in wait at the Havana harbor, and Cuban officials acting in the best interests of their island would attempt to attach part or all of the situado. The crown, which had interests of its own, might have sent them instructions to impound the situado for use in Spain.

With creditors and crown outfoxed, the situador might still face a long wait until the coast guard reported the seaways clear of corsairs and the fleet was ready to sail northward through the Bahama Channel. There is no telling how much of the Florida situado in both supplies and specie was lost en route.[42] Buccaneers grew so bold in the late seventeenth century that they sometimes waited at anchor outside the St. Augustine harbor. To elude the enemy, Floridians crossed their bar at low tide; or they sailed in September and October under great danger of storms. The likelihood of disaster was compounded by defective ships. The *Nuestra Señora del Rosario* capsized in the very harbor of San Juan de Ulúa with 3,000 pesos' worth of supplies aboard. Another vessel, apparently being bought on time, was lost off Key Largo and the crown strongly advised that payment be stopped on it.[43] A lost subsidy might be ordered replaced, but the sum could only be added to the arrears the Mexico City treasury already owed to the presidio.

Safely unloaded in St. Augustine, the situador faced a personal obstacle: the rendering of his accounts. The royal officials checked his purchase invoices against goods delivered, comparing prices with affidavits; they examined his expense receipts and counted the money he turned over. The total of invoices, receipts, and cash must equal the amount of situado in his notarized papers of transmittal. For any shortage he was personally liable. The closing of a situador's accounts might be delayed years waiting for all papers to arrive and be in order.

When the situador was expected, the officials went into action.

The public and governmental notary presented an up-to-date muster; the master of construction turned in the number of days' labor owed to soldiers. From these and his own records the accountant certified the gross amount due each person on plaza. The factor or his steward (later, the treasurer-steward) supplied the total each soldier had drawn from the royal warehouse against his wages. The accountant deducted this figure, plus the compulsory contributions to service organizations and the notes presented by preferred creditors, to arrive at the net wages the treasurer should count out from the coffer. Merchant Antonio de Herrera once brought the royal officials a list of 182 men in his debt for clothing and small loans. Although Governor Salinas authorized payment via payroll deduction Herrera was exiled shortly afterward. A few years later he reappeared by special, unexplained permission of the Council, and the soldiers were soon in debt to him again. Salinas, pleading their poverty, paid him with surplus situado funds. Governor-elect Rojas y Borja, of a more accommodating temperament, before he ever left Spain advanced Herrera directly from ensign to sergeant major of the garrison—an unlikely promotion for which the loan shark must have paid handsomely.[44]

Any time a situador brought actual cash, St. Augustine became a busy place. Tables were set up in front of the guardhouse, and as the roll was called each man came by, picked up his wages, and took them to the next table under the eyes of his officers to pay his debts to local merchants, artisans, and farmers, whose order in line reflected their current favor with the administration.[45] For the next few nights, while the soldiers had money in their purses, there was exuberant gambling in the guardhouse.[46] The influx of currency threw the town into a short-lived flurry of economic activity during which St. Augustine resembled Jalapa during the fair, or opening day at the silver smeltery.

Everyone on the payroll was supposed to get food and clothing at cost, but the original price became encrusted with surcharges.[47] From time to time the crown ordered that the soldiers not be charged import or export duties, nor the cost of supplies for the situador's vessel, nor the cost of ship repairs and replacements.[48] They were not to absorb the expense of supplies spoiled or mislaid, nor the 15 or 16 percent for handling, which may or may not have included the two reales per mark (nearly 8 percent) charge for changing silver.[49]

Neither were they to have passed on to them the cost of loss and leakage, given in the form of percentages called *mermas* to the shipmaster, the steward, and presumably anyone else who transported or stored crown merchandise. According to Pilot Andrés González, the Council of the Indies allowed mermas of 3 percent on flour, 4 percent on biscuit, 4 percent on salt, and 10 percent on maize. Given the density of rat population on the ships of the time, such allowances to a shipmaster may not have been excessive. Vázquez de Espinosa estimated that more than 4,000 rats were killed aboard his ship during a transatlantic crossing in 1622, not counting those the sailors and passengers ate.[50]

If there was any substance behind the prohibitions against add-on charges—and there is no reason to think otherwise—then prices "at cost" were costly indeed. Ex-Governor Hita Salazar, who had been governor of Vera Cruz before coming to Florida and who remained in St. Augustine as a private citizen after his term, once gave his experienced view of the situado. In spite of all the funds it contained—and he listed them: the 350 plazas for soldiers, the subsidy for friars, the allotment for administrative salaries, the 1,500-ducat Indian allowance, and the 1,500 ducats for bonuses—the common soldier still paid twice what he should have for shoddy goods he did not want, bought by profiteers with his own money.[51] If private merchants could obtain no foothold in town, and no one could leave who was in debt to the exchequer, then it is no wonder that by the 1680s garrison strength in Florida was being filled with sentenced malefactors and persons regarded as racial inferiors.[52] The entire garrison below officer level was existing under the most inexorable debt peonage.

6

The Royal Revenues

HE royal revenues that treasury officials in the Indies gathered
were varied. The Mexico City coffer, from which Florida
received the situado, provides a good example. In 1598 its major
accounts receivable were, in order of descending value: tribute, taxes
on bullion, the monopoly of mercury, import and export taxes, sales
tax, the tax of the crusade, the monopoly of playing cards, and the
sale of offices. Grouped by category, the revenues of mines supplied
the largest share of that treasury's yearly income, tribute came next,
and commerce third. The impecunious crown soon exploited further
sources of revenue: the clearing of land titles, the legitimizing of
foreigner and mixed blood status, and voluntary contributions.[1]

On an infant colony such taxes were imposed lightly if at all, yet
after a reasonable length of time a normal treasury was expected to
begin producing revenue.[2] This did not happen in Florida, where all
the royal revenues put together were not enough for regular forwarding to the king. Still, the funds generated were sufficient to
cover a number of ecclesiastical and provincial expenses, to aid in
provisioning the garrison, and to occupy the royal officials' time. The
crown's incomes fell into five categories:

1. Ecclesiastical: tithes and indulgences.

2. Crown properties: lands, productive enterprises, slaves and
convicts, royal offices and monopolies.

3. Shipping: freight charges and customs duties.

4. Barter, salvage, and booty: the king's treasure taxes.

5. Personal levies: tribute and donations.

In the Indies the tithes (*diezmos*) were meticulously divided. One-quarter of the revenue went to the bishop, one-quarter to the cathedral chapter. Of the remainder, two-ninths went to the crown, four-ninths to local clerics, and three-ninths to the construction of churches and hospitals. Therefore, although the tithes were collected and administered by the treasury officials, they were of little or no profit to the crown.[3]

In theory, Indians had been legally exempt from tithing since 1533, but in practice this varied. Florida missionaries argued that even a native owed his tithes and firstfruits—to them, not to the crown or the bishop.[4] We will return to the subject of Franciscan exactions under the heading of tributes. The legitimate tithes administered by the royal officials in St. Augustine came from Spanish Christians.

To encourage production, new settlements of Spaniards in the Indies were usually free from tithing for the first ten years. While the adelantado's contract did not specify this, it probably held true for Florida.[5] The tithes first gathered were so minimal that they enjoyed a certain independence-by-neglect. At the end of the sixteenth century the royal officials mentioned that they were collecting them in kind, auctioning the produce like any other royal property and using the proceeds to pay their own salaries. As can be seen in Table 4, the tithes of 1600 amounted to 840 pesos, three-fourths of which came from sales of maize, and the remainder from miscellany (*menudos*), probably other preservable produce. If the tithes of this period were collected at the rate of 2½ percent, as they were later in the century, this suggests a titheable production worth over 33,000 pesos. Treasurer Juan Menéndez Marquez noted in 1602 that the tithes of 1600 had been auctioned immediately after harvest; the tithes of 1601 (which he did not disclose) only appeared to be higher because he and the other officials had stored the maize until its price had risen by half, then had the presidio buy it to ration slaves and soldiers.[6]

Around this time the crown ordered that the tithes go for four years toward construction of a parish church, a disposition that was gradually extended to twenty years. After that, church construction and maintenance were subsidized by 2,000 ducats from the vacancies of New Spain bishoprics, and the Florida officials were permitted to use 516 ducats of the local tithes to pay secular clergy salaries, letting the remainder accumulate. Whenever the fund reached 4,000 or 5,000 reales the crown sent instructions on how to spend it. In the early

TABLE 4
VALUE OF TITHES AND TITHEABLE PRODUCTION
(IN PESOS)

Year	Arrobas of Maize	Tithes from Maize	Misc. Tithes (Menudos)	Tithes from Livestock	Total Tithes	Titheable Production
1600	—	651	189	—	840	33,600
1631	⎫	569	166	—	735	29,400
1632	⎬ 2,691½	569	135	—	704	28,160
1633	⎭	569	167	—	736	29,440
1648	847	847	70	220	1,137	45,480
1649	881	881	146	227	1,254	50,160
1650	1,468	1,468	120	265	1,853	74,120
1651	1,469	1,469	304	250	2,023	80,920
1652	1,391	1,391	116	152	1,659	66,360
1653	1,012	1,012	130	135	1,277	51,080
1654	1,024	1,024	142	176	1,342	53,680
1655	802	802	100	224	1,126	45,040
1656	743	743	150	193	1,086	43,440
1657	1,043½	1,043½	141	171	1,355½	54,220

NOTE: Of the 2,691½ arrobas of maize from 1631 to 1633, 406½ were sold at 5½ reales and 2,285 at 5 reales. The total of 1,707½ pesos has been averaged on a yearly basis and rounded off to 569 pesos. From 1648 to 1657 the tithes of maize were bought at 1 peso the arroba.

1620s and again in 1635 the bishop of Cuba inquired about his fourth of the Florida tithes. The crown, which was making up the difference in his income, referred his query to the Florida governor and royal officials, asking them whether their provinces were not suffragan to that bishop. They replied that don Juan de las Cabezas Altamirano had brought credentials as the bishop of Florida and Cuba when he made his visitation in 1605, but he had not asked for tithes, nor had any been sent to Cuba since.[7] Orders must have followed to send the bishop his fourth, for several years later the royal officials mentioned that tithes were no longer being administered as a royal revenue.[8]

In 1634, before this happened, Accountant Nicolás Ponce de León summarized what the tithes had been amounting to. The tithes of maize collected between 1631 and 1633 had come to 2,691 ½ arrobas, or about 897 arrobas a year. Of this, 406 ½ had been sold at 5 ½ reales the arroba and the rest at 5 reales, making a three-year total of 1,707 ½ pesos in tithes of maize, which averaged to 569 pesos a year. For the tithes from miscellaneous sources the accountant gave yearly figures, which totaled 468 pesos for the same period. Total tithes averaged 725 pesos a year, indicating a titheable production of around 29,000 pesos a year between 1631 and 1633, less than in 1600.[9]

In the 1640s there were great expectations from a wheat farm started by Governor Salazar Vallecilla on the Apalache-Timucua border. There would be other farms and much revenue, he and the royal officials thought, enough to establish an abbacy in St. Augustine similar to the one in Jamaica and keep all the tithes at home. Ponderous inquiries were set in motion, without result. Governor Rebolledo, in 1655, joined the campaign. Florida tithes now amounted to 2,000 pesos annually, he said, exaggerating, and if that sum was not adequate to support an abbot, he would gladly dispense with his sergeant major. No Cuban bishop had visited Florida in fifty years.[10] The crown responded by asking for a report on the tithes of the previous ten years. Tithes of maize from 1648 to 1657 came to an average of 1,068 arrobas a year, which at 1 peso the arroba brought in 1,068 pesos. The increase in value over the average of 569 pesos a year between 1631 and 1633 was mainly due to the higher price per arroba. For the first time livestock (*ganado mayor*) appeared as a separate category. The average total tithes for the ten-year period came to 1,411 pesos. If tithes were 2 ½ percent of both crops and calves— something of which we cannot be sure—this indicated a titheable ranching and agricultural production of some 56,000 pesos a year.[11] This was evidently insufficient to support an abbot, for that idea was dropped.

When don Gabriel Díaz Vara Calderón came on episcopal visit in 1674–75, he arrived in St. Augustine four days after a flood and charitably devoted the tithes laid up for him to relieving the hungry.[12] Soon after the bishop's visit, the treasury officials were ordered to begin sending the canons of the cathedral chapter their designated fourth of the tithes and explain why this had been neglected. They protested that no one had ever asked for them, and that anyhow tithes in Florida were grossly overvalued. When the livestock was auctioned, soldiers bid four or five times what it was worth, charging the amount to the back salaries they never expected to see. In this way cattle worth less than 1,000 pesos had been sold for 4,400, giving a false impression of the provinces' resources. In order to correct this overpricing, the treasurer and accountant meant in future to purchase the tithes of livestock as they did the tithes of maize, for rationing the soldiers. They would pay the local clerics, the bishop, and the cathedral chapter in drafts against the situado. The three ecclesiastics serving the parish church and the soldiers' chapel were paid around 900 pesos a year.[13] If half of the tithes were sent to Cuba, the total revenue must come to 1,800 pesos a year in order to cover clerical salaries, necessitating an annual titheable production of somewhere near 72,000 pesos.

This level of production Florida's Spanish population was unable to maintain. In 1697 the crown inquired why the bishop was not receiving his tithes. The royal officials answered briefly that in Florida the tithe was paid in the form of grain and was distributed to the soldiers. The year 1697 had been one of famine, when even the parish priest's private store of maize had had to be requisitioned, to his great indignation. As the bishop himself said, in times of hunger all men quarreled and all had reason.[14]

The crown's other ecclesiastical revenue in Florida came from the *cruzada,* or bulls of the crusade, which Haring has called "the queerest of all taxes."[15] This was a semicompulsory indulgence whose proceeds had been granted by the popes to the Spanish crown in recognition of its crusading activities. Royal officials and other dignitaries in the Indies paid two pesos a year, regular Spanish subjects one peso, and Indians and blacks two reales.[16] The cruzada must have been permitted to go for local purposes in Florida, for the indulgences were independently requested by the royal officials, a priest, and perhaps a governor. Governor Marques Cabrera once received 5,000 of them, neatly divided between bulls for the living and for the dead.[17] A cleric known as the minister or subdelegate of the Tribunal of the Holy Crusade did the preaching, and another cleric served as the notary.[18] By the end of the seventeenth century the market was glutted. The royal officials asked that no more indulgences be sent to Florida, where the people were poor and the last two shipments were sitting unsold in the warehouse. Ignoring pressure from the parish priest and the Council of the Indies, they refused to publicize the bulls any further.[19]

The second category of treasury income was provided by crown properties. Aside from the presidio's ships, which are treated later in this chapter, crown properties producing income consisted of lands, productive enterprises, slaves and convicts, royal offices, and monopolies.

Wherever Spaniards settled in the Indies they first recognized the lands belonging to pacified Indian towns, then founded their own municipalities, each of which was provided with several square leagues for the use of its vecinos. Other grants of land were personal. Pedro Menéndez, as part of his contract with the king, was entitled to claim an immense area 25 leagues on a side—more than 5,500 square miles, by Lyon's calculation.[20] He was also privileged to give out large tracts (*caballerías*) to gentlemen and smaller ones (*peonías*) to foot soldiers. Although many of these grants were in Santa Elena, when the two presidios were combined the settlers from Santa Elena were given lands in and near St. Augustine as though they had been there from the start.[21] All of the remaining, unused lands (*tierras baldías*) in the ecumene became part of the royal demesne (*realengo*). Anyone wishing to use a portion of it for some productive purpose, such as a cattle ranch (*estancia de ganado* or *hato*), applied to the governor. If the center or the headquarters of the proposed ranch was no nearer than 3 leagues from any native village and did not encroach upon another holding, the petitioner might be issued a provisional title.[22] Possession was conditional: land lying vacant reverted to the crown.

For over a century whatever taxes were paid on these lands held in usufruct went unreported. Treasury officials later claimed that the governors had collected fifty Castilian pesos per ranch. In the 1670s Governor Hita Salazar instituted a regular quitrent along with an accelerated land grants program to raise money for the castillo. Hacienda owners were charged four reales per *yugada*, which was the area a yoke of oxen could plow in one day, with a minimum of five pesos.[23] The governor also offered to legitimize earlier land titles and make them permanent. A clear title to a ranch cost fifty pesos per *legua cuadrada*, though it is not certain whether this was a square league, a league on the side of a square, or a radial distance in a circular grant.[24] The chiefs of native towns followed suit, selling their extra fields or leasing them to Spaniards.[25]

As it was a royal prerogative to grant lands in perpetuity, the government in Madrid annulled all titles issued by chiefs or governors, at the same time inviting more regular applications. Between 1677 and 1685 land sales and title clearances (*confirmaciones*) in Florida brought in 2,500 pesos to be applied to castillo construction.[26] The crown also disallowed part of the governor's new taxation schedule. Lands granted at the foundation and still held by the heirs were not to be taxed, ever. Land distributed after then could be taxed, but at no more than Hita Salazar's 4 reales the yugada, later reduced to 1 real.[27] Disposition of the revenues from lands beyond the confines of St. Augustine was a royal prerogative as much as granting the lands was. For several years the income was assigned exclusively to castillo construction, but starting in 1688 a modest sum was allowed for the expenses of holy days.[28]

In some parts of the Indies another kind of title clearance was going on: foreigners could legitimize their presence by a payment (*composición*). Several times the crown asked the officials in St. Augustine for a list of resident foreigners, including Portuguese, but as there is no evidence that the aliens paid anything extra into the treasury, this was probably for reasons of military and antischismatic security.[29]

The crown made one brief foray into agricultural production in Florida. In 1650 Governor Salazar Vallecilla's experimental wheat farm had been in operation for five years. Six square leagues were under cultivation; buildings, granaries, and corral were complete; and the property inventory included two experienced slaves, eight horses and mules, eleven yokes of draft oxen, and the necessary plows and harrows. The governor had even sent to the Canaries for millstones and a miller. Accountant Nicolás Ponce de León thought that in New Spain such an hacienda would be worth over 20,000 pesos. Unfortunately Governor Salazar Vallecilla died in the epidemic of 1649–50. When his son Luis, anxious to leave Florida, tried to sell the wheat farm, either no one wanted it or no one could afford it. Ponce de León, as interim governor, bought the hacienda for the crown at a cost of 4,259 pesos in libranzas that he estimated to be worth one-third less. He predicted that the farm would pay for itself within three years. The fiscal of the Council of the Indies, reading of the purchase, noted that even if the hacienda took longer than that to show a profit it would be valuable if it encouraged the production of flour in Florida. The Council sent word for the royal officials to administer this royal property without intervention from governors, making yearly reports on its progress.[30]

Before word got back of the crown's approval, the hacienda had vanished. Ponce de León had survived his friend Salazar Vallecilla only a short time. Locally elected Interim Governor Pedro Benedit Horruytiner had been persuaded by the Franciscans that Spanish settlement in the provinces had provoked the Apalache rebellion of 1647. At their request he had dismantled the wheat farm and sold off its inventory without waiting for the due process of auction. Wheat continued to be grown in Apalache and Timucua, as well as rye and barley, but not for the presidio. Most of the grain was shipped out by the chiefs and friars to Havana.[31]

In 1580 the crown gave permission for the treasury officials to obtain thirty able-bodied male slaves left over from the building of a stone fort. From time to time these were replenished.[32] When there was disagreement among the officials as to which of them was to manage the slaves, they were informed that the governor should do it, while they kept track of expenses. Their complaints that the governor used the slaves for personal purposes were ignored. When the slaves were not needed on the fortifications they were hired out and their earnings paid for their rations.[33] The same policy applied to the convicts sentenced to Florida: their labor bought their food. One illiterate black convict who had become a skilled blacksmith during his term in St. Augustine elected to stay on as a respected member of the community.[34] Native malefactors were sent to some other presidio unless there was a labor shortage in Florida. Whether in Havana or St. Augustine, their sentence lengths were often forgotten and their prison service then became indistinguishable from slavery.[35]

Slaves and convicts not only saved the crown money but were themselves a source of income. The timber they logged and sawed, the stones they quarried and rafted across the harbor from Anastasia Island, the lime they burned from oyster shells, the nails and the hardware they fashioned—not all was used in the construction of the castillo and government houses. Some was sold to private persons and converted into a revenue of the crown.[36]

Royal offices were a form of property expected to produce income every time they changed hands. Treasury offices became venal for the Indies in the 1630s; other offices already being sold were ecclesiastical benefices and military patents, which at least once included the Florida captaincy general.[37] In many of its overseas realms the crown sold municipal offices as well, but not in Florida. When a royal cédula dated 1629 arrived asking for a list of the offices it might be possible to fill in that land, Accountant Juan de Cueva responded that there were no new settlements; the only town of Spaniards was the one at the presidio.[38] One office frequently sold or farmed out in the Indies was that of tribute collector (*corregidor de indios*). For reasons that will be seen, this office did not exist in Florida. The St. Augustine treasury received revenue from the auction of lesser posts such as public and governmental notary or toll collector on the Salamototo ferry, but this income was inconsequential and almost certainly never reached the crown.[39]

The half-annate (*media anata*) was a separate revenue derived from offices and other royal grants: the return to the crown of half the salary of one's first year of income. Except in the case of ecclesiastics, it superseded the earlier *mesada,* or month's pay paid by a new appointee. Presented as an emergency measure following Piet Heyn's seizure of the treasure fleet, the half-annate was decreed in 1631, empire-wide, for every beneficiary of the king's grace, from a minor receiving a plain soldier's plaza, to the royal *infantes,* the king's sons. According to the *Recopilación,* the half-annate was increased by half (making it actually a two-thirds-annate) from 1642 through 1649.[40] But Governor Luis de Horruytiner, coming to Florida in 1633, paid the two-thirds amount, not the half. It was permitted to pay the tax in two installments, signing a note at 8 percent interest for the second half, due one year later. This is what Horruytiner did.[41]

For the rather complicated bookkeeping of this tax the St. Augustine treasury was authorized to hire a clerk of the half-annate, but collection of the royal kickback did not proceed evenly. The auditor who came to Florida in 1655 found that three-fourths of those liable for the half-annate still owed on it.[42] In 1680 it was decreed that the governors of Florida were exempt from the tax because His Majesty had declared their post to be one like Chile, known for active war (*guerra viva*). Four years later the treasury officials were included under this exemption because of valor shown during a pirate attack. What half-annate those in office had already paid was refunded.[43] The tax was not reinstated for this category of officials until 1727. Regular officers, however, in spite of a 1664 law exempting those on hazard duty, continued to owe the half-annate on their original appointments and for every promotion.[44]

One more revenue from royal offices was the unpaid salary money (*vacancias*) due to the death or suspension of royal appointees. As we have seen, the vacancies of bishoprics in New Spain formed a regular fund upon which the crown drew for extraordinary expenses. The same held true for Florida, except that the money was absorbed locally the way vacant plazas were. Surplus salaries due to vacancies were sent to the crown one time only, in 1602.[45]

A final type of revenue-producing royal property was the monopoly. The king had a tendency to alienate his monopolies by giving them out as royal favors (*mercedes*). Pedro Menéndez's contract, for example, promised the adelantado two fisheries in Florida, of fish and of pearls. Since the pearl fishery did not materialize, this clause meant, in effect, that only the governor or his lieutenants had the right to fish with a drag net or a seine, and this privilege was enforced. When the dispute over the Menéndez contract came to a formal end in 1634, the family's one remaining property in Florida was this fishery.[46]

Another monopoly which produced no revenue for the crown was gambling. To the official circular extending the monopoly of playing cards in the Indies, Governor Ybarra responded that people in Florida did not use them.[47] Some years later Sergeant Major Eugenio de Espinosa was granted the right to run a gaming table in the guardhouse, a monopoly he passed on to his feckless son-in-law.[48]

Beginning in 1640, paper stamped with the royal coat-of-arms (*papel sellado*) was required for legal documents in the Indies. A governor's interim appointment, for instance, must be written up on twenty-four-real paper for the first page and one-real for each page thereafter. Ordinary notarized documents began on six-real paper. Indians and indigents were entitled to use paper costing a quarter-real, or omit the stamp altogether. Perhaps this was why St. Augustine notaries seldom bothered to keep a supply of stamped paper, although when they used the unstamped they were supposed to collect an equivalent fee.[49]

One further crown revenue from a monopoly came from the three reales per beef charged at the royal slaughterhouse. Governor Marques Cabrera instituted this fee in the 1680s to pay for construction of the slaughterhouse and raise money for the castillo. It was one of his little perquisites to be given the beef tongues.[50]

The third category of royal revenues in Florida came from shipping. In St. Augustine, founded as the result of a naval action, ships were highly important. The townspeople were descendants of seafarers, and their only contact with the outside world was by sea. The bar at the entrance to their harbor was shallow at low tide, especially after the great hurricane of 1599, which altered many coastal features. Use of the harbor was consequently restricted to vessels under 100 tons or flat-bottomed flyboats on the Flemish model.[51] Some of the galliots, frigates, barges, pirogues, launches, shallops, and tenders belonging at various times to the presidio were purchased in Spain, Vera Cruz, or Havana, but a surprising number were constructed locally, perhaps in the same San Sebastian inlet where present-day inhabitants build shrimp boats. The people of St. Augustine referred to their boats fondly by name (*Josepfe, Nuevo San Agustín*) or nickname (*la Titiritera, la Chata*). Storms, shallows, and corsairs guaranteed that no vessel would last forever, but woe to the master who by carelessness or cowardice lost one!

One source of the crown income from shipping was freight (*fletes*). Freight charges in the Caribbean were high. Gillaspie estimates that between 1685 and 1689 shipping costs on flour represented 35 percent of its cost to the presidio. Whenever possible, the royal officials and the governor would buy a boat to transport the supplies rather than hire one. And since it cost 300 ducats a year to maintain the presidio boats whether they were in use or not, and the seamen had to be paid and rationed in any case, the vessels were kept in service as much as possible.[52] In them the chief pilot and other shipmasters carried loads of supplies out to the missions and maize back to the town. They patrolled the coast, putting out extra boats after a storm to look for shipwrecks, survivors, and salvage. They also made trips to Havana, Vera Cruz, Campeche, and across the Atlantic.

On any of these trips the shipmasters might execute private commissions and carry registered goods for those willing to pay the freight. Governor Méndez de Canzo's first report to the crown from St. Augustine suggested that the mariners be paid from these ship revenues. The crown responded by requesting the governor to report on all the presidio vessel income, what it was converted to, and on what spent. Accountant Bartolomé de Argüelles replied on his own. The governor, he said, saved himself 1,000 ducats a year in freight by the use of His Majesty's flyboat.[53]

A second crown revenue from shipping was the import and export duty on trade: the *almorifazgo,* which later officials would write *"almojarifazgo."* It was a complicated tax whose rate could be varied in numerous ways: by the class of goods, by their origin, by whether or not they were being transshipped, by the port of exit or entry (colonial or Indies), by special concessions to the seller, carrier, or consignee, and, perhaps most, by the individual interpretations of corrupt or confused officials. The year after St. Augustine was founded the duties on Spanish imports were doubled from 2½ to 5 percent ad valorem on articles leaving port in Spain, and from 5 to 10 percent on the same articles at their increased value in the Indies. The tax on wine more than doubled, changing from a total of 7½ percent to 20. Products of the Indies leaving for Spain paid 2½ percent at the port of origin and 5 percent upon arrival.[54] At the time, all this was theoretical as far as Florida was concerned. The adelantado and his lieutenants had been exempted from the almorifazgo for the three years of his contract, and the first settlers for ten years.[55]

The export tax apparently began in 1580, the year the Florida provinces were given permission to send two ships a year to the Canaries or Seville. At the same time the crown granted up to 300 ducats from the situado to build a customs house on the wharf in St. Augustine—a suggestion that became a command three years later.[56] The governor and royal officials used the proceeds of the export almorifazgo to pay their own salaries until 1598, when the crown assigned that income for the next four years to the parish church. The rate at which the tax was then being collected is unknown. In 1600 the auditor set it at 2½ percent. Export almorifazgo revenue came mostly from the sassafras and peltry of the Georgia coast. Realizing that St. Augustine was not a convenient shipping point, the royal officials sent a representative to San Pedro (Cumberland Island) to record cargoes, collect the tax, and see that the Indians were not cheated.[57]

Several general exemptions from the almorifazgos operated to the benefit of people in Florida. The belongings of royal appointees going to the Indies were exempt up to an amount stated in their travel licenses. Everything for divine worship and educational purposes was shipped tax-free, including the supplies and provisions for friars, and any kind of book. Colonially produced wheat flour and similar staples paid no tax in the port of origin. In 1593 a specific exemption was provided for the Florida presidio: nothing consigned to it from Vera Cruz was to be charged customs.[58]

A reduction in expense was not a revenue. The royal officials at the treasury in St. Augustine were supposed to be charging import almorifazgos of their own: 10 percent ad valorem on cargoes direct from Spain, 5 percent on the increase in value of Spanish goods transshipped from another colonial port, and 5 percent ad valorem on any colonial goods, even from another port in Florida. During the sixteenth century this almorifazgo was haphazardly applied. Accountant Argüelles reported that Governor Méndez de Canzo did not pay taxes on half of what the presidio boats brought him, yet it is evident that the royal officials did not know what percentage to charge.[59]

Auditor Pedro Redondo Villegas, coming to Florida in 1600, ordered that almorifazgos be collected on all imports regardless of point of origin, seller, carrier, consignee, or kind of goods. In his view, supplies bought with situado funds were as liable to entry duties as the goods purchased by individuals. The treasury officials in St. Augustine, as purchasing agents for the garrison, were accustomed to buy naval supplies tax-free from the skippers of passing ships. Their defense was that if the treasury charged the skipper an almorifazgo, he added the amount of it to his price and the cost was passed on to the soldiers, which they could ill afford. But when the auditor insisted that even naval supplies were subject to import duties, the treasury officials acceded without further protest; the revenue was to be applied to their salaries.[60] At San Juan de Ulúa, the port for Vera Cruz, the officials imposed an import almorifazgo of 10 percent on Spanish goods, based on the appraised value of the goods in their port. The Florida officials assumed that their own import tax on the same goods should be 10 percent of the increase in value between the appraisal at San Juan de Ulúa and the appraisal they made in St. Augustine. Redondo Villegas, rummaging about in Juan de Cevadilla's old papers, found what was probably the tax schedule of 1572–74 saying that the proper percentage was 5 if the goods had paid 10 percent already.[61] Presumably this was the rate the royal officials adopted for Spanish merchandise that did not come directly from Spain. They collected it in a share of the goods, which they exchanged preferably for cash at auction.

Auditor Redondo Villegas had gone too far. In 1604 the crown repeated the presidio's 1593 exemption with clarifications for his benefit:

> Because they are needy and prices are high and their salaries are small I order that they not pay taxes of almorifazgo in those provinces even when it is a contract with some private person, and this goes for what may be loaded in Seville also, or in another part of these kingdoms, on the situado account.[62]

In other words, goods charged against the situado were not to have export duties levied on them at the point of origin, or import duties in Florida. The royal exchequer was not so distinct from the presidio that the one should tax the other.

The strong position taken in this cédula lasted for two years. In 1606 the crown ordered that the export tax be paid on all wine shipped to the Indies, even that going as rations for soldiers. The royal officials in St. Augustine, for their part, levied the import almorifazgo on all merchandise brought in by private persons to sell to the soldiers, over the protests of the company captains, the governor, and at times, the crown.[63]

The first customs house was evidently destroyed in the fires or flood of 1599. To replace it, the officials asked for and received an addition to the counting house. They also were allowed a customs constable on salary and a complement of guards when there were goods on hand for registration or valuation.[64] The people of St.

Augustine put their ingenuity to work getting around the hated tax. By law, no one was supposed to board or disembark from an incoming ship ahead of the official inspection, under pain of three months in prison. Interim Accountant Sánchez Sáez, syndic and close friend of the Franciscans, may have been the one who suggested that the friars board vessels ahead of the royal officials. In the name of the Holy Office of the Inquisition they could seal boxes of books containing schismatic material, and only they could reopen these sealed boxes. Books were nontaxable items, and the friars, secure against inspection, could introduce high-value goods in the guise of books, untaxed. This was a common practice in the Indies. Governor Ybarra put a quick stop to the friars' presumption.[65]

Due to a shortage of ships, the crown was often forced to allow trade to foreign vessels. The earliest reinforcements ever to arrive in the new Florida colony, in the Archiniega expedition of 1566, shipped out in Flemish ships whose owners refused to embark from San Lúcar without licenses to load return cargoes of sugar and hides in Cuba and Santo Domingo.[66] The Flemish operated legally; other visitors did not. A foreign-owned ship coming to trade without registration was subject to seizure and confiscation, yet most of the merchant ships visiting St. Augustine may have been foreign. In 1627 the treasury officials accused Governor Rojas y Borja of being in collusion with Portuguese merchant Martín Freile de Andrada and of allowing open trade with the French.[67] By 1683 the crown, totally unable to supply its colony on the North Atlantic seaboard, was forced to approve Governor Marques Cabrera's emergency purchases from a New York merchant he called Felipe Federico. This Dutchman first gained entrance to the harbor as an intermediary returning the governor's son and another lad captured by pirates. Captain Federico and his little sloop, *The Mayflower*, became regular callers at St. Augustine. Others followed suit.[68]

The penalty for bringing in contraband goods even in Spanish bottoms was confiscation. The law provided that after taxes a sixth of the value went to the magistrate, a third of the remainder to the informer, and the rest to the king's coffer.[69] In many parts of the Indies this inconvenience was circumvented by the sloop trade in out-of-the-way harbors. In Florida, which had operated outside the mercantile law from the start, such evasions were necessary only when someone important was out of sorts. While Governor Salazar

Vallecilla was under suspension, a ship he had sent to Spain came back with a largely unregistered cargo of dry goods and wine. His confederates hid what they could before the return of Treasurer and Interim Co-Governor Francisco Menéndez Marquez, who was out in the provinces pacifying Indians, but the treasurer was able to locate 30,000 pesos' worth and apply price evaluations retroactively to what had been sold. For doing this, he declared, his honor and his very life were in danger. The governor and his henchmen were all Basques, Francisco said meaningfully, and the accountant behaved like one.[70] Francisco was probably disgruntled at having been left out of the distribution. He was not ordinarily so solicitous of the king's coffer. He and the same accountant, Ponce de León, had been jointly overdrawn 960 ducats from the almorifazgo account between 1631 and 1640, and during most of that time Ponce de León was not in Florida.[71]

The legal trade with Spain suffered as much from overregulation as from taxes. A cédula of 1621 had licensed the presidio's two little ships-of-permission to export pelts up to a value of 3,000 ducats a year—1,000 ducats above the former limit. By 1673 the Floridians did not find this small a cargo worth their while, yet the crown refused to raise the limit further.[72]

The royal bureaucracy, rigid about rules, was capricious in enforcement. In 1688 Accountant Thomás Menéndez Marquez, Francisco's son, reported that Captain Juan de Ayala y Escobar was bringing in unregistered goods and evading duties and that the governor, Quiroga y Losada, refused to take action. Unwittingly, Thomás brought down on himself the royal displeasure. If he and the other officials ever let this happen again, the crown warned, they would be punished severely. When they had knowledge of fraud they were to act independently of viceroys, presidents, and governors; how to do so was left unexplained. The governor escaped without reproof, and Ayala y Escobar was commended for his willingness to make dangerous voyages on behalf of the presidio.[73]

The royal officials complained that they could not be present at all the ports in Florida. Governor Vega Castro y Pardo allowed them to station subordinate customs officials at the San Marcos harbor in Apalache, but these did not stay. The governors' deputies in Apalache were directed to collect duties from visiting ships; in 1657 the friars of that province claimed that this directive had not produced a single real. Perhaps the royal officials should have visited these western ports or named new representatives, but it was not to their advantage. During the governorship of Cendoya another outlet, the San Martín (Suwannee–Santa Fe), was officially opened for exports. Havana merchants with Florida connections began sending sloops and ketches upriver to the landing that served don Thomás Menéndez Marquez's cattle ranch of La Chua. Back in Havana these merchants paid taxes of one real per hide or jug of lard, and one-half real per arroba of dried meat or tallow. Don Thomás (the same who later became accountant) himself had a frigate which visited the mouth of the San Martín and also carried rum to Apalache. This Gulf Coast trade was of no benefit to the Florida coffer. By that date the Cubans thought of Apalache and Western Timucua as colonies of theirs rather than provinces of Florida. Marques Cabrera made one last attempt in the 1680s to collect customs in Apalache. The Havana merchants in turn refused to supply or even visit St. Augustine, and accidents befell the boats the Florida governor sent to them.[74]

The *alcabala* (sales tax) so violently resisted elsewhere in the Indies was never collected in St. Augustine. The town was primarily a missions center and presidio, and friars, Indians, and soldiers all had alcabala exemptions of long standing. The crown tried to withdraw the privilege of the military in 1621, but there is no sign that anyone in Florida paid any attention.[75]

The fourth type of royal revenue was the *quinto,* a tax on treasure. There were two kinds: the true fifth was ordinarily associated with mines or pearl fisheries, but could be applied to other sources of regular extraction; the other quinto, actually a half, was also called the "tax on *hallazgos*" (finds). It was the royal share of salvage and of booty, which could be either the spoils of legitimate war or of the systematic looting of graves. When both quintos were applied to the same treasure, with the fifth taken out first and the tax on hallazgos from what remained, the king's share was 60 percent. Another source of treasure and valuable trade goods was *rescate* (ransom), the Spanish term for more-or-less compulsory trade with Indians not subject to the crown. The natives of Florida's lower coast gathered amber along the beaches. They also did most of the salvaging that was done, and were rich in bullion, costly commercial goods, and castaways used for sacrifice or slaves. All of these possessions were available through rescate. The natives to the north traded in peltry and medicinal herbs.

The quinto on rescates was the same as that on hallazgos: one-half.[76]

To encourage the search for mines the royal contract with Menéndez allowed ten years (from the date of first smelting) during which the quinto on bullion was to be reduced to a tenth. In spite of all efforts, however, no mines were discovered, either of minerals or of gems. Soldiers told tales around the campfire of the great Moyano diamond, but the multicolored mountain from which it came was never seen again.

A more likely source of wealth was pearls. In his exploration of the Southeast, De Soto discovered a cache of freshwater pearls belonging to the Lady of Cofitachique and his men packed them into their saddlebags by handfuls. Their story was one to be remembered, and Menéndez saw to it that his contract included the rights to a pearl fishery.[77] Pardo and Moyano, exploring the interior at the adelantado's command, were presented with many fine specimens, but the Cusabo revolt of 1576 put an end to their plans. It was not until eighty-two years after De Soto's theft that Governor Rojas y Borja followed up the promise of the pearls. An avid treasure seeker, he sent out three consecutive expeditions, two of them under the joint leadership of a Spanish ensign and a Christian chief. After many hardships the explorers relocated Cofitachique and the lagoon of pearl-producing mollusks.[78] But again, exploiting the fishery would have meant extending the conquest, and this the Spanish crown in 1628, the year Piet Heyn captured the treasure fleet, was unready to do. Once more the road to Cofitachique was forgotten. Governor Moral Sánchez, in the eighteenth century, said that the Indians sported freshwater pearls but refused out of their evil natures to say where they got them.[79]

Salvage, booty, and barter—these were the paths to riches that appealed to Spanish Floridians, the ones toward which they devoted their valor, their knowledge of the coasts, terrain, and natives, and the ships at their disposal. Until far into the seventeenth century some of the king's advisors retained their sanguine expectations. One of them recommended keeping people in Florida just to gather in the amber, gold, and pearls. He estimated that a fort could be supported on the quintos of amber and sassafras alone.[80]

Sassafras and sarsaparilla, then known as china root, were popular specifics for syphilis. Found on the Florida coast from Cumberland Island to the Savannah, they were one treasure that brought the

Spanish more problem than profit.[81] Between 1595 and 1610 particularly, large numbers of French ships visited the Indians to trade
for medicinal herbs, sometimes leaving factors to accumulate the
next season's cargo. The presence of French traders divided the
natives into Hispanophile and Francophile factions and was the cause
of prolonged war, both civil and internecine.[82] The relatively well
known Guale Rebellion of 1597 was only one phase of this long
conflict. During an interval of comparative peace the question arose
whether products obtained from the Indians subject to the crown
were liable to the king's fifth and the tax on hallazgos and rescates.
The Florida officials persuaded themselves that they were not, and
thereafter collected only the 2½ percent almorifazgo on sassafras or
pelts.[83]

"*Ambar*" was the most precious product naturally available. At
twenty-five pesos the ounce, a pound of it in a tooled leather case
made a princely gift to a high official in New Spain. Whether it was
ambergris or fossilized resin is still a matter of genial debate. The
author leans toward the latter, jewel amber, partly because of the
well-founded arguments of Eugene Lyon, and partly from reading in
a report attributed to Pedro Menéndez Marquez that "from Cape
Canaveral to Santa Elena there is a quantity of *ambar* thrown up on
the coast. There are whale fisheries there but it does not come from
whales. It is believed to be resin produced by the sea, which hardens
in the air."[84]

According to the Quaker merchant Jonathan Dickinson, the wild
Indians just south of St. Augustine combed the beaches for amber
and would trade five pounds of it for a mirror, an axe, a couple of
knives, and three or four twists of tobacco. A greater share of the
amber came from the Indians below Cape Canaveral. They would
send the governor word of a find, and perhaps a small sample, and he
would dispatch a presidio boat to them with trade goods. The royal
officials were supposed to commission someone to go along with the
crew to weigh and record the amber as it was brought in.[85]

The initial treasure tax on amber was 50 percent, the same as for
pearls. This was probably excessive. Governors either sent out the
boats without informing the treasury officials, or instructed the
officer-in-charge to conceal most of the treasure. For six months
Governor Rebolledo kept two boats down the coast with a troop of
soldiers who were regularly rotated. In return for 600 ounces of

amber worth 15,000 pesos he gave the Indians tools, some of them made from scrap iron (mortars, cannons, muskets, arquebuses, and one anchor) and the rest from 60 quintals of good pig iron. For all the iron he paid the treasury only 500 pesos. Sometime during his term the tax on amber was reduced to a fifth, but when Rebolledo paid anything he paid 6 percent.[86] The citizens of St. Augustine disliked the way governors monopolized the amber trade. Friars objected to the way knives and axes were traded freely to heathen tribes they were forbidden to visit "even in dreams." The royal officials said that when Indians were prevented from bargaining, Florida received no quintos at all.[87] Traders from Cuba and the other islands poached on the peninsular preserves, and European interlopers were attracted to the amber coast much as they had been to the sassafras one.[88]

In 1592 the crown forbade anyone to approach the salvaging and amber-trading Indians without presenting himself to the Florida governor beforehand for permission, and again afterwards to pay his quintos to the Florida treasury. The penalty for skipping this routine was confiscation of all booty, and a 2,000-ducat fine. Governor Ybarra asked the crown to concede to him a third of the proceeds in these cases on account of the trouble the smugglers caused him. The Council replied that judge and informer together could keep one-third, but the fine could be no more than 600 ducats. Nobody in the coastal trade was likely to have 2,000 ducats, they told the governor, and no one honored a law that was unenforceable. It was the original ordinance, however, with the 2,000-ducat fine, that remained on the books.[89]

Quintos were also paid on salvage. Salvors worked at their own expense in the sixteenth and seventeenth centuries as they do now, receiving the right to a wreck in return for half of what they recovered. This might or might not benefit the treasury. When the Portuguese Juan Fernández de Cea and his caravel of sailors recovered 2,390 pounds of Jean Ribault's bronze cannons off the coast of Florida, Pedro Menéndez Marquez, then lieutenant governor of Cuba, accepted 1,115 pounds of the cannon without telling the crown.[90] Incidentally, the guns of St. Augustine (never known to kill anyone but their gunners) were extremely valuable. Governor Méndez de Canzo, the artillery expert who defeated Drake in the harbor of San Juan, Puerto Rico, advised the king to withdraw the ordnance from St. Augustine altogether because it attracted corsairs. He was convinced that Drake had stopped by Florida in 1586 only for the treasure chest and the guns.[91]

The most important treasure to be salvaged from wrecks, then as now, was gold and silver. When Governor Salinas went in person to the Bahamas, after the hurricane and fleet disaster of 1622, Treasurer Juan Menéndez Marquez accompanied him to take charge of the bullion they expected to recover. If Indians beat other salvors to a wreck it was sometimes possible to barter with them for part of the treasure. Not only did Floridians do this but also Cubans, Dutch, and English, fighting one another for the privilege.[92] Some wrecks required sophisticated equipment. Don Marcos Luzio, a military engineer from New Spain, recovered 298 marks in silver bullion from the hull of the vice admiral's flagship *Las Maravillas,* which went down in 1656 in the Bahama Channel, seventy leagues from Providence Island. Of that salvage operation 143 marks were put into the Florida coffer. Pirates found all but 10 marks 1 ounce of the silver when they sacked St. Augustine in 1668, and it was probably the reason why they came. Buccaneers of mixed nationality were fully aware of the progress of salvage. Those who attacked St. Augustine in 1683 under Sanche de Agramont and Thomas Pain rendezvoused afterward at the old *Las Maravillas* site.[93]

The two men who were royal officials in 1683 never explained why 10 marks of silver were lying under some papers outside the king's coffer when both of them were abed. Maybe the total was not 10 marks, but more. It was convenient to blame pirates for missing money. Pedro Redondo Villegas had secret information that someone had removed 19,000 ducats from the treasure chest just before Drake captured it, and this may have been true. A member of the English raiding party wrote that the coffer he saw had already been broken open and ransacked.[94]

A secondary source of bullion was buried treasure. It could be the hoard of an Indian chief, the secret cache of a pirate band, or the place where survivors of a wreck had hidden money that was too heavy to carry and would legally belong to the salvors and the king. This source of treasure the crown willingly considered. Twice after the capture of Fort Caroline, Philip II commissioned persons to check out the stories of French prisoners, both of whom claimed to be the sole survivor of a treasure-burying incident. In the second case the cache was supposed to be 35,000 ducats, and the king reminded the governor of Cuba, to whom the matter was entrusted, to collect the quinto.[95] Another time an Indian led the Spaniards to a chest he had found full of money.[96]

While the authorities were most interested in artillery and bullion, they did not neglect other possibilities. Governor Zúñiga told the assembled chiefs of Guale that native beachcombers who discovered anything of value must tell the deputy governor, who would tell the governor, who would tell the king. The Quaker castaways of 1696 found that the wild Indians of Ais had stores of silk, linen and woolen cloth which they doled out to the Spaniards by the yard in exchange for tobacco.[97] Sometimes after a shipwreck unidentified clothing and other property washed up on the beach. Money from the sale of it usually went to the church, which was charged with masses for the drowned men's souls.[98]

The prizes of war were another source of the quinto. Ships were captured from corsairs as well as lost to them. Pedro Menéndez de Avilés took thorough advantage of a six-year letter-of-marque entitling him to any prizes he or his men might take, subject to the crown share of one-third.[99] In 1605 Governor Ybarra asked the king to grant him a French ship his men had captured in Guale, plus the quintos on the booty if His Majesty was so minded. The most valuable of his prizes were the rich noblemen aboard, French and English, but the crown refused to let them be ransomed, not even the great corsair Beltran Rogue from St. Malo, worth it was said 200,000 ducats. Instead, Inquisition examiner Francisco de Carranco was sent to St. Augustine, and with the aid of Bishop Altamirano managed to restore all but Rogue to the bosom of the church before Ybarra hanged them as corsairs and the town's confraternities devotedly buried them.[100] Ybarra was allowed 1,500 ducats from presidio funds for the ship, which the royal officials said was not worth 500 pesos.[101]

The booty of war in Florida, besides ships and captives, was likely to be furs and skins. Before Spaniards or Hispanic Indians left on campaign they collected testimony on the legality and justice of the proposed war so there would be no question about their right to divide the spoils.[102] The share to the royal coffer might be waived to reward heroism. In 1686 five Guale Christians, retreating by canoe from Alejandro Thomás de León's luckless corsairing expedition against Charles Town, were captured at the mouth of the Altamaha River by English fur traders on their way back to Carolina with a boatload of otter, beaver, bear, and buffalo pelts and deer skins. In the night the Guales got free, laid hands on the muskets, and killed four of the traders. They then brought the boat and the peltry down to St. Augustine. The Spanish governor, Marques Cabrera, determined to his satisfaction that the fur traders had been encroaching on Spanish territory. To encourage other Hispanic Indians to similar exploits, he rewarded the Guales with the entire prize and relieved them of labor service—something he said they appreciated more than the booty and of which the crown, when informed, heartily approved.[103]

Contemporary observers of the Spanish empire in America remarked on the favored status of the Florida Indians. Compiler Juan Diez de la Calle noted in 1646 that there were no encomiendas, workhouses, or mines in Florida, and he understood that the Indians there paid no tribute and did no service except a little paid labor in the soldiers' gardens. Governor Rodríguez de Villegas, an on-the-scene observer, commented that the Indians of Florida were "the least worked and the best treated in the Indies."[104]

Efforts to institute a tribute in Florida were only sporadically successful. No formal tribute system existed on which to build, beyond the communal work bees and a loose sharing arrangement when one town used another's hunting and gathering grounds.[105] Pedro Menéndez and most of his lieutenants, including Pedro Menéndez Marquez, tried to limit their demands on the natives to carrying baggage and providing food when they were on the march.[106] They even obtained a six-year grant from the crown entitling Florida to the surplus Indian tribute from Yucatán: maize, blankets, honey, chickens, and wax. In 1580 Captain Thomás Bernaldo de Quirós negotiated a treaty of tribute and vassalage with the Indians of Guale, and other tribute arrangements may have existed with the natives of the lower coast.[107] Later in the sixteenth century Chieftainess María of Nombre de Dios village—a real doña Marina with a Spanish soldier for a husband—had each of the forty-eight vecinos in her district bring the Spaniards one arroba of maize. The royal officials auctioned it off at four reales the arroba but advised the chieftainess not to require this in future because her people were poor. The officials knew that the unconverted and unconquered were watching. They should not resist becoming subjects of the king on account of a little maize.[108]

Nonetheless, when Governor Avendaño visited the districts of San Juan, San Pedro, and Guale he imposed a one-arroba requirement on the pacified natives of those places, covenanting with the chiefs not to let the soldiers take any more. Alonso de las Alas, the factor, did the collecting. Avendaño, on his way back from this visit, collapsed on the beach from a pulmonary hemorrhage and died.[109] His replacement, Méndez de Canzo, had scarcely arrived in St. Augustine when the Guales rebelled, killing five friars—half of the missionary contingent in Florida. The new governor moved the loyal Indians of San Pedro temporarily nearer the Spaniards and reduced their tribute to a token six ears until their fields should begin producing. Other chiefs who came to render obedience were promised the same concession. Méndez de Canzo eventually brought the insurgents under control by driving them from their villages and burning their crops. As pacification proceeded he restored the missions, returned the people to their homes, and reinstated the tribute. To assure his food supply he called in natives and paid them to clear land and grow maize near St. Augustine.[110]

Father Francisco Carranco of the Inquisition exceeded his authority in Florida, in Bishop Las Cabezas Altamirano's opinion, by imposing a second tribute for the support of the friars.[111] The details of this exaction are not known, nor how long it lasted. To the regret of everyone, the natives close to St. Augustine did not long survive conversion. An epidemic between 1614 and 1617 reduced their numbers by half. A revolt took further toll when Governor Rojas y Borja hanged the chieftainess of Santa María (St. Marys Island) and sentenced some of her supporters, ears docked, to hard labor on the fort in Havana. Two who were eventually pardoned found that while they had been in exile their countrymen from St. Augustine to Guale had died out almost completely.[112]

Although the royal officials kept the required books of annual tax rolls, no more was said of tribute to the crown. The requirement seems to have been commuted to paid service in the repartimiento, maintaining the transportation and communications system, and supporting the provincial garrisons. In 1701 one village of Guales living at San Juan del Puerto was expected to send workers to St. Augustine, run a ferry across the St. Johns River, and supply sixty brewings of cassina a month to the caretaker garrison at Santa María.[113] As population declined, the burden of serving and feeding the Spaniards fell more and more heavily on the common Indian. From all such duties the chiefs and their families were excused; their class continued to receive the Indian allowance, while their pretensions, if anything, increased.[114] When the chiefs near St. Augustine began leasing their villages' old fields to Spaniards the crown hurriedly forbade the practice, not this time because it alienated native lands—which the crown was concerned to protect—but because it infringed on the royal prerogative of imposing tribute.[115]

The maize production that the Franciscans exacted of their parishioners was the true tribute in Florida, one with an importance underscored by fifty years of bitter controversy. The friars were determined to sell the grain outside of Florida to pay their debts and finance the adornment of their churches. The governors were resolved to co-opt it for the garrison or to tap the profits. In the end it was military necessity that won. During the governorship of Torres y Ayala the chiefs of Apalache built a fort in San Luis at a cost of 304 pesos for the hardware, blacksmiths' wages, and workmen's rations. The money, according to the royal officials, came from the "1695 and 1696 tithes of those provinces."[116]

A different sort of personal levy was the *donativo,* a special-purpose contribution to the crown from those Spaniards whose rank or lineage exempted them from direct personal taxation. There were fifty-seven such persons in Florida to contribute to the king's 1698–1700 campaign for the upkeep of the Windward Squadron. Although the governor apologized that St. Augustine was a city without money, some of the donations were sizable. The interim accountant contributed from his salary 100 pesos, the artillery captain, 500 pesos. The crown took no chance on second thoughts: the viceroy was told to take the salary deductions from the situado.[117]

From Florida, in the late seventeenth century, the king could expect little else. One by one his ordinary revenues had been whittled away. The tithes were used for local stipends. The indulgences were gathering mold. Land taxes and slave or convict labor were applied mainly to the fortifications. There was no crown-owned productive enterprise. Half the officials were exempt from the half-annate. The usual monopolies were either granted out or unapplied. The limited almorifazgos were used by the officials for their salaries. There was no alcabala. Nothing had been said about quintos for years. The buccaneers who ranged the seaways prevented both barter and salvage. There was no tribute. To the crown's puzzled inquiries about its revenues the royal officials in 1699 made a blunt reply. The Florida treasury, they said, had only one income: the situado.[118]

7

Political Functions of the Royal Officials

]H[OWEVER independent of viceroys or audiencias, the governor of the provinces of Florida was still subject to the crown. The king expressed his will in two ways: by direct orders and general laws, and by encouraging rival authorities within the governor's jurisdiction.

A steady stream of cédulas signed "I the king" arrived to regulate every aspect of government. These orders could be addressed to the governor, the royal officials, one of the officers, or any other individual or group with reason to receive one. Each cédula was supposed to be presented to the cabildo for validation. The governor, royal officials, and public and governmental notary in turn received the written orders of their prince with reverence, kissing them and raising them overhead in ancient ceremonial fashion. Copies were made of those that were private property, then the royal orders were added to the Books of the Cédulas kept in the counting house.[1]

Receipt of a cédula did not guarantee compliance. Not every royal order was applicable: some were *sobrecédulas* (general decrees) sent to part or all of the kingdoms, presidencies, and captaincies general of the Indies. A sobrecédula in 1580 directed the governor of Florida, whose people could scarcely venture out of their forts, to make careful and widespread measurements during the coming lunar eclipse, for the purpose of establishing longitude.[2] The copyists who produced these form letters frequently referred to Florida as an

101

island—a natural mistake since the colony was in the administrative category of the Windward Isles (Islas de Barlovento).[3]

Even an applicable cédula might not be obeyed. Governors were known to check the mail pouch and hold out any dispatch they did not want the royal officials to see. In such a case the governor might correspond privately with the crown to get the order rescinded or delayed. Governor Aranguíz y Cotes in 1663 withheld the cédula that moved the appellate courts in civil, criminal, and exchequer cases from the Council of the Indies to Mexico City. Governor Marques Cabrera delayed three years to publish the 1680 cédula allowing land titles to be cleared by a payment.[4] The royal officials were no more anxious than the governor to obey a distasteful order. Their standard maneuver was to tell the king that either by an inadvertent error or for some sinister reason he had been misinformed.[5] No one flatly told the Spanish monarch that he was wrong.

The long-awaited *Recopilación de leyes de los Reynos de las Indias,* published in 1681, was an attempt to codify the laws of the Indies out of more than 400,000 royal cédulas. Florida's nine-volume set may have arrived at the St. Augustine cabildo in 1685, when it began to be cited locally.[6] There is no reason to suppose that these general laws were obeyed any more promptly or literally than the king's direct orders.

The second means of keeping a governor in line (or of hampering him, depending on the point of view) was the recognition of separate, sometimes conflicting authorities within his jurisdiction. One of these was the church. St. Augustine's parish church and secular clergy were suffragan to the bishop of Cuba, yet episcopal authority rested lightly on the colony. Bishops came to Florida only two times during the Habsburg era, in 1606 and 1674.[7] The first of these visits coincided with the appearance of an examiner from the Inquisition, Father Francisco de Carranco, to deal with a shipload of heretic corsairs. Once the auto-da-fé was over, Father Carranco left, and Florida received no further representative of that most independent branch of the church until late in the seventeenth century.[8] The first resident minister of the Holy Tribunal, Father Pedro de Luna, refused even to present his credentials to civil authorities. When Governor Marques Cabrera tried to get him to take action against a curate who had given sanctuary to an English pirate, Luna answered sharply, "I will not use the Holy Office to harass and vilify a dignified priest and bring scandal to Catholic breasts.... The Holy Tribunal is to be venerated. By cédulas of His Majesty and apostolic bulls it comes under no other jurisdiction."[9]

The friars were not subject to the bishop of Cuba; among them, authority flowed the other way. The Franciscan Custody of Santa Elena, created in 1609 and elevated to a province three years later, directed the missionaries in Cuba as well as Florida.[10] The friars valued their ecclesiastical independence highly and, extending it to civil matters, regarded themselves as defenders of all the citizens from autocracy. As Father Alonso del Moral said in 1676: "Everyone else here ... is subject to the governors, for everything passes through the governor's hands and everyone is subordinate to his will and orders."[11] Governor Treviño Guillamas found their attitude exasperating: "The friars and their rages give me all kinds of trouble, trying to intrude on the royal jurisdiction."[12]

The church was not the governor's only rival within his own territory. Treviño Guillamas went on: "And with some of the royal officials I have the same difficulties as with friars, for they are of such a condition and nature: they want to have what is not theirs and to keep what is someone else's."[13] A watchful crown had provided its treasury officials with a number of formal means for exercising power. Of the four functions of nonecclesiastical government into which Spanish administrative correspondence was properly divided, we have so far concentrated on Hacienda, or the exchequer; the royal officials were also active in Capitanía, Justicia, and Gobierno. They were importantly involved with the garrison; they were the judges in cases of the exchequer, and they were members of the city council.

The proprietors of the treasury in St. Augustine were not powerless before the governor's military role of captain general. They were able to exert influence on him in a number of ways: first, they were inactive officers of the garrison; second, one of them usually served as the military purchasing agent and collector of funds; finally, they were the official accountants, payroll officers, and stewards. When it came to dealing with the military, the royal officials were privileged and powerful.

In Florida, inactive officers were available for temporary assignment on coastal patrols, emergency details, leadership in the militia, or the deputy governorship of provinces. Known as *reformados* (officers without command), these men drew the pay of privates plus a small supplement from the bonus fund. It was an arrangement similar to the royal grant of reduced pay (*entretenimiento*) to an officer on leave, to keep him in the reserves. In most parts of the Indies reformados did guard duty; in Florida they were generally exempt.[14] At times the governor's prerogative to name officers got out of hand. Pedro Benedit Horruytiner, elected governor by his fellow officers in the hectic atmosphere of a plague year, handed out fifty-five patents including twenty-three for captain. Almost no one was left for guard duty. Governor Quiroga y Losada operated a smooth patronage system whereby men from Havana enlisted in St. Augustine, were rapidly advanced to ensign, given reformado status, and sent home as officers.[15]

All the royal officials born in or acclimated to Florida were reformados. Some had served with distinction for years and found it hard to settle down over their dusty books. In the succession of Menéndez Marquez officeholders, the accountant Pedro was also an admiral. Juan served as treasurer during an interlude in a long career of Indian fighting. Francisco took occasional leave of the treasury to pacify rebellious provinces. Juan II rallied the soldiers and saved the fort during the Searles pirate raid. He eventually returned to active service as a sergeant major in Havana and became a Knight of the Order of Santiago. Antonio was an expert on the southern coastal waterways, whom the governor took in search of the buccaneer Agramont. Francisco II was the dashing captain of Florida's first cavalry company.[16] Men like this were not backward about speaking their minds. The Junta de Guerra once had to remind them that it was the captain general's responsibility, not theirs, to inform the crown on military matters.[17]

Governor and treasury officials were supposed to act jointly on purchases for the garrison. The agent could be an outside merchant bringing a cargo of wine from the Canaries, one of the presidio's own shipmasters picking up a load of flour in Havana, or a procurador going to Spain at his own expense to execute commissions for the officers. The preponderance of supplies reaching Florida in any given year, however, came in care of the situador, who was, more often than not, one of the treasury proprietors. The hazards of his journey and the payroll preparations for his return made by the other officials have been described in Chapter 5.

As officers of a treasury associated with a presidio, the royal officials had two other duties that would not have been given them elsewhere: keeping the personnel records of the garrison and accounting for what was stored in the warehouses and arsenal. It was the accountant, as records specialist, who performed the act of "entering and erasing plazas" from the muster given him monthly by the governmental notary.[18] He maintained the individual service records in which every man's career was recorded from induction to retirement, with supplementary material rich in information about Indian wars, pirate attacks, explorations, salvage, and sea voyages. Officers tried to influence what went into their files. Captain Francisco de Salazar asked to have stricken from his record the fact that mutinous troops had once forced him to act as governor.[19] In the 1680s a controversy arose between Accountant Thomás Menéndez Marquez, who had been copying the soldiers' entire records for them on request, and Governor Marques Cabrera, who wanted to keep the contents of the files confidential. The crown ruled that the accountant could release only the bare facts of dates and posts served.[20]

Once a month the royal officials and the governor were supposed to make a joint inspection of the warehouses and arsenal, then observe the rationing. The company captains and corporals also stood by while the steward doled out each man's monthly rations and the notary recorded them. Since the soldiers had once complained of receiving fourteen-ounce pounds, the weights and measures were kept in evidence: the pint-capacity covered copper container for liquid measurements, and the balance or the steelyard with weights for dry ones.[21]

Not all of those supplied from the warehouse stood in line at St. Augustine. Certainly not the treasury officials, who drew rations on the grounds that they too served as soldiers.[22] Exact records were kept of the whereabouts of the garrison. When the chief pilot came in to fit out a launch for coastal patrol, he was given the rations for his seamen. Detachments of soldiers at the watchtowers along the coast carried a month's supply of provisions as they left. For the garrisons stationed in Timucua and Apalache the steward arranged a canoe pick-up point or sent out a supply train. Enrique Primo de Rivera, who obtained a contract in the 1680s for hauling provisions to the provinces, made the king's road passable to carts from present-day Tallahassee as far as Gainesville. Sometimes the officials found it more practical to issue trade goods to the soldiers and let them buy their own food from the Indians—or maybe this was the way to get rid of an overstock.[23] Items of every kind were carried, not only for the soldiers but for their women and children. The overseer of slaves and the master of construction used the buildings to store blankets, coarse clothing, and baskets full of maize and beans for the royal slaves, convicts, and repartimiento Indians. The Franciscan custodian kept the friars' provisions and the church supplies there until time to deliver them to the missions. According to Accountant Nicolás Ponce de León, everyone in town lived off the royal storehouses.[24]

In order to make effective collections from the debtors to the crown the treasury officials in the Indies were elevated to the dignity of royal judges (*jueces oficiales reales*) in 1567. In some regions they established autonomous courts and constabularies, but not in Florida, where after the first or second abandonment of Santa Elena the only bailiffs or justices were adjutants of the governor. In vain the crown warned, "It is our will that our officials ... do the attachments, imprisonings, sales and auctionings of property and other judicial proceedings that are necessary to collect what is owing to us," and "Let the bailiffs of that land execute the orders of the royal officials in the things relative to the treasury without delay."[25]

After 1621 the overseas treasury officials, who had become somewhat high-handed, were no longer supposed to call themselves judges or engage in law enforcement. If this ruling ever reached Florida, it was ignored. The treasurer, accountant, and factor continued to style themselves royal judges and to carry staves of justice.[26] If they had no private constabulary, there were other means of collection. Anybody wanting to leave the provinces was supposed to obtain their fiscal clearance. If a debtor to the crown had managed to escape to another jurisdiction they could pursue him, with royal consent, and require the help of the law.[27] In practice, they found that only a situador or a royal appointee like themselves was likely to get so deeply in debt to the crown as to be followed out of Florida. The last resort, if a debtor was in prison or deceased, was religious pressure. Letters of excommunication (*paulinas*) were taken out and read in the main churches of Havana and St. Augustine, calling on anyone holding property of the debtor, owing him money, or knowing of someone who did, to declare it forthwith or call down the wrath of God upon the whole town. After the letter was read, a solemn procession of parishioners in black veils, carrying a cross draped in black, marched back and forth across town chanting the *Laus Deo*.[28] Little was recovered by this means, which suggests either that there was little to recover or that a Spaniard prized his purse as ardently as his soul.

The role of the royal officials in Capitanía was functional, in Justicia it was mostly honorary, in Gobierno it was both. As regidores of the cabildo they held the only truly political offices in Florida. They were interpreters of local rights and the king's law as the clergy were of the law of God. They advised the governor in all matters concerning the town and the provinces. Until mid-century they were his regular substitutes. Officially or unofficially, the proprietors of the treasury were the underlying government of Florida.

Founding a town automatically meant creating a municipal government and governing body. There was an active city council in St. Augustine from the first day, and corresponding ones in San Mateo and Santa Elena, with regidores and justices (*alcaldes*) named by the adelantado. When these first officials had served their terms they were replaced by election; their offices had been elective in the Indies since 1523.[29]

It has often been written that there was no cabildo in Florida after the departure of Pedro Menéndez.[30] It is true that there was no municipal government house, no complement of municipal bailiffs and justices after the first twenty years or so, and perhaps no separate chest for municipal revenues, but a cabildo did exist, serving as both the council for the "noble and loyal city of St. Augustine," and the "assembly of the republic" (*ayuntamiento de la república*).[31]

Before council memberships were made venal in the Indies, the officials of the exchequer in a capital city automatically sat as regidores on its cabildo. In Florida this privilege was never revoked; cabildo memberships were awarded concurrently with titles to treasury office and did not become separately salable.[32] The most exceptional thing about the seventeenth-century cabildo in Florida is that except for the royal officials there were no regidores, none elected by the cabildo and none appointed by the governor. This is why the council had no need of separate headquarters, separate meetings, or even a separate chest or book of resolutions. Cabildo membership was exactly the same as that of a general treasury council, down to the ex-officio notary, and the busy royal officials saw no point in distinguishing between the two except on formal occasions.

The regidores, also called deputies and even governors, were representatives of the king as certainly as was the governor. To them he presented his commission and evidence of bond on arrival. At civil ceremonies they walked at his sides carrying their staves of office and—St. Augustine not having a royal standard bearer—one of them bore the standard of the city. One served as minister of protocol.[33] The regidores were responsible with the governor for the welfare of the land. In concert with him they must endeavor to make the earth fruitful and the idle productive. With him they were charged with the pacification, conversion, and right treatment of the natives, the construction of churches, and decent provision for divine worship.[34] They were, in short, his advisory council. If as reformados the royal officials felt entitled to give their military opinions, as sole members of the municipal council and provincial assembly they spoke even more assuredly on behalf of local interests. They regarded themselves and were called by others "the fathers of the country."[35]

A cabildo considered all matters of public concern within its *término*. There were three senses in which the geographical term was understood. In its largest meaning, the término stood for the whole territory claimed by the crown, the entire space not incorporated in another Spanish municipality. The término was also the area of pacified settlement and communication network, the hinterland known to historical geographers as "ecumene" and to Spanish Floridians as "the provinces."[36] In its third and most limited meaning, the término was the city and its immediate environs (market, lots, gardens, and the common woods and pastures)—the region also known as the *jurisdicción* or *concejo*.

When it came to total area claimed, St. Augustine had one of the largest términos in the New World during the seventeenth century, when the nearest incorporated Spanish town by sea was Havana, and the nearest by land, Santa Fé, New Mexico. In a captaincy general like Florida, known for active war, governors were not disposed to take civilian advice about how to deal with invasions and rebellions, explorations or conquests.[37] In these cases the *junta de guerra* superseded the civil cabildo, and the royal officials' right to participate might be questioned. Sergeant Major Aranda y Avellaneda refused to give his opinion on a Guale border problem in 1684, saying that with the accountant and treasurer present it was no council of war.[38]

The crown was equally reluctant to trust creole regidores with military authority, which is why it did not want them serving as interim governors. They did so nonetheless. Until 1650 the governors all had cédulas permitting them to appoint an interim substitute for eventualities of absence, incapacity, or death, yet after the sudden death of Governor Martínez de Avendaño no one could find such a provision in his papers, and the regidores allowed a junta to acclaim them interim co-governors. Sometimes they succeeded to power by selection. When Governor Ybarra went on visita to Guale and San Pedro he left Treasurer Juan Menéndez Marquez in charge. (When Ybarra returned it was necessary to have the notary read the treasurer his duties and ask him not to interfere in the king's justice.)[39] Governor Fernández de Olivera on his deathbed called a junta and appointed the accountant and treasurer to govern in his stead. Governor Rodríguez de Villegas, when he was dying, named Accountant Nicolás Ponce de León governor of peace, in charge of the exchequer and of justice, and Sergeant Major Eugenio de Espinosa governor of war. The officials did not always wait to be appointed. Instructed to suspend Governor Salazar Vallecilla for not finishing his galleon, they could find no one so qualified to take his place as themselves.[40]

The crown endorsed these assumptions of power with reservations. Rodríguez de Villegas was charged at his posthumous residencia with having given the post of governor of peace to the accountant, knowing it was incompatible with his duties. And the Council of the Indies was advised to fill the vacancy left by Salazar Vallecilla without delay, as the "province" stood in grave danger "governing itself at the hands of royal officials."[41]

In 1621 Governor Salinas was told to appoint a captain to serve during his absences, not a royal official. Then, beginning with Eugenio de Espinosa in 1632, each successive sergeant major received a standard cédula naming him interim governor-elect in military matters—a provision which conflicted with the cédula to the governors and caused confusion whenever the governorship fell vacant. Espinosa was a murderous old man obviously unfit to govern. The next sergeant major, his son-in-law Nicolás Ponce de León II, was weakly and fearful.[42] The problem of gubernatorial succession was researched several times, by both the Florida accountant and the fiscal of the Council, but the crown's invariable public position was "Let there be no innovation."[43] Its private arrangements were more flexible. Once, when the sergeant major's health was failing, the governor of Havana was sent secret orders to choose a successor ad interim for Florida if it was left without a governor. Within the captaincy general itself, the military aspect of the governorship continued to be given precedence over the civil. But when relations with foreign neighbors called for diplomatic contacts, the governor sent as his representative a royal official, which meant a regidor.[44]

From the time Santa Elena was abandoned in 1587 until Pensacola was founded in 1698, St. Augustine was Florida's only incorporated town. There was talk of organizing another cabildo with annually elected regidores and magistrates in Apalache, particularly after Governor Aranguíz y Cotes put a thirty-man garrison at San Luis and Spaniards began to move there and call themselves its vecinos. But Spanish population in the province never grew large enough to support a second city. The many schemes to encourage settlement—Canary Island farmers, Campeche weavers, cotton and hemp plantations—were little more than grant proposals that Madrid was unable to find.[45]

The concerns of the cabildo within the provinces were mainly with Indian governance, labor, and production. There was some initial difficulty determining who was to govern the Indians: their chiefs, the friars, or the governor and his advisory council. During the governorship of Méndez de Canzo the friars complained that the chiefs had abdicated their order-keeping powers and the governor refused to assume them, forcing the Franciscans to move into the vacuum. A few short years later Father Gerónimo de Celaya was preaching that Governor Ybarra had no jurisdiction over the natives whatever.[46] Spells of cooperation alternated with bitter disputes, but eventually the tribes were organized into administrative provinces. Each province was supplied with ecclesiastical and military authorities who were not supposed to interfere in civil government. The republic of Spaniards had its parallel in the republic of Indians, living in polity under their own municipal governments, with chiefs for magistrates and elected elders (*principales*) for regidores.[47] The chiefs and their advisors, whether from one town or a council of towns, answered to the governor and the regidores alone.

The regidores kept records of the repartimiento Indians whom the chiefs sent, at first to clear land and work in the soldiers' maize fields, then to do more and more of the unskilled work in St. Augustine. The labor draft was not meant to be onerous. It was part of no one's plan for the Indians to die off leaving an increasingly heavier burden on those who remained. The regidores also kept track of the frontier missions that did not yet supply tribute or labor, advising the governor where friars should be sent or withdrawn. When it was necessary to discipline chiefs, the regidores gave the governor their moral support or, to his chagrin, withheld it. When he went on his once-a-term visita to check on Indian defenses, morality, and grievances, he sometimes asked the regidores to accompany him. Between times they could be sent to the provinces themselves to solve disputes between Indian towns and Spanish settlers, problems of native succession, and questions of debts owed by Spaniards.[48] When chiefs came to visit the capital, the regidores advised the governor on the proper gifts to be made them from the Indian allowance, did the disbursing of the goods, and made the report to the crown.[49]

Governor Méndez de Canzo had allowed the ancient post of protector of the Indians to lapse. When in the mid-seventeenth century the crown issued general orders for every administrative district to have such an official, to be called the defender, the possibilities of salary and patronage were quickly taken up.[50] Accountant Juan Menéndez Marquez II said that the defender should be someone like parish priest Francisco de Soto, able to stand up to governors. In an almost identical letter Governor Guerra y Vega recommended the same man. The governor's mistress and the accountant's wife were both Sotos and probably relatives of the candidate.[51] The friars had a different idea. The defender should be their own provincial, who alone had authority apart from the governor's and no private interests to pursue. The Franciscan commissary general, asked for his opinion, particularly opposed giving the appointment to the treasurer or accountant, even though, as he said, "they are the most notable subjects upon whom this responsibility might be laid, for they have business enterprises of their own and are always thinking of their dealings and investments and would thus acquire even greater control over the Indians."[52] At length Governor Marques Cabrera named Sergeant Major Domingo de Leturiondo defender of the Indians, augmenting his salary by a plaza, since there were no tributes from which to pay him. The Council disapproved. It was unnecessary to create a new salaried position when the defense of the Indians was the responsibility of the local magistrates and bailiffs, they said, ignoring the fact that there were no magistrates or bailiffs per se in Florida.[53] The post of defender became an intermittent office activated by the governor in cases of Indian mistreatment, crimes, and rebellions. It was oftenest held by a regidor.[54]

Within the local jurisdiction the cabildo carried out most of the activities of a modern city or county council: zoning, licensing, quality and standards control, utilities, recording of deeds (but not vital statistics, which were recorded by the parish priest), property appraisal, probate, street cleaning, nightwatch, mapping and surveying, maintaining public order, leasing public lands, attracting government installations and funds, highway and waterway maintenance, public recreation, and even, to a degree, health, education, recreation, and welfare. The cabildo had other duties no longer assigned to local authorities, such as enforcing curfews, fixing prices, punishing concubinage, managing public auctions and markets, reducing specie drain, raising a militia, registering and naturalizing aliens, sending a district representative to the metropolis, and worrying about an adequate food supply.[55]

In spite of the many obligations of its council, the city of St. Augustine did not have a large budget. The royal officials explained in 1621 that their municipality had no means of raising money (*arbitrios*) because it was "a closed presidio without vecinos except for the soldiers, with no fruits of the land, no offices to sell, and no fines to apply." This they told the crown in order to dip into the situado for the money to build themselves houses.[56] St. Augustine did have a little disposable income from service fees, fines, and properties.

City employees were paid by the fees (*posturas*) for their services. The notary charged to copy or notarize papers; he and the town crier kept a percentage of the goods sold at auction; the butcher at the slaughterhouse charged by the carcass; ferrymen collected by the boatload. Obligatory inspections of quality or of measures at the market stalls and wineshops were also done for a fee.[57] Since not even the regidores were paid a salary they took turns by the month inspecting taverns. Every time a cask of wine was decanted the regidor in attendance collected twelve reales: eight for himself and four for the confraternity of the Most Holy Sacrament.[58] It was a pleasant task, providing not only an extra peso but a show of generosity and a sociable cup of wine.

Justice also paid for itself. The costs for the notary, guards, and informers, as well as for the governor or regidor who sat as judge on the case, were paid out of the fines and confiscations imposed by the court. The fort served as the jail, and relatives of the prisoners provided the food. The regidores, vecinos of the town themselves, were not rigorous in the collection of debts to non-Floridians. When Juan García, backed by his kinsman the governor, foreclosed on the pitiful shacks of soldiers and charged them collection costs (*décimas y costas*), Accountant Argüelles shook his head in disapproval. Such severity was something new in Florida, which in 1598 was a land as yet without sustenance or productivity.[59]

The Spaniards founded municipalities as a means not only of government but of distributing land. They marked out a tract several leagues square and in the center, or some other logical spot, laid out the main plaza, with spaces for public buildings and the church. A grid pattern of streets was imposed and the blocks divided into house lots (*solares*) for the first settlers, with the choice lots near the plaza. On the outskirts of town were the commons (*ejidos*), consisting of arable fields (*suertes*), pastures (*dehesas*), and woods (*montes*). For his yearly planting each vecino received an allocation of the fields that after the six-month growing season would revert to commons, onto which the cattle were turned to feed on the dry stalks.[60]

A municipality usually reserved part of its lands for some kind of profitable use, the income of which was called a *propio*.[61] The town of St. Augustine, bounded by the sea, a swamp, an estuary, and a creek, seems to have possessed no lands for income. Its only identifiable propios came from the horse-drawn gristmill, which after paying off its own construction brought in 200 ducats a year.[62] The quitrents which Governor Hita Salazar imposed on farmers were at first applied entirely to castillo construction. In the 1680s the town began receiving a small revenue from land use, but as a royal favor, not a right. Charles II, who took a personal interest in holy day celebrations, assigned 55 pesos a year from the quitrents to buy wax tapers for the parish church on the Day of Corpus Christi. Perhaps by coincidence, 55 pesos was the arbitrary limit upon direct local taxation cited in the *Recopilación* in 1681.[63]

In addition to fees, fines, and rentals, a municipality had two sources of emergency revenue: *sisas* and *servicios*. Sisas were excise taxes imposed on certain foodstuffs for a specific purpose and a limited time. In order to build a church, Governor Rojas y Borja declared a "tribute" on vegetables, maize, and fish. The regidores disapproved of his action because the tax was regressive, falling most heavily on the poor, and also because they had not been consulted.[64] Servicios, like the donativos discussed in Chapter 6, were a levy on the higher echelons of society. As one of his fund-raising efforts to put the castillo into defensible order, Governor Hita Salazar gathered 1,600 pesos from the treasury officials, officers, and ranchers.[65]

While no mention has been found of a separate coffer for municipal funds in general, there was a chest for the property of the deceased. Men of all social classes died in Florida, far from their legal kin. A soldier seldom left anything except the wages owed him, which went almost automatically to the church.[66] Other people's property was forwarded to the House of Trade to be held for the appearance of heirs. The king would make use of the funds in the meantime. For the Archiniega expedition of 1566, Philip II borrowed 26,000 ducats from the goods of the deceased, to be replaced from the first shipment of treasure from the Indies.[67] If no heirs could establish a claim, the property escheated to the crown and was used for alms. The same king ordered the House of Trade in 1583 to support the parish church in Florida out of the goods of the deceased.[68]

In general, when someone of means died intestate or at a distance from his heirs, the regidores of St. Augustine inventoried his belongings, converted them into something storable in a chest, such as money, plate, or jewels, and delivered them into the keeping of the senior regidor, who was known for this purpose as the keeper of the goods of the deceased (*tenedor de bienes de difuntos*).[69] In a place short on specie it was not easy to accomplish the conversion of houses, slaves, and personal property into liquid capital. Also, if the deceased had been a person with responsibilities toward the treasury his accounts would have to be settled before his belongings could leave the provinces. All this delayed the forwarding of estates and led to the complaints of heirs.[70]

When the royal coffer was empty and the presidio in need, it was as tempting for the governor as for the king to borrow from the goods of the deceased. Méndez de Canzo used 1,500 ducats of his predecessor's estate to cover a shortage in the situado. It was also possible for the senior regidor to supply what was missing from one chest out of the other. Treasurer Juan Menéndez Marquez borrowed a gold chain and some wrought silver from the goods of the deceased to conceal a deficit in the royal coffer. Alonso Sánchez Sáez was even more brazen. During the confusion of the Drake assault he opened the chest of the deceased and pocketed 3,000 reales. When a general letter of excommunication was read to cover such an eventuality, he wrestled with his conscience for "many days," then put the money back.[71]

Ever since the Revolt of the Comuneros in 1520 the Spanish government had looked with suspicion upon representative assemblies. This did not mean, however, that Madrid was unreceptive to representatives from the colonies. Friars in their chapter meetings elected a procurador or advocate to present their problems to the crown, and the cabildo did likewise. In 1659 Salvador de Cigarroa went to Spain and obtained justice for himself and his colleagues against the crooked auditor Santa Cruz.[72] Domingo de Leturiondo's trip in 1672 resulted in the lifting of several trade restrictions and an increased authorized strength for the presidio. Juan de Ayala y Escobar served as procurador numbers of times in the dangerous war years from 1683 to 1706, carrying messages from Indian chiefs as well as Spaniards.[73]

It was typical of the intermeshing of authority in colonial government that while the regidores could be the governor's political rivals, there was no way for them to be independent of him. He had a vote in the cabildo, and although the majority was supposed to carry, membership was so tiny that a single vote had unusual weight. It was to counteract the autocracy of Governor Menéndez Marquez that the officials of the treasury asked permission in 1580 to name additional regidores.[74] It was denied, and half a century later the royal officials, and also the regidores, were reduced from three to two. A crafty executive could split the unity of two regidores by favoring one. And when there was an unexpected vacancy in the treasury offices it was the governor's privilege to supply an interim appointee to sit in the cabildo and vote as directed.

Governor Marques Cabrera regarded a cabildo with a membership of only three, counting himself, and no other magistrates or officers of the law, as no cabildo at all. In order to have a true deliberative body he appointed two more regidores: Pedro Benedit Horruytiner and Domingo de Leturiondo, men of integrity, knowledge, and experience.[75] He said he wanted to avail himself of the law permitting him to audit the accounts with the aid of two regidores and a notary, and he could hardly do so with the two regidores who were treasury officials.[76] This reform of the governor's was probably welcomed no more enthusiastically than his earlier ones, about which the friars were grumbling:

> Everything is turned upside down with this new sort of government which Your Grace is trying to introduce everywhere and in everything with these [new orders], not realizing that any innovation in government will cause disquiet and the deterioration of political practices that have long been the custom.[77]

There is no indication that Marques Cabrera's increased number of regidores was approved.

It was possible for a governor to force his will on the cabildo by controlling the public and governmental notary who was their recording agent. He would say that the regidores were troublemakers trying to provoke lawsuits and would order the notary to stop proliferating their papers under pain of a heavy fine. It was a crude but effective method of getting on with government business.[78] When a governor wanted to ride roughshod over the rights of the citizens or the cabildo he had every means to do so, for his adjutants were the only police power in town. A genuinely political governor, however, simply replaced the notary with his own attaché, after which he did not need to attend either treasury or cabildo councils to know everything that happened. When all else failed, a governor who found the existence of a cabildo inimical to his intentions announced that it was invalid in a town of soldiers and dissolved it.[79] In such a case the royal officials simply waited him out. His term was limited and his residencia was coming, whereas they had been appointed for life.

The governor understood that if he dissolved the cabildo the treasury officials would report his mismanagements in detail throughout his stay. A common letter of complaint began: "The governors pay little heed to the royal officials and we have no preeminences nor rights of intervention, nor are we allowed our authority as regidores." At this point the officials filled in their specific grievance: "The governor is consenting to trade in this city with Portuguese and Frenchmen," or "The governor is forcing us to sign prepared libranzas." Then they attached the standard conclusion:

> In all the cases that arise, whether in matters of the exchequer, the city or conversions, he takes action apart from us, and if we present the objections that occur to us he says that we have no intervention whatsoever, and if we ask for this in writing he refuses it, abusing us and speaking disrespectfully to us and threatening us if we do not go along with his opinions.[80]

Perfunctorily the Council would warn the governor to treat the royal officials well and not to place hindrances in the way of their work, then would file the regidores' letter with the other complaints awaiting his residencia.

The crown may have relied too heavily on the institution of the residencia, considering the way it was conducted. The officials of the Florida treasury urged that a regular judge be sent from the Royal Audiencia of Mexico City to take a residencia, for "with the incoming governor justifying the outgoing, no one dares demand his rights."[81] The bribes involved were practically institutionalized. Governor Rebolledo boasted that 4,000 or 6,000 pesos would clear him of any charge. Ex-Governor Hita Salazar said that Marques Cabrera purposely delayed his proceedings because Hita Salazar had not given him 3,000 pesos as the other ex-governor and an ex-governor's widow had.[82] A bad residencia in St. Augustine was proof of nothing but poverty and a lack of friends.

Auditor Redondo Villegas believed that the worst evil in Florida was the trouble between the royal officials and the governor.[83] Such a view would be easy to exaggerate. There was after all no point in repeating, letter after letter, that things were going well, especially when governmental business in Florida did not operate smoothly within the law. At such times as the creole royal officials and the peninsular governor were in agreement about matters of the treasury, the military, justice, and municipal and provincial government, they formed an impenetrable power bloc to forward their joint interests and made no report on these to the crown. From St. Augustine, official silence was tantamount to collusion.

8

Accounting and Accountability

THE bookkeeping system at the royal treasury was both thorough and cumbersome. Perhaps because a copyist was paid by the number of folios, no value was placed upon brevity. Each number was written twice, in words and in numerals. At the beginning, accounts were kept in a variant of Roman numerals in which an "e" might stand for a ten, and the numbers from two to four began with one to three undotted "i's" and ended with a dotted "j" whose elongated tail curved under the adjoining letters.[1] In that age before commas, a bookkeeper inserted other symbols for clarity. The number 1,000 was represented by a "U," as in Accountant Argüelles' statement that the English armada coming upon Cartagena had 26 ships and VIU men, meaning 6,000, or Auditor Redondo Villegas' reference to the year 1600 as IU600. The symbol for a million was "Q" or "q^{os}," standing for *quentos*. The number 17,913,725, for example, could be written 17q^{os}913U725. A *quento escaso* was 100,000.[2] Roman numerals began going out of use in 1580, but for another fifty years or more a numeral could be written either way.[3]

The smallest integer was the maravedí, equivalent to approximately 0.1 gram of silver. Gold as well as silver coins could be expressed in maravedís, making it easier to reflect fluctuations in the bimetallic ratio. Perhaps this is why the crown was requiring, by the late 1570s, that all accounts be recorded in that unit.[4] There were 34 maravedís to the real, 272 maravedís (8 reales) to the peso, and 375 maravedís (11 reales) to the ducat. During the sixteenth century large

118

figures were customarily stated in terms of ducats. Starting around 1600, amounts to be collected on the situado were stated in pesos. The separate subsidies within the situado, however, continued to be expressed in ducats for another third of a century, and fines and bonds were cited in that coin even longer.[5] The *escudo,* whose value was set at 400 maravedís in 1566, was worth 1.1 pesos, or 300 maravedís, in the late seventeenth century. It was not a common coin and usually entered Florida as part of a pension or salary awarded elsewhere.[6] Since all these coins had separately varying exchange rates and availability, contracts designated the one in which they were to be fulfilled, and the added expressions *de contado, efectivos,* or *acuñados* meant "in cash."

The form of bookkeeping practiced in sixteenth- and seventeenth-century colonial treasuries was not double-entry, although this method was known.[7] The crown preferred the "charge-discharge," or *cargo-data,* system based upon personal liability.[8] In this system one was "charged" when he accepted responsibility for a certain amount of money or quantity of property. He was "discharged" when he produced equivalent funds or items of property or acceptable evidence of their correct and authorized expenditure. At the end of an accounting period or, in the case of situadores and shipmasters, after the voyage, one sought discharge by "rendering" his accounts to the proper authority, who was said to "take" them.

The "charge-discharge" system, while it emphasized personal liability, also fostered a sense of proprietorship. What was a private responsibility could be of private advantage. Even with intentions that were upright it was possible to confuse one's own money and property with that of the crown. "Charge-discharge" accounting style did not facilitate a running balance. Both cargo and data entries might appear on the same page with cargo at the top and data below; more often they were on separate pages, in separate sections, or even separate books. Knowing that someone else would be going over their accounts and calling in their deficits, some of the royal officials never balanced their books at all.

In 1578 Visitador Alvaro Flores de Quiñones was furnished with a list of the books being kept in Florida. The treasurer and the factor each kept two books, one of data and the other of cargo. The treasurer's accounts were of monies and credit received and expended; the factor's, a running inventory of goods by classification. Two other books of primary importance were the book of the coffer and the book of resolutions. Five secondary books contained salary contracts and service records, musters, probate records, ship registries and merchandise evaluations, and the accounts of situadores and others temporarily charged with monies or supplies. Other books were added as required. St. Augustine's various ledgers and the supporting vouchers and receipts (*cartas de pago*) were stored in boxes and cupboards at the counting house. Auditors and their assistants brought special one-hole punched paper (*papel agujereado*) on which to make copies, which they tied with red tape of wool or linen and forwarded to the Council of the Indies.[9] When the Council was finished with them, the copies went to the Castle of Simancas near Valladolíd, set aside by the Emperor Charles V as an archival repository.[10]

There were three, sometimes four levels of accountability for an official to surmount on his way to formal quittance (*finiquito*): rendering his accounts, the local audit, the review audit, and in some cases, an appeal to a higher court. As one might expect for a treasury both isolated and poor, the Florida arrangements for accountability were irregular, often unclear, and complicated by continuous changes and combinations of levels. Perhaps this is why Hoffman found that among the treasuries of the Antilles and the circum-Caribbean, the Florida treasury was outstanding for its unreliable accounts and infrequent audits.[11]

Provision had been made for appeals, or fiscal litigation, long before there was a permanent settlement on the peninsula. Only a few days after Pánfilo de Narváez landed at Tampa Bay in 1528, a royal ordinance listed the Florida treasury officials among those whose appeals were to go to the audiencia of Mexico. This disposition was repeated in 1533, when Florida was regarded as one with the western Gulf Coast province of Pánuco. In more general legislation, the New Laws of 1542 specified that treasury officials in the Indies should send an annual financial summary to the accountants of the Council. The Ordinances of 1554 called for audits every three years and gave detailed procedural instructions, which were largely ignored while the crown made a short-lived experiment in Peru with a special board of accountants. In 1563 the Ordinance of the Audiencias amended audit intervals to be yearly, and the following year the procedural orders were reissued. By 1570 most Caribbean treasuries were being audited on a regular basis.[12]

The Florida treasury was an immediate exception. For the first eleven years it was hardly a treasury at all. Its books were tied in first with the personal accounts of Menéndez, then with the subsidy to the Indies Fleet. When Florida received a subsidy of its own, the adelantado and his numerous nephews treated it as part of their personal funds. Auditing was done at the convenience of crown-appointed investigators, usually officials from the Fleet. One of these, Treasurer Andrés de Eguino, discovered in 1569 that Steward Juan de Junco, Menéndez's earliest treasury appointee, had false scales with which he systematically cheated the king's soldiers. Junco's confederates at once initiated a cover-up. Lieutenant-Governor Las Alas refused Eguino the use of a boat to visit the fort on Cumberland Island and interview the substitute treasurer there. Magistrate Martín de Argüelles ordered Eguino to surrender the book containing his evidence. When the visitador tried to transport Junco and several key witnesses to Spain, Pedro Menéndez Marquez, at that time acting governor of Cuba, treated his proposal with derision.[13]

Havana and St. Augustine, one week apart in good sailing weather, had been forced into frequent contact by the necessities of defense and supply. For several years it appeared that the Florida settlements, younger than either Havana or Santiago by half a century, were going to take the lead, especially when the two governorships were combined in the person of Pedro Menéndez in 1567, and Havana became little more than a supply depot for the adelantado's Florida garrisons and Indies Fleet. It received a subsidy for troops the same year Florida did, but for only a third as many. In the Menéndez clan, loyalties were wholly personal. The Asturians' allegiance to Philip II did not extend to cooperation with his servants or compliance with his bureaucracies. In 1573 the king moved to establish royal control by appointing Dr. Alonso de Cáceres, a distinguished member of the audiencia of Santo Domingo, to investigate Pedro Menéndez Marquez's term as Cuban lieutenant governor.[14]

At the time, the outside investigator was the crown's chosen means of detecting frauds and recovering treasury deficits. There were three kinds of investigation: a *pesquisa* was a secret inquiry into almost anything; a *residencia* was a judicial inquiry into a bonded official's completed term; and a *visita* was the investigation of an entire local bureaucracy and its activities, past and present. In practice the three were not strictly differentiated. Dr. Cáceres first conducted a pesquisa and came up with fifty counts on which to try Menéndez Marquez. As judge of the residencia he found him guilty on thirty-eight of them and referred his case to the Council. Cáceres had also been ordered to go to Florida for a one-month visita, but he never embarked on it. Menéndez Marquez and Esteban de las Alas were heard to boast at the door of a tavern that they would put the judge ashore at Tequesta and let the Indians see that he did no further harm, and it was possible that they meant it.[15]

Without visiting Florida, Cáceres nonetheless formed an opinion on how it was being managed. In a lengthy report which avoided direct accusation of the adelantado, he explained that the numerous lieutenant governors and officials in the Florida forts were kinsmen or close connections of the Menéndez clan in Cuba, all of them doing as they pleased what would profit them. No one outside their group could ship salt meat or any other foodstuff to Florida, for no skipper would load it. The clan monopolized shipping, priced the supplies, figured the payroll, and took each other's accounts, "and so they remain with everything."[16]

After the revelations of the residencia judge the governorships of Florida and Cuba were separated. The new governor in Havana was sent 200 slaves and the money to complete El Morro.[17] Menéndez Marquez, badly needed in the Fleet of the Indies, spent the next three years as an admiral. The Council never communicated his sentence of exile and suspension to him; it hung over his head for the rest of his career.[18]

Baltasar del Castillo y Ahedo, onetime accountant of the Menéndez armada, was commissioned in 1575 to visit the forts in Florida, inspect the artillery, and report on the governor and officials. His services were cheap (200,000 maravedís a year instead of the 3,000 ducats the Council would have had to pay someone else), for the reason that he, too, was under sentence of perpetual exile and loss of office, for trafficking as an armada official.[19]

Before Castillo y Ahedo could get to Florida, Indians massacred two of the proprietors and one acting official when they landed on the island of Sapala en route between forts. Doña Mayor de Arango, widowed by the death of Treasurer Pedro Menéndez the Younger, lamented to the crown that everything the royal officials had with them had been stolen by the Indians: their belongings, the account books, and, by inference, the money they were taking to pay the soldiers. Others said that the Indians had not touched the king's silver, which was on a different boat. Enough books and supporting materials were produced for Castillo to expand his visit into an audit. It was a frustrating experience; as he said, "In Florida I did not find, nor was there ever, an account which was clear."[20] Doña Mayor left for Havana with 4,000 ducats, which the shipmaster buried for her in the floor of his room. Someone else brought her another 800 ducats. When the auditor realized how much was missing he returned to Havana and put doña Mayor under house arrest. With him, he hoped, was sufficient evidence to indict the whole Menéndez clan, living and dead. In the last resort, he said, everything was chargeable to the adelantado. Pedro Menéndez Marquez, busy in the Indies Fleet, had been only peripherally involved. The Council sent him to reconquer the Florida provinces from the Indians (who were apt to ally themselves with French corsairs) and told Castillo not to interfere with his finances.[21]

Regular (as opposed to patrimonial) administration of the Florida accounts began in 1577 as a consequence of the Castillo visit, but was slow to develop. In 1580 the crown attempted to tighten its control on all overseas treasuries and impose new taxes. Juan de Cevadilla and Lázaro Sáez de Mercado were the appointees who brought the orders to St. Augustine, promising, "From now on, the amount being spent will always be known, and the care that is taken of the exchequer." The Florida treasury, they discovered, was not as stable as it should be. Their predecessors kept them waiting three months to take office. Governor Menéndez Marquez denied their authority as royal judges, as administrators of the situado and supplies, and as regidores. He refused to allow them a notary or bailiff to assist with the inspection of ships. He would not let them have a key to the royal warehouse nor show them the payroll for construction of the fort. He tried to make them receive goods without the proper affidavits. He had soldiers building huts half a league from town, and he would not tell the royal officials why. The crown took up these complaints over the next three years in a steady stream of admonitory cédulas. The most significant of these approved the new treasury proprietors' plan to take turns being situador, converting them almost involuntarily from servants of the crown into Florida entrepreneurs.[22]

In the drafty halls of Spanish government the left hand did not necessarily know what the right was doing. In 1585 Menéndez Marquez, under suspended sentence for fiscal malfeasance, received a letter which read:

> It is very inconvenient that ordinarily there is no explanation given to my Council of the Indies of the manner in which the subsidy is distributed and spent at those forts, and the rest of what comes into the hands of those officials. So I have ordered that every year the accounts be taken and sent to the Council.
>
> When you receive this cédula have the officials present themselves, the treasurer and accountant and factor, and ask a sworn report from them of the time they have not accounted for, and examine the books. If they are overdrawn, charge it to them and their bondholders and properties and put it into my coffer. At the beginning of every year take the same accounting from them and report to my Council.

It was the same form letter that would be sent five years later to Interim Governor Gutierre de Miranda. [23]

The approved procedure for taking accounts was this: Once a year the governor, with the help of a notary and two regidores as outlined in the Ordinances of 1554, counted the cash in the treasure chest, inventoried the supplies in the warehouse, and struck a balance in the books between receipts and disbursements, deciding one by one whether the entries were legitimate and adequately documented. The royal officials were expected to explain any discrepancy and settle any deficit within three days.

Certain difficulties were inherent in this plan. It was unhandy to render accounts yearly when the subsidy to which the accounts were tied did not come every year. It was unseemly to take accounts with the help of regidores, when the only regidores in Florida were the three treasury officials. Taking accounts was also time-consuming and called for a degree of interest and skill. Menéndez Marquez, quondam merchant, royal accountant, and smuggler, was capable, if not entirely trustworthy, but most Florida governors were ordinary career officers. [24] Méndez de Canzo could not comprehend why one could not make entries into closed books. Pedro de Ybarra, when he got his form letter, answered curtly, "I cannot take accounts. I am a soldier." [25] A final problem was that whereas financial summaries went to the Council, fiscal appeals did not. Treasurer Juan de Cevadilla argued that the 1533 cédula referring Florida-Pánuco appeals to Mexico still applied, and the crown did not disagree. The fact that Pedro Menéndez had obtained a contract codicil to explore and take possession of the coast as far as the southern Pánuco border seemed to support the treasurer's claim.[26]

Cevadilla died in New Spain owing the treasury more than 21,000 ducats; five years later there had still been no audit of his books because the auditor assigned to do it was in prison. The treasurer's widow, Petronila de Junco (niece of Juan of the notorious scales), entreated the crown to send someone else, as she was being detained in St. Augustine against her will. When a cédula arrived ordering the governor to attend to her, treasury officials Bartolomé de Argüelles and Juan Menéndez Marquez were serving as interim co-governors due to the death of Martínez de Avendaño. Finding time and Petronila on their hands, they had already started balancing the books of both her husband and her father, deceased Factor Rodrigo de Junco. Cevadilla owned nothing that could be attached, Argüelles reported, and Junco's accounts were impossible to take because his estate was in Oviedo, most of his bondholders were dead, and Drake had burned the books. As a gesture, the officials put their colleagues Factor Las Alas and Steward Fernández Perete on half-salary until they should account for what funds had passed through their hands.[27] When Governor Méndez de Canzo arrived to take office, Argüelles and Menéndez Marquez finished the accounts and closed the books.

The auditor who reopened them was Pedro Redondo Villegas, accountant of the royal munitions foundry in Cuba, who was asked to go to Florida in 1598 in place of his colleague who was in prison. The instructions given him were to:

1. Investigate the condition of the royal soldiers, artillery, and forts.

2. Correct accounting procedures at the treasury.

3. Audit the accounts of the royal officials and anyone else through whose hands royal monies or supplies had passed.

4. Recover deficits from the individual's property, bondholders, heirs, and successors.

As duly commissioned judge of accounts (*juez de cuentas*) he had the magisterial power to subpoena witnesses and notarial records and to execute property judgments without recourse. Appeals from his decisions were to go, not to the Mexico City audiencia, but to the Council.[28]

During his absence from home, Redondo Villegas received his regular salary of 100,000 maravedís, out of which he paid 200 ducats to a substitute. In Florida he was given an additional 60 escudos a month, plus 20 escudos for an assistant. Governor Méndez de Canzo supplied him with a residence, 6 escudos a month for expenses, a plaza with unspecified supplements for his Cuban clerk, and, when that clerk went back home, the services of a youth from the governor's own household, dignified with the title of taker of accounts (*tomador de cuentas*). The auditor and his assistants charged 2 reales per folio for copying the audited accounts with the verifying annotations in the margins. Not counting his perquisites of house, assistants, or expense account, Redondo Villegas cleared 790 escudos a year by being in Florida. The royal officials claimed that this was why he prolonged his stay, copying unnecessary papers and opening accounts long closed, while payment was stopped on their salaries.[29]

The royal officials particularly disliked his changes in their bookkeeping system. In obedience to a cédula which they had been ignoring, the auditor required them, beginning January 1, 1600, to keep a duplicate of the treasurer's record of drafts against the situado. He also refused to accept any precedent from the Indies Fleet without a cédula endorsing it for Florida; anything the treasury officials had allowed without such validation—whether free medicines, extra rations, office supplies, or tax exemptions—he threatened to charge to them personally. They were also forced to report the 60,000 pesos surplus in their coffer.[30]

Part of the reason Redondo Villegas was overstaying his welcome was that the king had extended his commission and told him to renew collections on the Cevadilla and Junco accounts, which he had determined amounted to 23,258 and 1,606 ducats respectively.[31] As part of that process he threw Gil de Cevadilla and Juan de Junco the Younger in prison and coerced testimony from them against other parties. One of these was Captain Hernando de Mestas, a favorite envoy of the governor. On his way back from Spain in 1599, Mestas had been captured off Puerto Rico by French corsairs, who rifled through his trunk. Among the items they took was a Council receipt for 4,000 ducats collected from Juan de Oribe Apalúa, one of the

Cevadilla bondholders. Without this receipt, Mestas was unable to prove he had given the Council the money. Accountant Argüelles, himself in trouble for his easygoing collections, may have known that Mestas was a secret informer. Five days after Argüelles wrote that the auditor had him under pressure, he, the governor, and the auditor were all on good terms and Mestas was in irons in the castillo. An unannounced search of the captain's house had produced two incriminating letters addressed to the Council. The governor, furious, held Mestas incommunicado under pain of death. Redondo Villegas slapped a demand on him for the 4,000 ducats. If the prisoner did not sign a confession that his secret reports on the governor were untrue, the king's auditor offered to break his bones with an iron bar and make him no man. [32]

The ship carrying Redondo Villegas' precious papers went down in the Bahama Channel, but the governor's new envoy, Fabricio López, saved the account copies and they eventually reached Spain. A letter that Mestas managed to slip out of prison got there, too, with one parting shot. With ungrammatic emphasis the captain warned the king to disregard Méndez de Canzo's tales of a hill of diamonds in the interior (*tierra adentro*), for "the perfect diamonds is the situado!" [33] What became of Captain Mestas is unknown; the governor was recalled to Spain and suspended from His Majesty's service for eight years, not for conniving with an auditor, but for having appointed his ten-year-old son Antonio a company captain. [34] The Cevadilla account was finally reclosed eleven years after the treasurer's death. Argüelles, Menéndez Marquez, and Las Alas each spent years in Spain in litigation. Argüelles received his quittance in 1605; Menéndez Marquez was proposed for a 1,000-ducat reward and given the governorship of Popayán; Las Alas' reputation was rehabilitated after his death. [35]

The problem of audit and appeals was never solved to suit the royal officials. In 1605 Philip III created three Tribunals of Accounts in the cities of Mexico, Los Reyes (Lima), and Santa Fé (Bogotá). They were to serve as intermediaries between the local treasuries of their audiencias and the Council in Spain, compiling the annual financial summaries and sending out roving auditors. The tribunals were empowered to give quittance in cases of fiscal litigation, thus serving as a final court of appeals. Two auditors independent of the tribunals were appointed, one to reside in Caracas and the other in

Havana. In 1609, the poorer and more distant coffers, which included Española, Puerto Rico, and Cuba, were subordinated to the closest tribunal and its roving auditors. Florida was too insignificant to be mentioned.[36] The 1605 decentralization, far from being the end of territorial autonomy, or a turning point in the fiscal organization of the Florida treasury, for years had no measurable effect on it whatever. St. Augustine was a jurisdiction unto itself. The Florida officials, receiving the situado from the Mexico City treasury, declined to answer to the Mexico City tribunal. They asked that in their case the old system be followed of a visiting auditor and appeals direct to the Council.[37] So it was, perhaps by default.

To understand the next chapter in treasury history we must once again digress to the relationship between Florida and Cuba, two colonies grudgingly interdependent. The gradual pacification of the peninsula, accomplished by Florida-based soldiers and friars, brought benefits to the island. Cuban fishermen searched the Florida coastal waters; Cuban traders bartered with the southern Indians for amber and salvage; Cuban armada suppliers floated ships' masts down the San Martín and other Gulf rivers.[38] Meanwhile, the younger colony was going into debt. As early as 1595 St. Augustine's obligations in Havana equaled half a year's situado. As the situados fell into arrears Cuban merchants became reluctant to advance goods on credit. The crown ordered the governor of Cuba to furnish St. Augustine with emergency supplies, but this did not keep prices from rising. As the presidio went deeper and deeper into debt it began to take as long to bargain with suppliers in Havana as to collect the situado.[39] Santo Domingo's Dr. Cáceres had thought that the only way to correct Florida's problems was to break the Menéndez stranglehold on shipping and have someone in Havana administer the situado.[40] Investigators and auditors from Cuba were even more convinced that this was the solution. Yet when a Cuban official at last received supervisory powers over the Florida situado it was not to regularize counting house procedure or to solve a difficulty in the balance of trade: the measure was decreed out of the financial distress of the crown.

For some time after 1628, when Piet Heyn captured the silver fleet at Matanzas, the empire's fiscal affairs were in extraordinary disorder. The effect on Florida was that situados fell so far behind and were so slowly paid that no money seemed to come into the coffer at all.

When the situados were coming more regularly, with a good share in money, the royal officials made some effort to keep up with their bookkeeping. But as year after year passed and Florida seemed to be forgotten, they grew lax about everything except which of them should go next to Mexico City.

Unfortunately for morale in St. Augustine, the loss of the silver fleet coincided with a cutback in the number of proprietors and the introduction of a new tax. The protests of the first accountant appointed after the reduction, Ponce de León, were summarized for the Council in 1631:

> The Florida counting house is one of the busiest in the Indies and of the most personal labor, because it keeps the accounts and records of all that is spent and distributed on the infantry of that presidio to give them rations of comestibles—something not done anywhere else—and the same for the religious who attend that province, and the mariners who serve there, and the Indians, to sustain and clothe them, all of which requires a great quantity of paperwork. There has also been added to the counting house the offices of overseer and factor, which were consumed, and all the paperwork that went with these offices Your Majesty has ordered to be the accountant's responsibility. Now in addition, Your Majesty orders that papers and new books be kept on the accounts and records of the tax of the half-annate.

The accountant's conclusion was ominous: if he was not given another assistant the books were going to get behind.[41] As we have seen in Chapter 4, a clerk of the half-annate was approved in the bureaucracy's good time, which by then was too late.

Treasurer Francisco Menéndez Marquez was as reluctant to assume the duties of steward as the accountant was to do the work of factor-overseer; only his tactics were different. In 1630 he had his orphaned siblings, five sisters and one little brother, ask the crown for a yearly grant of 100 ducats each from the vacant salary of the factor-overseer. The proposal was denied.[42] At the same time, he named Alonso Menéndez y Posada (not the seven-year-old brother by that name but their sixty-year-old uncle) to the office of steward, which he reactivated.[43] The crown ignored the move.

In 1638 the king, in desperate straits, ordered General Carlos de Ibarra to sequester the situados bound for Caribbean garrisons, and followed this with an order for the situadores of the Windward Isles to report to Accountant Pedro Beltrán de Santa Cruz in Havana each year on their way back to their respective presidios, telling him what payments they had made and what cash they carried. To give him magisterial authority over them, Santa Cruz was named a judge of accounts.[44]

Florida Accountant Ponce de León worriedly wrote to the crown. He and Governor Horruytiner, he said, were keeping Treasurer Francisco Menéndez Marquez in prison for his frauds in collecting the situados for 1631 and 1632. They had learned that the incoming governor and the new auditor, who was a vecino of Havana and a close connection of the treasurer, meant to release him. If the treasurer, intent on revenge, was to be let out of prison, the accountant wanted to be transferred to another post where his life would be in less danger. Menéndez Marquez was indeed released, and in 1641 Ponce de León found occasion to go to Mexico City, where he stayed.[45] After several years had passed, Auditor Santa Cruz appointed Pedro Benedit Horruytiner, son of former Governor Luis Horruytiner, in Ponce de León's place.[46] Horruytiner and Menéndez Marquez reported that the books had not been properly kept since 1632. Many papers were unsigned, others were in rough drafts innocent of comprehensibility or totals, and a number of supporting vouchers were missing. It would take full-time work by someone, he thought, to bring up to date the accounts of royal slave earnings, almorifazgos and tithes, ship registries, and the record of each soldier's wages and withdrawals.[47]

According to the rule of collegial responsibility, this delinquency of the accountant's was just as much the fault of the treasurer. Most of the lapses mentioned involved duties of the steward, and now that the treasurer had been retitled "treasurer-steward" it might have been assumed that he would take care of them. Francisco Menéndez Marquez shrugged off the responsibility, saying that since the office of steward had been added to his duties without any allowance for an assistant, he had more work than he could do without keeping the accountant's books. The crown's reaction to this impertinence was oddly mild: whatever it cost to put the books in order was to come from the royal officials' salaries or property, and not be a charge on the treasury.[48]

Before receiving this letter, Francisco had already named another relative, Juan Ruíz Mejía, to the office of steward at a salary of 200,000 maravedís—a low sum, he said, since the steward had to hire assistants. The treasurer argued that it was time for a new royal office:

> The separation of this steward's office is very much in Your Majesty's service, so the treasurer can be free to attend to the balancing and settlement of the other business of his office and that of the counting house. For that matter, the place of factor-overseer was most important to the service of Your Majesty ... in this presidio. The governor who advised Your Majesty otherwise could have had no other motive than less opposition to his money making.

The crown was unmoved. The treasurer-steward might divide his own salary with an assistant if he liked, and the king stood disposed to honor and reward his servants, but no new royal offices were to be created.[49] The pleas of later treasurers received the same response.

Pedro Benedit Horruytiner, overwhelmed by the disorder in the counting house, asked for a formal investigation (*visita de caja*) and audit. His request came inopportunely. The crown had just made a pronouncement about the general uselessness of such investigations and ordered that they be curtailed. In no case was the salary of a visiting auditor to be charged to the royal exchequer; it must come out of fines and condemnations.[50]

Perhaps because the culprits at the Florida treasury had no property worth the condemning, Santa Cruz did not find the time to visit St. Augustine in the 1640s. Instead he proposed a remedy for the treasury's problems, which he thought of in terms of the situado. It should not be necessary for the Florida governor and royal officials to send a situador to Mexico City. The officials of that coffer should deliver the Florida subsidy to the treasury at Vera Cruz to be sent, registered on one of the flagships of the fleet, to the officials in Havana. There were merchants in Vera Cruz and Havana who would supply the Florida presidio with provisions and clothing at reasonable prices and at their own risk. Comments on this proposal by the fiscal of the Council show that the officials in Havana were trusted no more than those in St. Augustine. The fiscal thought it would be as well to contract for presidio clothing. As for collecting and transporting the situado, the governor of Florida should farm out the position of situador to the lowest bidder and let him worry about how to get it to St. Augustine. In accordance with this laissez-faire attitude, Governor Salazar Vallecilla awarded the mission of situado collection to four vecinos of Vera Cruz. Instead of sending clothing, they filled the presidio with wine and rum, and the frauds they committed were spectacular even for Florida. The crown ordered the auditor to proceed against the Vera Cruz villains and everyone with whom they had had dealings. Santa Cruz's investigation took him to St. Augustine, fifteen years after he had been appointed its auditor, and there he saw for himself the state of treasury records.[51]

In 1653, when the auditor arrived, Treasurer Francisco Menéndez Marquez had been dead for two years and Pedro Benedit Horruytiner was the elected interim governor. The books of the counting house were in worse shape than they had reported. The accounts of the masters of presidio vessels had not been taken since 1624. The taxes on ship tonnage had not been collected, nor the half-annate. The papers of Steward Alonso Menéndez y Posada had accumulated untouched from 1630 to 1649, and the clerks had to divide them into three batches for recording. The books of the soldiers' wages and deductions had not been kept since 1646. The auditor and his assistants felt like the seven maids with seven mops:

> It was a terrible job to bring that up to date. Eight persons worked on it, and every book had over 400 folios covering the infantry and the friars. Since there is only one supplier of clothing and staples, and the outlet for merchandise is the royal warehouse, where everything necessary to life is dispensed against [the soldiers'] salaries—everything for women and children as well as themselves—the treasury and presidio are in total confusion. No one knows what he is owed nor what he owes, not even the royal officials, and the usual thing is to give people more than is owed them.[52]

Francisco had had good reason for letting the books get behind. When he died he had run up a deficit totaling 16,165 pesos. In a place as poor as Florida, embezzlement on such a scale was remarkable. The heirs of the estate paid all but 4,000 pesos of the debt immediately and Santa Cruz gave them six years to pay the balance, using 8,000 pesos worth of cattle, horses, and hogs as collateral. If the auditor was Francisco's kinsman he gave no indication of it: the first payments (1,950 pesos in libranzas and silver plate) he applied to his own expenses.[53]

The auditor continued to claim that Florida's problems stemmed from situado mismanagement at every step, from the choice of situador, through the bribes in Mexico City, to the kind of transportation to Florida. He pressed one of his earlier solutions. A fourth of the situado for Florida could be saved if it were brought to Cuba by the general of the galleons and turned over to the royal officials in Havana, who could either send it on or let the Florida officials come after it the way those of Santo Domingo and Puerto Rico did. The Council of the Indies again ignored the Cuban accountant's efforts to have a greater say in the Florida subsidies. Its fiscal asked the viceroy to investigate the charges of bribery and told the auditor to go on with his collections.[54]

In 1657, the year after the auditor returned to Havana, Florida Accountant Santos de las Heras came into the harbor with situados rumored to amount to over 200,000 ducats. Using the 1639 cédula authorizing him to keep track of all situados passing through Havana, the auditor demanded a report on what Las Heras carried. The accountant-situador refused. At that time the governorship of Havana was divided between a political and a military governor. Santa Cruz and the political governor confined Las Heras in the cabildo building; the military governor released him and let him sail. When Santa Cruz tried to take testimony as to how much money was really going to the St. Augustine coffer, the military governor forbade the local notaries to assist him in any manner.[55]

Santa Cruz's star was going down. Governor Rebolledo and the royal officials in St. Augustine were even then gathering testimony, and in 1659 they sent Salvador de Cigarroa to Madrid as a procurador to expose him at court. The accusations Cigarroa made in Madrid were serious: Santa Cruz claimed to have had eight assistants and to have finished the work in ten months, whereas he had actually had two assistants and had not finished. His marginal entries were not in correct form. He had charged people for copies of his judgments and refused to provide any. In all his time as auditor he had neither given receipts for payments against debts nor put anything into the treasure chest. He had released fiscal offenders from prison by a private arrangement: they gave him a portion of what they owed and he reported the debt uncollectible. He had laid a charge of 4,500 pesos for expenses (including 2,500 pesos for the purported assistants) upon the Florida treasury and had tried to embargo the situado on its way through Havana to pay it. From various persons he had extorted 8,000 pesos in libranzas, wrought silver, jewels, and other valuables. After the time of his audit no one could be found to accept (in other words, to buy) a bonded office, for fear of him and his false reports. In response to these charges and to complaints emanating from Cuba, the Council ordered the investigation and punishment of Auditor Pedro Beltrán de Santa Cruz. The visita was entrusted to the bishop of Cuba; when he died without having done it, the task was handed on to his successor. In 1666, thirteen years after his trip to Florida, the auditor was still awaiting trial and the Floridians had still not received a copy of his audit.[56]

The treasury officials asked in 1660 to present their audits for review and send their appeals to the seven auditors of the tribunal of accounts in Mexico City. This request was quickly approved, but as it was tied in with forwarding criminal appeals to the audiencia, Governor Aranguíz y Cotes withheld the cédula. It was repeated to the next governor five years later and evidently put into effect. Pedro Benedit Horruytiner, whose association with the discredited auditor was not held against him, was named lieutenant auditor for Florida with a salary of 500 pesos from the situado surplus.[57] No such arrangement seemed to last long. During the regency of Queen Mariana (1665–75) a reorganization took place. All the treasuries of the Windward Isles, including Florida, were told to present their audits and summaries to the royal auditor in Havana. The officials in St. Augustine objected that this would be impossible as no one exercised the local office of lieutenant auditor. Some years later, Governor Hita Salazar promised for them that summaries would be sent triennially to the correct tribunal, which he acknowledged to be the one in Cuba.[58]

The governor who came in 1680, Marques Cabrera, was a religious mystic who had written a book titled *Espejo de buen soldado* (*Mirror of the Good Soldier*).[59] He was much interested in accounting, appointed himself judge of accounts, and spent months going over the papers of interim stewards, accountants, situadores, shipmasters, and construction foremen. To no one's surprise he uncovered many irregularities. In the books of the treasurer he found taxes and fines ten years delinquent.[60] Unfortunately for the crown, before the governor could implement fiscal reforms he was overtaken by events. A local cabal proved too much for his unstable emotions and he fled in a panic to Havana. Ten years later his unpaid salary was still under embargo.[61]

The governor who succeeded him, Quiroga y Losada, was interested in building, not bookkeeping. He asked the crown to relieve him of the chore of taking accounts and give it to a lieutenant auditor. Such an official was eventually appointed, for among the dignitaries in St. Augustine on the day Philip V was acclaimed was an auditor of accounts, but this was long after Quiroga y Losada's term.[62] Rather than have the accounts be taken in Havana he did them himself, and on the basis of his investigations put the accountant and several others in prison. This action, which had little effect on them, was disastrous for the governor. The influence of Cuba was then at its height. Havana vecino Laureano Torres y Ayala, having spent nearly four years in the powerful position of governor-elect, was about to embark on a six-year term as governor. One of Torres y Ayala's first acts in office was to release the accountant, who had made him an illegal two-year salary advance out of money owed to Quiroga y Losada.[63] The principal Florida families—Menéndez Marquez, Florencia, Hita Salazar, and Horruytiner—united with their man from Havana to ruin his predecessor. Quiroga y Losada's residencia dragged on for fifteen months in St. Augustine, then was moved to Cuba, where Notary Juan de Argote charged the unlucky man 3,500 pesos for the paperwork alone. While the ex-governor was in Mexico City appealing before the audiencia, Argote attached his wife's gowns and jewels, down to her favorite earrings and the rings from her fingers. Seven years after Quiroga y Losada's term was over he faced long appeals before the Council, and the chest containing his irreplaceable residencia papers had disappeared between the Canary Islands and Cádiz.[64]

In this last decade of the Habsburg era the four levels of treasury accountability stood theoretically as follows: Accounts were rendered to the governor or a lieutenant auditor, who also did local audits. Financial summaries of various kinds were sent to the Council, the viceroy of New Spain, and the tribunal of accounts in Havana. Audit reviews were the responsibility of that same tribunal, which was also the court of appeals. In practice, accounts were taken and local audits were done by persons with local ties. Reviews and appeals, like the situado, were firmly in the hands of a powerful Cuban–Floridian creole clique.[65]

It had been the crown's desire ever since St. Augustine was founded to bring its treasury there into line with minimal royal policy, ordinary honesty being considered an unrealistic goal. But the obstacles to sound financial accounting and accountability were self-perpetuating and perhaps insuperable. Most officials charged with correcting the situation preferred to profit by it; those who tried to do otherwise were destroyed by the local power structure. Given the royal officials' chronic absenteeism, lackadaisical performances, and misappropriations, if not outright fraud, the crown treated them with a lenience that approached indifference.

Conclusion

THERE should have been no Spanish colony in Florida. Philip II's reluctant attempts to colonize on the continent were his response to the hateful French principle of effective occupation. The king enforced his costly claim because interlopers were not to be tolerated, and although Florida was a land without riches, cities, or decent harbors, his advisors were sure it guarded the passage to the East. Once the French were driven out, Spanish presence could be maintained by settlements or, if necessary, a caretaker garrison and a handful of friars.

Florida, however, proved difficult to conquer and settle and even more difficult to govern. For the first fifteen years treasury affairs were in a state of chaos. Accounts of the garrison were mingled with the personal accounts of Pedro Menéndez and his extended family or with the ship accounts of the Indies Fleet. Officials were appointed and did not serve, or served and were not confirmed, or were confirmed and then killed by Indians. Some came on loan from the Fleet without the formality of titles. The beginnings of rational, nonfamilial accounting were seen in 1580, but the benefits of it were lost in accidents of war. The year of Drake's raid, 1586, saw the coffer stolen, the treasury headquarters destroyed, the books burned, and the branch office of Santa Elena abandoned. The French continued to be a problem. Undeterred by the capture of Fort Caroline or the massacre of Matanzas, they resumed their seasonal trading, and the Indians' desire for allies against the Spanish made them all the more welcome.

During the hectic sixteenth century, Florida enjoyed a moratorium on royal regulations as well as taxes. Had the crown enforced its laws on barter and trade, production, native labor, campaigns in the field, unauthorized expenditures, or conflicts of interest, the tiny colony could not have survived. The years from 1595 to 1605 saw a gradual change. For the first time governors were appointed from outside the Menéndez clan. Problems with the French and Indians came to a head. After campaigns against Guale, Surruque, and a tribe at the Savannah River, the nearer natives submitted to trade, tribute, and conversion. St. Augustine was redesigned and rebuilt, and laborers were summoned in shifts to grow maize. The visit of a royal auditor signaled a new century and a new era. The treasury was instructed to break with casual Fleet practices and infant colony exemptions. There would be tighter supervision of officials, precise procedures, and new taxes.

The history of the Florida treasury in the seventeenth century, as we have seen, is the story of the sabotaging of this plan. The question is, why? Was it due to defects of the Spanish imperial system? Those defects are well known. Historians seem to have often chosen the Spanish empire, like the Roman, for homilies on decline and fall. Some of the characteristics predisposing to collapse, such as venality of office, or monarchs whose interests clashed with those of the country, were common to all the courts of Europe. Others were more peculiarly Spanish, such as an increasingly enclave mentality in the face of assaults upon the Catholic faith and territory and, related to that, a growing inability to compromise with ideals, resulting in a wider than usual disparity between the lawful and the worldly and practical. Yet one could argue that these "Spanish" traits containing the seeds of eventual decline were the very qualities that had once made the empire possible and had given it vitality.

John Leddy Phelan, in his thoughtful administrative analysis, "Authority and Flexibility in the Spanish Imperial Bureaucracy," hypothesizes that the strength of the Spanish bureaucracy lay in this divergence between law and practice. Local officials with conflicting jurisdictions were forced to choose which of several standards to apply, knowing they could be held responsible for any of them. The system allowed flexibility and a degree of decentralization without weakening central authority. It was the reason why the bureaucracy, like the church, could maintain political and societal stability in the Indies for three centuries.

In Florida the tangled hierarchies of the government provided as many causes for conflict as the Floridians' common dependence upon Indian labor or their mutual absorption in the situado. From time to time a royal cédula would clarify some point of contention, but the crown was inattentive and erratic and left other points vague, as though to test the maneuvering skill and power base of the contenders. At any time the political clout of a royal appointee could have been measured by the disputed areas he had under his control. If the imperial bureaucracy made any contribution to political and societal stability, it was by supporting propertied officeholders. The system was decentralized and the system was flexible, but effective central authority did not exist.

The royal officials were at fault for their embezzling, graft, and gross neglect of duty. The crown, acting through the Council of the Indies, was also at fault for its spasmodic supervision, disconnected *ad hoc* decisions, inadequate support, and general lack of interest. But running deeper than the actions of any person or tribunal were the problems of the imperial bureaucracy itself: the cumbersome safeguards, the conflicting jurisdictions, the practice of filling offices by patronage or purchase, the ambience of conspicuous display, the commercial monopolies and their corollaries of lawbreaking and economic decay. And if all these had been magically corrected, there would still have been the problems proper to St. Augustine, a hardship post in a land known for bad climate, decreasing population, and active war.

Efficient and upright treasury administration was a chimera. Given the contemporary milieu and mores, that goal was probably as unattainable as justice for the Indians, which also concerned the crown, or fairness to soldiers, just beginning to enter the royal consciousness. Yet if one substituted for these goals the larger one of maintaining a foothold on the continent, the crown's attitude of capricious neglect might prove to have been the best one available.

The officials of the treasury were not so much Spaniards as Floridians. Their appointments had been royally confirmed and their privileges and obligations juridically outlined, but as everyone knew, these were technicalities. The king's Florida coffer was his in name only; they treated it as their own. Their profiteering, slipshod book-keeping, and nonchalance toward regulations were a model of maladministration, deplored by their bureaucratic superiors but never seriously chastised. There should have been no Spanish colony in Florida but there *was* one, and these sturdy individuals, wholly occupied in their struggle to keep up appearances, to take advantage of their privileges, to escape their obligations, to exercise control over their city and its provinces, and to perpetuate their hold on the king's coffer, were the colony's underlying government. They were making it survive.

Appendixes

APPENDIX 1

GOVERNORS AND ACTING GOVERNORS OF FLORIDA, 1565–1706

Name	Dates of Service Beginning	Ending
Pedro Menéndez de Avilés (died)	9–1565	9–1574
Esteban de las Alas (deserted)	10–1566	8–1570
Pedro Menéndez de Avilés II	8–1570	1571
Diego de Velasco	7–1571	4–30–1575
Diego de Velasco (arrested)	4–30–1575	2–24–1576
Hernando de Miranda (deserted)	2–24–1576	9–5–1576
Alonso de Solís (killed by Indians)	4–3–1576	7–1576
Gutierre de Miranda	9–5–1576	1577
Pedro Menéndez Marques (resigned)	3–6–1577	1594
Vicente González	11–22–1577	1578
Thomás Bernaldo de Quirós	1578	1579
Gutierre de Miranda	1582	1586
Francisco de Salazar	1583	1587
Juan de Posada	1588	1589
Gutierre de Miranda	1589	1592
[Rodrigo de Junco] (drowned en route)	[1592]	[1592]
Gutierre de Miranda (deposed by mutiny)	1592	1593
Francisco de Salazar (arrested)	1593	7–1594?
Francisco de Miranda	7–1594?	1594
Domingo Martínez de Avendaño (died)	1594	11–24–1595
Alonso de las Alas, Bartolomé de Argüelles, and Juan Menéndez Marquez	11–24–1595	6–2–1597
Gonzalo Méndez de Canzo	6–2–1597	10–20–1603
Pedro Pertrene	1598?	1598?
Juan García de Naiva	5–1598	1598

Continued

141

APPENDIX 1—*Continued*

Name	Dates of Service	
	Beginning	Ending
Pedro de Ybarra	10–20–1603	1610
Juan Menéndez Marquez	11–1604	12–1604
Juan Fernández de Olivera (died)	1610	11–23–1612
Juan de Arrazola and Joseph de Olivera	11–23–1612	1613
Juan de Treviño Guillamas	1613	8–2–1618
Juan de Salinas	8–2–1618	11–1624
Alonso de Pastrana	11–8–1622	?
Luis de Rojas y Borja	11–1624	6–23–1630
Alonso de Pastrana	8–17–1627	?
Andrés Rodríguez de Villegas (died)	6–23–1630	7–1631
Nicolás Ponce de Leon and Eugenio de Espinosa (Ponce seeks sanctuary)	7–1631	7–29–1633
Luis de Horruytiner	7–29–1633	1638
Damián de Vega Castro y Pardo	1638	4–9–1645
Benito Ruíz de Salazar Vallecilla (suspended)	4–9–1645	1646
Francisco Menéndez Marquez and Pedro Benedit Horruytiner	1646	1–8–1648
Benito Ruíz de Salazar Vallecilla (died)	1–8–1648	1651
Nicolás Ponce de León	1651	10–1651
Pedro Benedit Horruytiner	10–1651	6–18–1654
Diego de Rebolledo (arrested)	6–18–1654	2–20–1659
Alonso de Aranguíz y Cotes (died)	2–20–1659	11–2–1663
Nicolás Ponce de León II	11–2–1663	12–30–1664
Francisco de la Guerra y de la Vega	12–30–1664	7–6–1671
Manuel de Cendoya (died)	7–6–1671	7–8–1673
Nicolás Ponce de León II	7–8–1673	5–3–1675
Pablo de Hita Salazar	5–3–1675	9–28–1680?
Juan Marques Cabrera (deserted)	9–28–1680?	4–11–1687
Pedro de Aranda y Avellaneda	4–11–1687	8–20–1687
Diego de Quiroga y Losada	8–20–1687	5–15–1693
Laureano Torres y Ayala	9–21–1693	1699
Joseph de Zúñiga y Cerda	1699	1706

NOTE: Names of royally appointed governors are in boldface type; those of lieutenant governors are indented; all others were governors ad interim.

APPENDIX 2

PROPRIETORS AND SUBSTITUTES, STEWARDS, AND SITUADORS, 1565–1702

Year	Factor-Overseer	Accountant	Treasurer	Situador and Year
1565	[Hernando de Miranda]	[Pedro Menéndez Marquez]	[Esteban de las Alas]	
	Juan de Junco (ST)*			
1567	Alonso de las Alas (ST)			
1568	Francisco Pérez (ST)		[Florencio de Esquivel]	
	Juan Jiménez (ST)		[Andrés de Eguino]	
	Juan de la Bandera (ST)			
1569	Thomás Alvarez			
1570				
1571	**Hernando de Miranda**	[**Baltasar del Castillo y Ahedo**]	**Andrés de Eguino**	
	Diego Londoño de O.	[**Pedro Menéndez Marquez**]	Antonio Hernández	
			Pedro Menéndez de Avilés II	
1572	Bartolomé Martínez (ST)			
1573	**Diego Londono de Otalora**	Miguel Moreno de Segovia	Miguel Delgado	Pedro Menéndez de A. II (1573)
1574	killed by Indians	killed by Indians	killed by Indians	Pedro Menéndez Marquez (1574)
1575	Juan de Posada	Bartolomé Martínez		Pedro Menéndez de A. II (1575)
1576	Hernando de Quirós	promoted to governor		Miguel Delgado (1576)
		Lázaro Sáez de Mercado		Inigo Ruiz de Castresana (**1576**)
1577	[**Pedro de Errada**]	Nicolás de Aguirre	**Juan de Cevadilla**	
	Juan de Posada		Martín de Quirós	
	Juan Méndez (ST)		Hernando de Urteaga	
	Pedro de Arrieta (ST)		Juan López de Avilés	

*ST: Steward.

Continued

Note: Boldface names indicate proprietors. Names of stewards (ST) and substitutes are indented. An arrow indicates the beginning and end of a term of service for which dates have been definitely ascertained. Brackets indicate individuals appointed who did not serve. In last column, date represents either the year of the situador's journey or (in boldface) the year of the situado. A slash between two situadores' names indicates that they made separate trips; "and" between names indicates that they traveled together.

APPENDIX 2—*Continued*

Year	Factor-Overseer	Accountant	Treasurer	Situador and Year
1578	**Rodrigo de Junco** Juan López de Avilés Gil de Cevadilla Gaspar Fernández de Perete (ST)			Juan de Cevadilla (1578)
1579	in Spain			Juan de Cevadilla and Martín de Quirós (1579)
1580				
1581				Gil de Cevadilla and Rodrigo de Junco (1581)
1582	Pedro Guerra de la Vega in prison in Madrid	Alonso Sánchez Sáez dies in Havana		Juan de Cevadilla (1582)
1583				
1585	Juan de Junco			Juan de Cevadilla (**1585**)
1586			Bartolomé de Argüelles Juan López de Avilés in Spain	Juan de Cevadilla (**1586**)
1587	Juan Gómez Fialo (ST)		Gil de Cevadilla	Juan de Cevadilla (**1587**)
1588				Juan de Cevadilla (**1588**)
1589	Gil de Cevadilla (ST)			Juan de Cevadilla and Juan de Junco (**1589**)
1590		**Bartolomé de Argüelles**	dies in New Spain	Juan de Cevadilla and Juan de Junco (**1590**)
1591	Gaspar Fernández de Perete (ST) Gaspar Fernández de Perete	Juan de Quevedo	Juan López de Avilés	Bartolomé de Argüelles (**1591**)
1592	promoted to governor drowned at San Mateo Alonso de las Alas [**Pedro Guerra de la Vega**]		[**Juan de Posada**] drowned at San Mateo	Juan de Junco (**1592**)

Continued

APPENDIX 2—Continued

Year	Factor-Overseer	Accountant	Treasurer	Situador and Year
1593	**Alonso de las Alas**	in Spain	**Juan Menéndez Marquez**	Juan Menéndez Marquez and Juan de Junco (**1593**)
1594			imprisoned in Havana	Bartolomé de Argüelles (**1594**)
1595	Juan de Junco	in Spain		Alonso de las Alas (**1595**)
1596				Juan Menéndez Marquez (**1596**)
1597	suspended / Juan López de Avilés			Juan Menéndez Marquez (**1597**)
1598				Matheo Luis de Florencia (**1598**)
1599				Juan Menéndez Marquez (**1599**)
1600			Sebastian de Ynclán	Juan Menéndez Marquez (1600)
1601	Pedro López de S. Julian			
1602				Juan García (1602)
1605		in Spain on leave / Alonso Sánchez Sáez		
1606		asks for transfer		
1607		taken off salary		
1608		**Juan de Arrazola**		
1609		expelled		
1610	imprisoned		imprisoned	
1611	imprisoned / Andrés de Sotomayor	asks for transfer	imprisoned / Joseph de Olivera	
1612				
1613		Francisco Ramírez marries Arrazola's widow		
1614	dies on way to Spain	dies / **Francisco Ramírez**		
1616	**Juan de Cueva**			
1617				Juan de Cueva/Cristóbal de Quijano (1617)

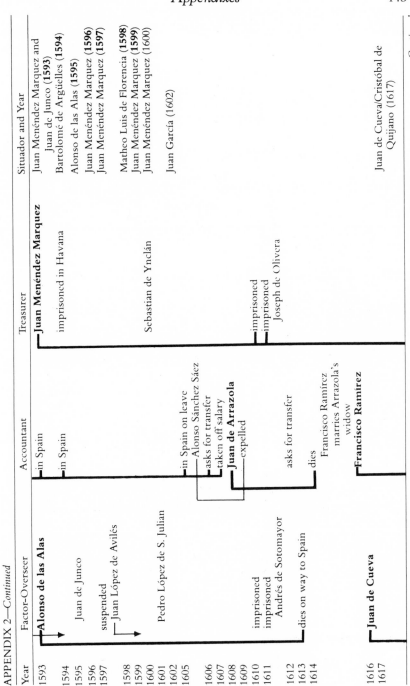

Continued

APPENDIX 2—*Continued*

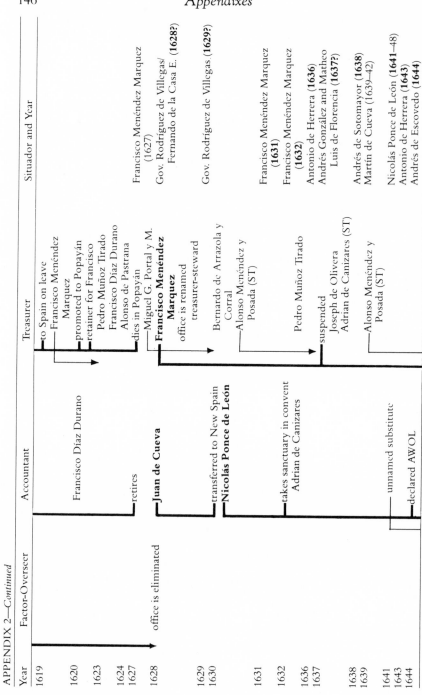

Year	Factor-Overseer	Accountant	Treasurer	Situador and Year
1619			to Spain on leave — Francisco Menéndez Marquez	
1620		Francisco Díaz Durano	promoted to Popayán	
1623			retainer for Francisco — Pedro Muñoz Tirado — Francisco Díaz Durano — Alonso de Pastrana	
1624		retires	dies in Popayán	
1627				Francisco Menéndez Marquez (1627)
1628	office is eliminated	**Juan de Cueva**	Miguel G. Portal y M. **Francisco Menéndez Marquez** — office is renamed treasurer-steward	Gov. Rodríguez de Villegas/ Fernando de la Casa E. (**1628?**)
1629		transferred to New Spain		Gov. Rodríguez de Villegas (**1629?**)
1630		**Nicolás Ponce de León**	Bernardo de Arrazola y Corral — Alonso Menéndez y Posada (ST)	
1631				Francisco Menéndez Marquez (**1631**)
1632		takes sanctuary in convent — Adrian de Canizares		Francisco Menéndez Marquez (**1632**)
1636			Pedro Muñoz Tirado	Antonio de Herrera (**1636**)
1637				Andrés González and Matheo Luis de Florencia (**1637?**)
1638			suspended — Joseph de Olivera — Adrian de Canizares (ST)	Andrés de Sotomayor (**1638**)
1639			Alonso Menéndez y Posada (ST)	Martín de Cueva (1639–42)
1641		unnamed substitute		Nicolás Ponce de León (**1641**–48)
1643		declared AWOL		Antonio de Herrera (**1643**)
1644				Andrés de Escovedo (**1644**)

Continued

APPENDIX 2—*Continued*

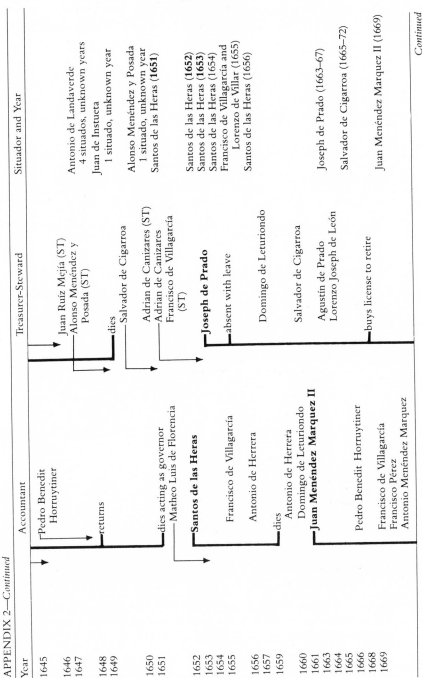

Year	Accountant	Treasurer-Steward	Situador and Year
1645	Pedro Benedit Horruytiner	Juan Ruiz Mejía (ST)	
1646		Alonso Menéndez y Posada (ST)	Antonio de Landaverde
1647			4 situados, unknown years Juan de Instueta
1648	returns	dies	1 situado, unknown year
1649		Salvador de Cigarroa	
			Alonso Menéndez y Posada
1650	dies acting as governor	Adrian de Canizares (ST)	1 situado, unknown year
1651	Matheo Luis de Florencia	Adrian de Canizares Francisco de Villagarcía (ST)	Santos de las Heras (**1651**)
1652	**Santos de las Heras**		Santos de las Heras (**1652**)
1653		**Joseph de Prado**	Santos de las Heras (**1653**)
1654	Francisco de Villagarcía		Santos de las Heras (1654)
1655		absent with leave	Francisco de Villagarcía and Lorenzo de Villar (1655)
1656	Antonio de Herrera		Santos de las Heras (1656)
1657		Domingo de Leturiondo	
1659	dies Antonio de Herrera Domingo de Leturiondo		
1660	**Juan Menéndez Marquez II**	Salvador de Cigarroa	
1661			
1663	Pedro Benedit Horruytiner	Agustín de Prado	Joseph de Prado (1663–67)
1664		Lorenzo Joseph de León	
1665	Francisco de Villagarcía		Salvador de Cigarroa (1665–72)
1666	Francisco Pérez		
1668	Antonio Menéndez Marquez	buys license to retire	
1669			Juan Menéndez Marquez II (1669)

Continued

Appendixes

APPENDIX 2—*Continued*

Year	Accountant	Treasurer-Steward	Situador and Year
1671	transferred to Havana		
1672	Pedro B. Horruytiner II		Gov. Cendoya (1672)
1673	**Antonio Menéndez Marquez**		Pedro Benedit Horruytiner II (1673–75)
1674	Salvador de Cigarroa	goes to Guadalajara / Francisco de la Rocha	
1678		ordered to return	Antonio Menéndez Marquez (1678)
1680	buys futura for Thomás		
1681			Antonio Menéndez Marquez (1681)
1682	Juan de Pueyo		Salvador de Cigarroa/Domingo de Leturiondo (1682)
1683		Francisco de Cigarroa	Antonio Menéndez Marquez (1683)
1684	dies in Havana / **Thomás Menéndez Marquez** / Francisco de Cigarroa / Juan Sánchez de Uriza / gets possession of office	Francisco de la Rocha	
1686		retired without pay	
1687		**Juan Fernández de Avila** / dies	Gov. Marques Cabrera (1687)
1688		Joachin de Florencia futura for Matheo Luis de Florencia	
1689	Juan de Pueyo		Thomás Menéndez Marquez (1689–93)
1690	ordered to return		
1692	ordered to return	**Matheo Luis de Florencia** / ordered to return	Alonso Díaz de Badajoz and Francisco de Cigarroa, years unknown / Matheo Luis de Florencia (1692–99)
1693	imprisoned		
1702			Thomás Menéndez Marquez (1702)

Glossary

adelantado—a conqueror or frontier defender, under personal contract to the king.

alcabala—an excise tax on goods.

almorifazgo—the customs duties on incoming and outgoing cargoes; also *almojarifazgo*.

arroba—a Spanish measure weighing about 25 pounds.

audiencia—the highest regional court of appeals, with some governing functions.

cabildo—the municipal corporation of a community; also a meeting of its governing body, or the building used for such meetings.

cédula—a written royal order with the force of law.

ducat *(ducado)*—a gold coin; more commonly, a Spanish monetary unit worth 275 maravedís or 11 reales.

encomienda—an allotment of tributes and services from an Indian community.

escudo—a Spanish coin worth first 350 maravedís, later 300.

fiscal—the crown prosecutor in cases of the exchequer.

futura—the right of succession to an office.

junta de guerra—a council of war.

libranza—a note payable against the situado.

maravedí—the smallest unit of Spanish account currency. There were 34 to the real, 272 to the peso, and 375 to the ducat.

peso—a Spanish colonial monetary unit, most commonly the Mexican silver coin worth 272 maravedís or 8 reales.

pipe *(pipa)*—a measure containing 126.6 gallons.

plaza—a man-space or man-pay in a garrison; also the place of military assignment.

presidio—a military outpost; also its associated town.

procurador—a presidio's commissioned representative to Spain.

real—a Spanish colonial monetary unit worth 34 maravedís.

reformado—a military officer without command.

regidor—a member of the cabildo; a city councilman.

repartimiento—literally, a division. Used to refer to the rotating labor service of the Indians.

residencia—the judicial inquiry following a bonded official's term of office.
situado—the yearly subsidy to the garrison; also called the *situación*.
situador—the commissioned collector of a situado.
termino—a cabildo's geographical jurisdiction.
vecino—a householder accepted to citizenship by the cabildo of a particular municipality.
visita—a crown-ordered visit of investigation; also a provincial circuit inspection.
visitador—the official commissioned to make a visita.

Notes

The names of document collections are given in full the first time they are cited. The following abbreviations have been used for subsequent references: AGI (Archivo General de Indias); CT (Contratación); EC (Escribanía de Cámara); IG (Indiferente General); JTC (Jeannette Thurber Connor Papers); JUS (Justicia); NC (Spanish Records of the North Carolina Historical Commission); PAT (Patronato); SD (Santo Domingo); ST (John B. Stetson Collection).

Unless otherwise noted, in all documentary references the address of origin is understood to be St. Augustine, and the addressee is the crown. The cities in Spain from which cédulas originated have been omitted. When the addressee of a cédula is given simply as "the governor" or "the royal officials," Florida is understood. Names have been standardized to what seems the most common spelling.

NOTES TO CHAPTER 1

1. The historical development of treasuries in the Indies up to 1605 is discussed in the first chapter of Ismael Sánchez-Bella, *La organización financiera de las Indias, Siglo XVI* (Seville: Escuela de Estudios Hispano-Americanos, 1968), pp. 9–69.

2. Eugene Lyon, *The Enterprise of Florida: Pedro Menéndez de Avilés and the Spanish Conquest of 1565–1568* (Gainesville: University Presses of Florida, 1976).

3. Ibid., app. 1, "Agreement between Dr. Vázquez of the Council in the Name of the King, with Pedro Menéndez de Avilés, March 15, 1565," pp. 213–19. The bounds of Florida in the 1565 contract did not include the northern Gulf Coast, called Amichel. This was corrected in 1573 by a codicil extending the adelantado's territory around the Gulf to the border of New Galicia: the River Pánuco, which he proposed to penetrate and settle (cédula to Pedro Menéndez de Avilés, 2–23–1573, in "Registros: Reales órdenes y nombramientos dirigidos a autoridades y particulares de la Florida. Años 1570 a 1604," typescript, [1907], P. K. Yonge Library of Florida History, pp. 27–31; hereafter "Registros").

4. Paul E. Hoffman, in "The Defense of the Indies, 1535–1574. A Study in the

Modernization of the Spanish State" (Ph.D. diss., University of Florida, 1969), p. 314, identifies this period as the "Huguenot Crisis of 1565–1568."

5. Lyon, *Enterprise of Florida*, pp. 85–87, 147, 183. The cost to the crown of the colony's first twenty years is the subject of Paul E. Hoffman, "A Study of Florida Defense Costs, 1565–1585: A Quantification of Florida History," *Florida Historical Quarterly* 51 (April 1973): 401–22.

6. Pedro Menéndez de Avilés, Santander, 5–12–1568, "Letters of Pedro Menéndez de Avilés and Other Documents Relative to His Career, 1555–1574," comp. and trans. Edward W. Lawson, 2 vols., typescript (St. Augustine, 1955), P. K. Yonge Library of Florida History, 2:345 (hereafter "Letters").

7. Pedro Menéndez de Avilés, Matanzas, Cuba, 12–5–1565, trans. Lyon, in *Enterprise of Florida*, p. 137.

8. Paul E. Hoffman, *The Spanish Crown and the Defense of the Caribbean, 1535–1574: Precedent, Patrimonialism, and Royal Parsimony* (Baton Rouge: Louisiana State University Press, 1980), pp. 122–32; Pedro Menéndez de Avilés, Santa Elena, 7–22–1571, "Letters," 2:439; idem, [Spain, ca. 11–2–1569], Archivo de Valencia de Don Juan, Consejo de Indias section, Envío 25-H, no. 162, courtesy of Eugene Lyon.

9. Testimony on the return of Las Alas, Seville, 11–3 to 12–22–1570, PAT 179/5 R4-2, in Jeannette Thurber Connor, trans. and ed., *Colonial Records of Spanish Florida*, 2 vols. (DeLand: Florida Historical Society, 1925, 1930), 1:292–319 (hereafter *Colonial Records*); titles to Pedro Menéndez de Avilés [the Younger], Pedro Menéndez Marquez, and Hernando de Miranda, 3–5–1571, and Diego Londono de Otalora, 5–3–1573, "Registros," pp. 13–19, 42–44; Juana de Morales, 3–5–1607, SD 25 ST 1087.

10. Lyon, *Enterprise of Florida*, p. 207; Hoffman, *Defense of the Caribbean*, pp. 107, 145–46.

11. Council, 10–21–1579, IG 739 JTC 7; Hernando de Miranda to Secretary Ledesma, [ca. 1594], IG 1373 JTC 7.

12. Council, 10–21–1579, IG 739 JTC 7.

13. Alonso de Cáceres, sentence against Pedro Menéndez Marquez, Havana, 2–20–1574, PAT 177, *Colonial Records*, 1:338–49; Council, 2–15–1578 and 10–21–1579, IG 739 JTC 7.

14. Report on the Battle of San Mateo, [between 9–1–1580 and 12–30–1580], SD 168 JTC 8; Lillian M. Seaberg, "The Zetrouer Site: Indian and Spaniard in Central Florida" (master's thesis, University of Florida, 1955), p. 105; Bartolomé de Argüelles, 8–3–1598, SD 229/24 JTC 3.

15. Bartolomé de Argüelles, Juan Menéndez Marquez, and Pedro López de San Julián, 1–23–1602, SD 229/43 JTC 3; Hoffman, *Defense of the Caribbean*, p. 161; Verne E. Chatelain, *The Defenses of Spanish Florida, 1565 to 1763* (Washington: Carnegie Institution, 1941), pp. 50–51, 140–41. The Florida *Contaduría* records in the Archivo de Indias are audited copies, not originals. See Paul E. Hoffman and Eugene Lyon, "Accounts of the *Real Hacienda*, Florida, 1565 to 1602," *Florida Historical Quarterly* 48 (July 1969):57–59, 63.

16. Michael V. Gannon, *The Cross in the Sand: The Early Catholic Church in Florida, 1513–1870* (Gainesville: University of Florida Press, 1965), pp. 38–39.

17. Juan de Posada, n.p., [ca. 1–1581], PAT 19/33 JTC 1; Bartolomé de Argüelles, 3–18–1599, SD 229/27 JTC 3.

18. Bartolomé de Argüelles, 5–15–1602, SD 229/46 JTC 3; Hernando

de Miranda, title of lieut. gov. to Gutierre de Miranda, 9–5–1576, SD 231 ST 628.

19. Juan de Cevadilla and Lázaro Sáez de Mercado, 3–6–1580, SD 229/5, *Colonial Records,* 2:270.

20. Pedro Redondo Villegas, 4–20–1601, SD 232/13 JTC 4; Bartolomé de Argüelles, 5–15–1602, SD 229/46 JTC 3.

21. Francisco Ramírez, Juan de Cueva, and Francisco Menéndez Marquez, 1–4–1621, SD 229/82 JTC 3; Juan Menéndez Marquez, [seen in Council 4–3–1620], SD 232/80 JTC 4; Juan Menéndez Marquez II, 1–25–1667, SD 229/130 JTC 3; Joseph de Prado and Juan Menéndez Marquez II, 6–30–1668, SD 229/134 JTC 3; Hoffman, *Defense of the Caribbean,* pp. 98–99, 159.

22. Letter of 4–5–1567, Mérida, "Letters," 2:323.

23. Santos de las Heras and Domingo de Leturiondo, 10–8–1657, SD 229/116 JTC 3; Gov. Marques Cabrera, 12–8–1680, SD 226/68 JTC 3, and 3–20–1686, SD 852 JTC 6; Thomás Menéndez Marquez and Joachin de Florencia, 7–6–1689, SD 234/101 JTC 4.

24. Christóval de Viso to secretary of the Council, Madrid, 6–27–1682, SD 226/89 JTC 3.

25. Hoffman, *Defense of the Caribbean,* p. 228; Gov. Zúñiga y Cerda to Gov. Chacón, castellan of el Morro, Havana, 10–3–1704, with enclosures of 1–11–1701 and 6–7–1704, SD 852/C JTC 6.

26. Joseph de Prado and Domingo de Leturiondo, 11–24–1660, SD 229/122 JTC 3; Gov. Marques Cabrera, 6–14–1681, SD 226 JTC 3, and 1–25–1682, SD 234/45 JTC 4.

27. Friars in chapter, 1–14–1617, SD 235/18 JTC 4; Francisco Menéndez Marquez, Juan de Cueva, and Francisco Ramírez, 1–30–1627, SD 229/87 JTC 3.

28. Herbert Eugene Bolton, *The Spanish Borderlands: A Chronicle of Old Florida and the Southwest* (New Haven: Yale University Press, 1921), p. 166; cédula to Bartolomé de Arguëlles, 8–18–1593, "Registros," p. 240.

29. Act on the Apalachicolas, 9–20–1681, enclosed with Gov. Marques Cabrera, n.d., SD 226/95 JTC 3.

30. Report on the Battle of San Mateo, [between 9–1–1580 and 12–30–1580], SD 168 JTC 8; Pedro Menéndez de Avilés, [Seville or Madrid], [ca. 2–1565], St. Augustine, 10–15–1565, and Santa Elena, 7–22–1571, in "Letters," 1:130, 233, 2:432–33; Gov. Ybarra, 5–10–1605, SD 224/76 JTC 2.

31. Gov. Rojas y Borja, 1–20–1625, SD 225 JTC 4, and 6–30–1628, SD 225 JTC 3.

32. Juan Menéndez Marquez, 4–13–1601, SD 232/11 JTC 4. The governor's visits and pacifications, according to the treasurer, were thinly veiled trips for amber and sassafras (idem, 4–21–1603, SD 232/27 JTC 4).

33. Anon., 11–20–1655, SD 225 JTC 3.

34. Joseph de Prado, 12–30–1654, SD 229/115 JTC 3; cédula to Gov. Marques Cabrera, 3–22–1685, SD 852/34 JTC 6; Herbert Eugene Bolton and Thomas Maitland Marshall, *The Colonization of North America, 1492–1783* (New York: Macmillan Co., 1932), p. 211. For information on St. Augustine's overseas trade regulations see William R. Gillaspie, "Juan de Ayala y Escobar, *Procurador* and Entrepreneur: A Case Study of the Provisioning of Florida, 1683–1716" (Ph.D. diss., University of Florida, 1961), pp. 21–23, 40–41, 82; Gov. Salinas, 8–19–1619, summary, SD 26 ST.

35. Gov. Hita Salazar, 10–30–1678, SD 845 JTC 5.

36. Diego Peña to Gov. Benavides, San Marcos de Apalache, 8–6–1723, SD 842/76 JTC 5.

37. Francisco de San Buenaventura, Bishop of Tricale, 4–29–1736, SD 863/119 JTC 6.

38. Ex-Gov. Hita Salazar, [seen in Council 2–8–1684], SD 839/84 JTC 5; Gov. Zúñiga y Cerda, 10–15–1701, SD 840/20 JTC 5.

39. See Chapter 5, pp. 63–65.

40. Pedro Beltrán de Santa Cruz, Havana, 11–28–1645, SD 229/102 JTC 3.

41. Cédula to the governor, 10–11–1681, in investigation of the trade goods, 12–7–1680 to 6–28–1683, SD 229/159 JTC 3. Two studies discuss the provisioning of Florida from Spain and other colonies: Lyon, *Enterprise of Florida,* deals with the period 1565–68; Gillaspie, "Juan de Ayala y Escobar," focuses on the purchasing agent's role between 1683 and 1716, but also summarizes previous difficulties and the measures introduced by a Habsburg government to relieve the necessities in Florida (see particularly pp. 17–24).

42. Francisco Menéndez Marquez and Pedro Benedit Horruytiner, 2–6–1647, SD 229/103 JTC 3.

43. Cargo manifest on the *Nuestra Señora del Rosario* out of Seville, [1607], SD 229/54 JTC 3; [Alonso de Cáceres], report, [Havana], [after 12–12–1574], PAT 19/33 JTC 1; Gillaspie, pp. 51–52; Juan de Cueva, Juan Menéndez Marquez, and Francisco Ramírez, 1–27–1617, SD 229/79 JTC 3.

44. Bartolomé de Argüelles, [1601], SD 232/1 JTC 4; Gov. Rojas y Borja, 2–13–1627, SD 225 JTC 3. For ship sizes during the Habsburg period see Jaime Vicens Vives, with Jorge Nadal Oller, *An Economic History of Spain,* trans. Frances M. López Morillas (Princeton: Princeton University Press, 1969), pp. 366–67.

45. Juan Menéndez Marquez, Juan López de Avilés, and Bartolomé de Argüelles, 9–13–1600, SD 229/41 JTC 3.

46. On Florida self-sufficiency see Gov. Fernández de Olivera, 12–15–1611 [or 1612], SD 229/67 JTC 3.

47. See Amy Bushnell, "The Menéndez Marquez Cattle Barony at La Chua and the Determinants of Economic Expansion in Seventeenth-Century Florida," *Florida Historical Quarterly* 56 (April 1978).

48. Gov. Salazar Vallecilla, 4–16–1645, summary, SD 225 JTC 3.

49. Francisco de la Rocha and Francisco de Cigarroa, 5–21–1686, in residencia of Gov. Marques Cabrera, EC 156-D/15 JTC 1; Gov. Marques Cabrera, 3–20–1686, SD 852 JTC 6; Gov. Quiroga y Losada, 12–20–1687, SD 839/114 JTC 5.

50. Three ranchers, 8–28–1689, SD 234/104 JTC 4; Alonso de Leturiondo, 4–29–1697, SD 235/143 JTC 4; Gov. Zúñiga y Cerda, [after 3–30–1704], SD 858/B-260 JTC 6; idem, proclamations, 11–5–1702 and 11–10–1702, SD 858/B-23 and 76 JTC 6; Charles W. Arnade, *The Siege of St. Augustine in 1702* (Gainesville: University of Florida Press, 1959), p. 36.

51. Charles W. Arnade, *Florida on Trial, 1593–1602* (Coral Gables: University of Miami Press, 1959), pp. 14–15; Hoffman, *Defense of the Caribbean,* pp. 216–23, 174, 229.

52. Bolton and Marshall, p. 23. Florida first appears in cartographic history on the Cantino map of 1502. See Carl Ortwin Sauer, *Sixteenth Century North America: The Land and the People as Seen by the Europeans* (Berkeley: University of California Press, 1971), p. 25.

53. In Jerald Milanich and Samuel Proctor, eds., *Tacachale: Essays on the Indians of Florida and Southeastern Georgia during the Historic Period* (Gainesville: University Presses of Florida, 1978), few of the contributors attempt to estimate population at contact for the tribes that are their specialties, and no overall estimate is proposed.

54. Arnade, *Florida on Trial*, p. 45.

55. Félix Zubillaga, S.J., *La Florida: La misión jesuítica (1566–1572) y la colonización española* (Rome: Institutum Historicum S.I., 1941), pp. 371–73; Bartolomé de Argüelles, 5–12–1591, SD 229/16 JTC 3; Fr. Francisco Pareja, 1–17–1617, SD 235 JTC 4.

56. Gov. Rodríguez de Villegas, 12–27–1630, SD 225/30 ST, cited by Brian George Boniface in "A Historical Geography of Spanish Florida, circa 1700" (master's thesis, University of Georgia, 1971), pp. 81–82.

57. Agustín and Juan, natives of San Juan del Puerto, [el Morro, Havana], 7–2–1636, SD 27/28 JTC 2; Francisco Menéndez Marquez and Pedro Benedit Horruytiner, 7–27–1647, SD 235 JTC 4.

58. Bushnell, "Menéndez Marquez Cattle Barony," pp. 419–20.

59. Int. Gov. Nicolás Ponce de León II, [before 11–29–1674], SD 226 JTC 3; Ex-Gov. Hita Salazar, 12–15–1680, SD 226/73 JTC 3; Joachin de Florencia visita of 1694–95, in residencia of Gov. Torres y Ayala, EC 157-A/91 JTC 1; Domingo de Leturiondo visita of 1677–78, in residencia of Gov. Hita Salazar, EC 156-A/87-90 JTC 1; Bushnell, "Menéndez Marquez Cattle Barony," p. 425.

60. Arnade, *Florida on Trial*, p. 41; cédula to Gov. Ybarra, 9–23–1603, "Registros," p. 355; Fr. Claudio de Florencia et al., 5–7–1707, SD 863/61 JTC 6; Parish Register Baptisms, 9–10–1597. For more on the Florencia family in Apalache see Amy Bushnell, "Patricio de Hinachuba: Defender of the Word of God, the Crown of the King, and the Little Children of Ivitachuco," *American Indian Culture and Research Journal* 3 (July 1979):2–10.

61. Joseph de Prado and Juan Menéndez Marquez II, 9–22–1667, SD 847/4 JTC 6.

62. Francisco de Florencia and Juan de Pueyo, 8–13–1706, SD 840/92 JTC 5.

NOTES TO CHAPTER 2

1. Eugene Lyon, "St. Augustine 1580: The Living Community," *El Escribano* 14 (1977):25.

2. Bartolomé de Argüelles, 8–3–1598, SD 229/24 JTC 3.

3. John Preston Moore, *The Cabildo in Peru Under the Hapsburgs: A Study in the Origins and Powers of the Town Council in the Viceroyalty of Peru, 1530–1700* (Durham, N.C.: Duke University Press, 1954), p. 277; Gov. Hita Salazar, 10–30–1678, SD 845 JTC 5.

4. Ignacio de Leturiondo, [copyist's date, 1707], in residencia of Gov. Zúñiga y Cerda, SD 858/4-206 JTC 6; anon., 1–19–1682, in residencia of Gov. Hita Salazar, EC 156-G/70 JTC 1; Ex-Gov. Quiroga y Losada, [Cádiz], [Council summary 10–19–1697], SD 840/TT1 JTC 5; Gov. Hita Salazar, SD 845 JTC 5; Juan Menéndez Marquez, 4–13–1601, SD 232/11 JTC 4; Gov. Méndez de Canzo to Gov. Ybarra, 1603, SD 232 JTC 4. The bishop of Cuba, Diego de Evelina y Compostela, warned

one governor that he would need the parish priest's good report and should keep on good terms with him. (A copy of the bishop's letter of 5–30–1697 is with Gov. Torres y Ayala, 7–2–1697, SD 235/145 JTC 4.)

5. Ex-Gov. Rojas y Borja, 7–27–1630, in residencia of Gov. Rojas y Borja, EC 154-B.

6. Juan Menéndez Marquez II and Lorenzo Joseph de León, 9–9–1666, SD 229/129 JTC 3.

7. Miguel Gerónimo Portal y Mauleón's lawyer, [1630], EC 154-B Escribanía; Juan Rodríguez de Cartaya, n.d., [sent from Junta to Cámara 5–7–1613], IG 1868 JTC 7.

8. Cargo manifest, [1607], SD 229/54 JTC 3. For Indian wages see Table 1, p. 39, in this volume.

9. Ex-Gov. Quiroga y Losada, Cádiz, [Council summary, 10–19–1697], SD 840/TT1 JTC 5; Salvador de Cigarroa, Madrid, 6–25–1659, SD 229/121 JTC 3; Sánchez-Bella, p. 265.

10. Cédula to Rodrigo de Junco, 4–17–1592, "Registros," p. 201; Catalina de Valdés, [1616], SD 232/76 JTC 4.

11. María Menéndez y Posada, Madrid, [before 11–3–1629], included with a petition of the heirs, Madrid, [before 6–30–1630], SD 6/42 and 44, JTC 2.

12. Don Patricio, Chief of Ivitachuco, and don Andrés, Chief of San Luis, [Apalache], 2–12–1699, in Mark F. Boyd, Hale G. Smith, and John W. Griffin, eds., *Here They Once Stood: The Tragic End of the Apalachee Missions* (Gainesville: University of Florida Press, 1951), p. 25.

13. Bartolomé de Argüelles, 5–15–1602, SD 229/46 JTC 3; Pedro Beltrán de Santa Cruz, Havana, 11–20–1655, SD 233/48 JTC 4; cédula re Petronila de Junco, 10–19–1594, "Registros," pp. 254–55; Juan Menéndez Marquez, [Council summary 5–24–1622], SD 229/85 JTC 3. See marriage of don Francisco de la Rocha, Parish Register Marriages, 6–25–1689.

14. Ignacio de Leturiondo, [copyist's date, 1707], SD 858/4-206 JTC 6. Gillaspie divided a 1689 census by the hearth count and estimated an average of 2.8 persons per family (pp. 6–7). This is probably too low; in a presidio there were many single men.

15. Parish Register Marriages and Baptisms, passim; Francisco Menéndez Marquez II will, 9–2–1742, included with the probate papers, 7–3–1743, SD 847/73½ ST. Luis Arana supplied a summary and Charles Arnade a transcript of this document.

16. Domingo de Leturiondo to Gov. Marques Cabrera, San Pedro [de Potohiriba], 11–28–1685, SD 839/82 JTC 5; María Menéndez y Posada, Madrid, [before 11–3–1629], included with a petition of the heirs, Madrid, [before 6–30–1630], SD 6/42 JTC 2; Pedro Menéndez de Avilés will, San Lúcar, 1–7–1574, "Letters," 2:460–65.

17. For the social importance of real estate owned by women see Charles W. Arnade, "The Avero Story: An Early Saint Augustine Family with Many Daughters and Many Houses," *Florida Historical Quarterly* 40 (July 1961):1–34. Two of the Thomás Menéndez Marquez daughters married ranchers with property contiguous to their father's (Bushnell, "Menéndez Marquez Cattle Barony," p. 427). For plaza and royal office dowries see Bartolomé de Argüelles, 3–18–1599, SD 229/27 JTC 3; cédula of 9–27–1681 to Enrique Primo de Rivera and a letter of his,

10–18–1695, both with 11–26–1690, SD 234/115 JTC 4; Joseph de Prado and Juan Menéndez Marquez II, 6–30–1668, SD 229/134 JTC 3.

18. Francisco Menéndez Marquez, [Seville?], [before 3–26–1629], EC 154-B Escribanía; Dr. Pedro Fernández de Pulgar, *Historia General de la Florida*, n.p., [after 1640], lib. 4, cap. 5, fol. 210, JTC 7; Alonso de Leturiondo, 4–29–1697, SD 235/143 JTC 4; Christóval de Viso to secretary of the Council, Madrid, 6–27–1682, SD 226/89 JTC 3.

19. Gannon, pp. 46, 79; anon., visita of Juan de las Cabezas Altamirano, Bishop of Cuba, 6–27–1606, SD 235 JTC 4; Fr. Antonio de Somoza, n.p., 5–2–1673, SD 235/97 JTC 4; Maynard Geiger, O.F.M., *The Franciscan Conquest of Florida (1573– 1618)* (Washington: Catholic University of America, 1937), pp. 218, 236–38.

20. Luis R. Arana, "The Spanish Infantry: The Queen of Battles in Florida, 1671–1702" (master's thesis, University of Florida, 1960), pp. 23, 80–90; cédula from the queen regent [Mariana], 12–24–1673, SD 235/100, included with Fr. Juan Moreno to Her Ladyship, n.p., [seen in Council 4–18–1673], SD 235/95 JTC 4; friars in chapter, correspondence with Gov. Marques Cabrera, 8–9–1685 to 8–14–1685, SD 864/3 JTC 6.

21. Antonio de Argüelles to Antonio Ortíz de Otalora, 6–11–1690, SD 234/110 JTC 4; Junta de Guerra, 3–8–1687, SD 833 JTC 4; Sánchez-Bella, p. 133; Gov. Marques Cabrera, 10–6–1686, SD 848/21 JTC 6, and Junta de Guerra reply, [after 1–13–1687], SD 848/21 JTC 6.

22. Pedro Beltrán de Santa Cruz, Havana, 11–20–1655, SD 233/48 JTC 4; Parish Register, passim; Bushnell, "Menéndez Marquez Cattle Barony"; Alonso de Leturiondo, 4–29–1697, SD 235/143 JTC 4.

23. Lyon, "St. Augustine 1580," p. 26; Gov. Treviño Guillamas, 10–12–1617, SD 232/77 JTC 4.

24. Thomás Menéndez Marquez, 7–1–1697, SD 839/136 JTC 5; Fr. Francisco Alonso de Jesús to Gov. Rojas y Borja, [seen by the governor 3–2–1630], SD 235/25 JTC 4.

25. Friars in chapter, 9–10–1657, SD 235 JTC 4; Boniface, p. 74; Ex-Gov. Hita Salazar, 12–7–1680, SD 226/65 JTC 3; fiscal of the Council, 8–30–1686, comments on Francisco de la Rocha and Juan de Pueyo, 4–1–1684, SD 229/164 JTC 3.

26. Pedro Beltrán de Santa Cruz, Havana, 11–20–1655, SD 233/48 JTC 4; Fr. Claudio de Florencia, 6–9–1707, SD 840/110 JTC 5; Int. Gov. Aranda y Avellaneda, 6–22–1687, SD 234/81 JTC 4.

27. Gov. Ybarra, 1–8–1604, SD 224/74 JTC 2; Juan Menéndez Marquez and Alonso de las Alas, 11–26–1609, SD 229/62 JTC 3.

28. Arnade, *Siege of St. Augustine,* pp. 42–44, 58–59.

29. Francisco Ramírez, Juan de Cueva, and Francisco Menéndez Marquez, 1–4–1621, SD 229/82 JTC 3; Parish Register Marriages, 4–20–1678 and 10–10–1691; Francisco Menéndez Marquez II probate papers, 7–3–1743, summary, SD 847/73½ JTC 6.

30. Pedro Sánchez Griñán, report, Madrid, 7–7–1756, JTC 7; Lyon, "St. Augustine 1580," pp. 23, 26; *Jonathan Dickinson's Journal or, God's Protecting Providence...*, ed. Evangeline Walker Andrews and Charles McLean Andrews (Stuart, Fla.: Valentine Books, 1975), p. 62; Moore, p. 155.

31. Francisco de la Rocha and Francisco de Cigarroa, 3–20–1685, SD 227 NC 6; Arnade, *Florida on Trial,* p. 74; Francisco Menéndez Marquez II will, 9–2–1742,

included with the probate papers, 7–3–1743, SD 847/73½ ST-Arana; Alonso de Leturiondo, 4–29–1697, SD 235/143 JTC 4; Gov. Zúñiga y Cerda, edict, 11–6–1702, SD 858/B-26 JTC 6.

32. Juan Menéndez Marquez, 4–13–1601, SD 232/11 JTC 4; cédulas to Juan de Cevadilla and Lázaro Sáez de Mercado, 4–13–1577, and to the governor, 9–19–1593, "Registros," pp. 76–96, 244–45.

33. Sánchez-Bella, p. 214; Juan Menéndez Marquez, Havana, 6–10–1600, SD 129 ST 811; Gov. Navarrete, 11–15–1749, SD 2541/101 JTC 7; Pedro Sánchez Griñán, report, Madrid, 7–7–1756, JTC 7; Gov. Ybarra to Fr. Benito Blasco, 12–7–1605, SD 232 JTC 4.

34. Santos de las Heras to the lord secretary, Mexico City, 3–15–1654, SD 229/113 JTC 3; Diego de Evelina Compostela, Bishop of Cuba, to Gov. Torres y Ayala, 5–30–1697, included with Gov. Torres y Ayala, 7–2–1697, SD 235/145 JTC 4; Bartolomé de Argüelles, 10–31–1598 and 3–18–1599, SD 229/25 and 27 JTC 3; Alonso de las Alas, 1–12–1600, SD 229/29 JTC 3; Parish Register Baptisms, 9–10–1597 to 3–7–1619 passim.

35. Cédula to doña María de Solís, 1–31–1580, "Registros," pp. 127–28.

36. Lyon, "St. Augustine 1580," pp. 25–26; Miguel Gerónimo Portal y Mauleón's lawyer, [1630], EC 154-B Escribanía; Parish Register Marriages, 4–20–1678; Florencia visita of 1694–95, EC 157-A/91 JTC 1.

37. In lawsuit of Hernan Ponce de León vs. Isabel de Bobadilla, 1–16–1546, IG 1963, and 12–4–1544, JUS 750 ST 55 and 54.

38. Cédula to the governor of Cuba, 8–10–1574, SD 2528 ST 256; Baltasar del Castillo y Ahedo, Havana, 2–12–1577, SD 125, *Colonial Records,* 1:228.

39. Gov. Méndez de Canzo, edict, 1–31–1600, SD 224/16 JTC 2; Parish Register Baptisms, 8–1–1640 and 8–3–1644.

40. Baptism of Lorensa, daughter of Captain Dionisio de los Rios, Parish Register Baptisms, 8–20–1675.

41. An unidentified document mentioning the slaves escaping to Ais is in JTC 1 between the Alvaro Mexía voyage description of July, 1605, and the report of the first Francisco Fernández de Ecija voyage, October, 1605, PAT 19/29.

42. Gov. Ybarra, 1–4–1606, SD 224/80 JTC 2; Bartolomé de Argüelles, 8–3–1598, SD 229/24 JTC 3; Francisco Menéndez Marquez, Juan de Cueva, and Francisco Ramírez, 1–30–1627, SD 229/87 JTC 3.

43. Parish Register Marriages and Baptisms, passim; Bushnell, "Menéndez Marquez Cattle Barony," pp. 418, 430; Francisco Menéndez Marquez II probate papers, 7–3–1743, SD 847/73½ JTC 6.

44. Alonso de Pastrana, [ca. 1616], SD 232/75 JTC 4; contract for sale of the Salazar Vallecilla estate, 10–16–1651, SD 233 JTC 4; Pedro Beltrán de Santa Cruz, Havana, 11–20–1655, SD 233/48 JTC 4; Salvador de Cigarroa, Madrid, 6–25–1659, SD 229/121 JTC 3; Int. Gov. Nicolás Ponce de León II, [1674], SD 226 JTC 3.

45. Gov. Méndez de Canzo, 9–22–1602, SD 224/70 JTC 2; *Recopilación de leyes de los Reynos de las Indias* [1681], facs. ed., 4 vols. (Madrid: Ediciones Cultura Hispánica, 1973), *lib.* 8, *tít.* 9, *ley* 6, 4–29–1605 (hereafter *Recop.,* 8:9:6); Francisco de San Buenaventura, Bishop of Tricale, 4–29–1736, SD 863/119 JTC 6; Fr. Alonso del Moral, [seen in Council 11–23–1676], summary, SD 235/104 JTC 4; Gov. Marques Cabrera, 12–8–1680, SD 226/66 JTC 3; Bartolomé de Argüelles, 10–21–1598, SD 229/25 JTC 3; Gov. Salinas, 11–20–1618, SD 225 ST 1106; Fr. Antonio de Somoza, n.p., 5–2–1673, SD 235/97 JTC 4.

46. *Recop.,* 8:9:19, 5–7–1570; Council, 9–25–1662, appended to Gov. Aranguíz y Cotes, 11–15–1661, SD 225 JTC 3; Chiefs of Guale, 10–16–1657, SD 235 JTC 4; Juan Menéndez Marquez II, 1–25–1667, SD 229/130 JTC 3; Fr. Juan Luengo, n.p., 11–30–1676, attached to and answering a memorial by Fr. Alonso del Moral, summarized 11–5–1676, SD 235/104 JTC 4.

47. Florencia visita of 1694–95, EC 157-A/91 JTC 1; Alonso de Leturiondo, report, Madrid, [ca. 1700], SD 853/14 ST-Hann; idem, 6–14–1690, SD 235/127 JTC 4; Gov. Marques Cabrera, 6–28–1683, SD 229/160 JTC 3; petition of the Florida soldiers, n.d., and cédulas of 2–9–1627 and 8–21–1629, filed with another petition of 1–14–1627, summaries, SD 233/5 JTC 4.

48. Juan Menéndez Marquez, Juan López de Avilés, and Bartolomé de Argüelles, 9–13–1600, SD 229/41 JTC 3. In the 1680s, when cattle were plentiful, the soldiers were issued fresh meat weekly instead of salt or dried, but they did not prefer it. See Salvador de Cigarroa and Francisco de la Rocha, 2–18–1680, SD 229/150 JTC 3, and Gov. Joseph de Córdova Ponce de León, Havana, 10–6–1683, SD 234/55 JTC 4.

49. Bartolomé de Argüelles, 5–12–1591, SD 229/16 JTC 3; Gov. Martínez de Avendaño, 7–9–1594, SD 127 ST 704; Juan Menéndez Marquez, 9–20–1602, SD 229/49 JTC 3; Pedro Beltrán de Santa Cruz, Havana, 11–20–1655, SD 233/48 JTC 4; Gov. Zúñiga y Cerda, 10–15–1701, SD 840/20 JTC 5; Gillaspie, pp. 48, 103.

50. Fernández de Pulgar, *Historia General de la Florida,* n.p., [after 1640], JTC 7; Fr. Juan Gómez de Palma, [Madrid?], [ca. 1640], British Museum MS 13976, fol. 87 or 89, JTC 7; Alonso de Leturiondo, 3–18–1689, SD 847/A1 JTC 6; Nicolás Ponce de León, 11–20–1637, SD 225 JTC 3.

51. Sánchez-Bella, p. 158; Arnade, *Florida on Trial,* p. 33; Bartolomé de Argüelles, 11–2–1598, SD 229/26 JTC 3; Juan Menéndez Marquez, 4–13–1601, SD 232/11 JTC 4.

52. Francisco Menéndez Marquez and Pedro Benedit Horruytiner, 5–17–1646 and 2–6–1647, SD 229/98 and 103 JTC 3; Int. Gov. Nicolás Ponce de León, 9–20–1651, SD 233/45 JTC 4; Santos de las Heras, Mexico City, 3–15–1654, SD 229/113 JTC 3.

53. Joseph de Prado and Antonio Menéndez Marquez, 3–21–1672, SD 229/136 JTC 3; Gov. Marques Cabrera, 6–28–1683, SD 234/55 JTC 4; Francisco de Lara, 12–12–1672, SD 233/92 JTC 4; Francisco de la Rocha and Juan de Pueyo, 4–1–1684, SD 229/164 JTC 3; Thomás Menéndez Marquez and Joachin de Florencia, 12–29–1693, SD 847/A2 JTC 6; Antonio Ponce de León, 4–29–1697, enclosed with Gov. Torres y Ayala, 8–26–1697, SD 847/A4 JTC 6.

54. Bartolomé de Argüelles, 11–2–1598, SD 229/26 JTC 3; cargo manifest, [1607], SD 229/54 JTC 3; Thomás Menéndez Marquez and Joachin de Florencia, 12–29–1693, SD 847/A2 JTC 6.

55. Captain Alonso de Pastrana, 2–29–1624, SD 26 ST 1167; Florencia visita of 1694–95, EC 157-A/91 JTC 1; Fr. Francisco Pérez, [seen in Council 7–28–1646], summary, SD 235 JTC 4; Alonso de Leturiondo, 4–29–1697, SD 235/143 JTC 4; Gov. Zúñiga y Cerda, 10–24–1701, SD 840/21 JTC 5.

56. Fr. Juan Gómez de Palma, [Madrid?], [ca. 1640], British Museum MS 13976, fol. 87 or 89, JTC 7; Juan de Pueyo visita of 1695, in residencia of Gov. Torres y Ayala, EC 157-A/91 JTC 1; *Francisco Pareja's 1613 "Confessionario": A Documentary Source for Timucuan Ethnography,* ed. Jerald T. Milanich and William C. Sturtevant, trans. Emilio F. Moran (Tallahassee: Florida Dept. of State, 1972), p. 68; Alonso de

Leturiondo, 4–29–1697, SD 235/143 JTC 4; Francisco Ramírez, Juan de Cueva, and Francisco Menéndez Marquez, 5–30–1627, SD 225 ST.

57. Pedro Sánchez Griñán, report, Madrid, 7–7–1756, JTC 7; Lyon, "St. Augustine 1580," p. 23; Alonso de Leturiondo, 4–29–1697, SD 235/143 JTC 4; idem, report, Madrid, [ca. 1700], SD 853/14 ST-Hann; [Alonso de Cáceres], report, [Havana], [after 12–12–1574], PAT 19/33 JTC 1; *Jonathan Dickinson's Journal,* pp. 55–56, 58, 61.

58. Pedro Menéndez Marquez, Havana, 5–15–1580, SD 224, *Colonial Records,* 2:302.

59. Fr. Francisco Martínez, memorial, [seen in Council 6–15–1658], summary, SD 235 JTC 4; Francisco Ramírez, Juan de Cueva, and Francisco Menéndez Marquez, 5–30–1627, SD 225 ST.

60. Francisco Ramírez, Juan de Cueva, and Francisco Menéndez Marquez, 5–30–1627, SD 225 ST; Thomás Menéndez Marquez and Joachin de Florencia, 12–29–1693, SD 847/A2 JTC 6; [Francisco Fuentes] to the Padre, San Luis, 11–27–1682, copy in the act on the Indian complaints, 10–30–1681 to 6–28–1683, SD 226/105 JTC 3; Alonso de Leturiondo, 3–18–1689, SD 847/A1 JTC 6, and 8–7–1697, SD 235/146 JTC 4; Fr. Francisco Martínez, memorial, [seen in Council 6–15–1658], summary, SD 235 JTC 4.

61. Juan de Pueyo and Juan Benedit Horruytiner, 11–10–1707, SD 847/11 JTC 6; Thomás Menéndez Marquez and Joachin de Florencia, 7–6–1689, SD 234/101 JTC 4.

62. Alonso de Leturiondo, 3–18–1689, SD 847/A1 JTC 6; Thomás Menéndez Marquez and Joachin de Florencia, 12–29–1693, SD 847/A2 JTC 6.

63. Bartolomé de Argüelles, 2–20–1600, SD 229/32 JTC 3; Gov. Zúñiga y Cerda, edict, 11–6–1702, SD 858/B-26 JTC 6; Ex-Gov. Hita Salazar, 12–7–1680, SD 226/65 JTC 3; chief of Guale to Gov. Marques Cabrera, Sapala, 5–5–1681, SD 226 JTC 3; Florencia visita of 1694–95, EC 157-A/91 JTC 1; [Manuel Solana to Gov. Zúñiga y Cerda], San Luis, [before 5–14–1703], in Boyd, Smith, and Griffin, eds., *Here They Once Stood,* pp. 46–48.

64. Alonso de Leturiondo, 4–18–1687, SD 234/75 JTC 4; Juan Pinto, declaration, in act against Gov. Marques Cabrera, 6–22–1687, SD 234/82 JTC 4; Bushnell, "Patricio de Hinachuba," p. 4.

65. Cargo manifest, [1607], SD 229/54 JTC 3; act against Fr. Alonso del Moral, included with Gov. Marques Cabrera, 6–28–1683, SD 226/105 JTC 3; Gov. Hita Salazar, 9–6–1677, SD 226/34 JTC 3; Francisco Menéndez Marquez, Juan de Cueva, and Francisco Ramírez, 1–30–1627, SD 229/87 JTC 3.

66. Juan Jiménez, 6–1–1627, SD 229 ST.

67. Acclamation of Philip V, 1–7–1702, and obsequies for Charles II, 3–28–1702, SD 840/45 and 50 JTC 5; Gov. Quiroga y Losada, 8–16–1689, SD 227/80 ST 2819.

68. Gov. Córcoles y Martínez vs. Joseph Benedit Horruytiner, 10–11–1712, summary, SD 848/60 JTC 6; cargo manifest, [1607], SD 229/54 JTC 3; Bartolomé de Argüelles, 10–31–1598, SD 229/25 JTC 3; Alonso de Leturiondo, 8–9–1697, SD 235/147 JTC 4.

69. Cédula to Gov. Menéndez Marquez, 7–11–1583, "Registros," pp. 155–56; anon., 6–27–1606, SD 235 JTC 4; Francisco Menéndez Marquez, 2–8–1648, SD 229/109 JTC 3; Juan Menéndez Marquez II, 7–4–1668, SD 233 JTC 4; Chatelain, p. 153n21.

70. *Recop.,* 8:3:9, 4–6–1588; Juan Menéndez Marquez, 4–13–1601, SD 232/11 JTC 4; Gov. Treviño Guillamas, 10–7–1614, SD 232/74 JTC 4.

71. Gov. Marques Cabrera, 3–20–1686, SD 852 JTC 6; cargo manifest, [1607], SD 229/54 JTC 3; Diego de Florencia, purchase order and goods receipt, Santa María de Galve, 12–2–1702, SD 858/B-255 JTC 6; Florencia visita of 1694–95, EC 157-A/91 JTC 1.

72. Lyon, *Enterprise of Florida,* pp. 105–6; Joseph de Prado, 12–30–1654, with comment by the fiscal of the Council, 7–3–1656, SD 229/115 JTC 3.

73. Pedro Sánchez Griñán, report, Madrid, 7–7–1756, JTC 7; Gov. Rebolledo, 10–18–1657, SD 233 JTC 4; Chatelain, p. 74; Florencia visita of 1694–95, EC 157-A/91 JTC 1.

74. Acclamation of Philip V, 1–7–1702, SD 840/45 JTC 5.

75. Leturiondo visita of 1677–78, EC 156-A/87-90 JTC 1; [Francisco Fuentes] to Gov. Marques Cabrera, postscript on a copy of the Fuentes letter to the Padre, San Luis, 11–27–1682, in act on the Indian complaints, 10–30–1681 to 6–28–1683, SD 226/105 JTC 3; Juan de Ayala y Escobar, edict, San Luis de Talimali, 2–22–1701, SD 858/B-233 JTC 6.

76. Alonso de Leturiondo, 4–29–1697, SD 235/143 JTC 4.

77. Sánchez-Bella, p. 163; Gov. Salazar Vallecilla, 5–22–1647, SD 229/107 JTC 3; Antonio Ponce de León, affidavit, 2–26–1687, and Fr. Domingo de Ojeda, 2–20–1687, SD 864/4 JTC 6. The three companies were of Spanish infantry, Indian archers, and Indian arquebusiers. See *A 17th Century Letter of Gabriel Díaz Vara Calderón, Bishop of Cuba, Describing the Indians and Indian Missions of Florida,* trans. Lucy L. Wenhold, Smithsonian Miscellaneous Collections (Washington: Smithsonian Institution, 1936), vol. 95, no. 16, p. 3.

78. Gov. Rojas y Borja, 11–6–1628, SD 233/9 JTC 4; Sánchez-Bella, p. 156; cédula to Gov. Marques Cabrera, 3–22–1685, SD 852/34 JTC 6.

79. The fiscal of the Council commented that it did not honor the church to advertise the town's location by night to pirates (Gov. Quiroga y Losada, act on bell ringing, 5–28–1689, and comment on that and the governor's letter of 8–16–1689, on 7–12–1693, SD 235 JTC 4).

80. Miguel Gerónimo Portal y Mauleón's lawyer, [1630], EC 154-B Escribanía.

NOTES TO CHAPTER 3

1. Titles and instructions to Juan de Cevadilla and Lázaro Sáez de Mercado, 4–13–1577, "Registros," pp. 76–96; same officials, 3–6–1580, SD 229/5, *Colonial Records,* 2:264.

2. Pedro Menéndez died without a secure hold on Florida and it never became a profitable colony, yet the crown settled 40,000 ducats, a fishery, and numerous honors on the heir to his entailed estate, Martín Menéndez de Avilés y Porras, a grandson of the adelantado's nephew Pedro Menéndez the Younger. See anon., n.p., 8–6–1648, SD 6/54-2 JTC 2, and Bushnell, "Menéndez Marquez Cattle Barony," pp. 411–12.

3. The story of Francisco's futura is in Juan Menéndez Marquez, n.d., with Council action of 4–10–1620, SD 232/80 JTC 4; Council summary and reply, 1–9–1627, to Francisco Menéndez Marquez, n.d., SD 229/86 JTC 3; Gov. Rojas y

Borja, 12–18–1627, SD 27 ST 1199; and residencia of Gov. Rojas y Borja, 10–9–1627 to 9–2–1630, EC 154–B Escribanía.

4. Gov. Rebolledo, 10–1657, SD 233/53 JTC 4.

5. Junta de Guerra, 3–8–1687, SD 833 JTC 4.

6. Francisco Menéndez Marquez and Pedro Benedit Horruytiner, 5–17–1646, SD 229/98 JTC 3.

7. Antonio de Argüelles to Antonio Ortíz de Otalora, 6–11–1690, SD 234/110 JTC 4.

8. John H. Parry, *The Sale of Public Office in the Spanish Indies Under the Hapsburgs,* Ibero-Americana no. 37 (Berkeley: University of California Press, 1953); *Recop.,* 8:21:1.

9. The laws governing the sale, renunciation, and confirmation of offices are in *Recop.,* 8:20–22.

10. Bushnell, "Menéndez Marquez Cattle Barony," p. 412; Council, 5–17–1614 and 7–10–[1614], SD 6 ST 1078, 1079.

11. Gov. Marques Cabrera, 3–20–1686, SD 234/64 JTC 4, and 10–6–1686 with Junta de Guerra reply, n.d., SD 848/21 JTC 6; Francisco Fernández de Madrigal to Francisco de Arce, Madrid, 11–23–1673, SD 851/23 ST 1858.

12. Cámara, 3–19–1689, SD 833/38 ST 2789; Juan de la Rosa, [San Luis], 12–24–1677, fol. 584, in the Leturiondo visita of 1677–78, EC 156–A/87–90 JTC 1.

13. The cédulas are dated 7–6–1579 and 4–21–1592, in "Registros," pp. 124, 204.

14. Many *títulos* are preserved in the "Registros." The title of regidor was first issued to Florida treasury officials 2–15–1527, CT 3309 ST 20.

15. *Recop.,* 8:26:2, 6–16–1593; Thomás Menéndez Marquez and Joachin de Florencia, 12–6–1693, SD 230/98 JTC 4; royal officials, 4–6–1696, SD 230/109 ST 3356. It was customary in the sixteenth century to allow three months travel time to some posts in the Indies (Sánchez-Bella, pp. 160–61).

16. Ex-Gov. Hita Salazar, [arrived 2–8–1684], SD 839/84 JTC 5; Nicolás Ponce de León, 11–20–1637, SD 225 JTC 3; Pedro Benedit Horruytiner, 11–10–1657, SD 233/55 JTC 4; Pedro Beltrán de Santa Cruz, Havana, 11–20–1655, SD 233/48 JTC 4. The laws regarding bonds are in *Recop.,* 8:4:1–8.

17. The oath for a royal official is given in *Recop.,* 8:4:9; the laws of collegial responsibility are in *Recop.,* 8:3.

18. Ibid., 8:4:62–63; Cámara reply on 5–14–1685 to Gov. Marques Cabrera, 5–30–1684, SD 226/116 JTC 3; Juan de Cevadilla, 10–25–1585, SD 231 ST 522.

19. *Recop.,* 8:4:50–53.

20. Instructions to De Soto and permissions to the treasury officials, 5–4–1537, CT 3309 ST 20.

21. *Recop.,* 8:4:45–49, 2–15–1528 to 10–4–1600.

22. Council, Madrid, 6–4–1580, IG 739, *Colonial Records,* 2:316; Bushnell, "Menéndez Marquez Cattle Barony," pp. 423–24, 428.

23. Sánchez-Bella, pp. 149–54.

24. Lyon, *Enterprise of Florida,* pp. 25, 50.

25. For a discussion of Florida tribute see Chapter 6, pp. 97–99.

26. Council, 10–21–1579, IG 739 JTC 7; Juan Menéndez Marquez, Juan López de Avilés, and Bartolomé de Argüelles, 9–13–1600, SD 229/41 JTC 3; "Registros," pp. 76–243 passim; Nicolás Ponce de León and Francisco Menéndez Marquez, n.d., and Council reply, 8–3–1631, summary, SD 27 ST.

27. See Council re widow of Pedro Menéndez de Avilés [the Younger], 9–20–1584, IG 740 ST 499.

28. Juan Menéndez Marquez, Juan López de Avilés, and Bartolomé de Argüelles, 9–13–1600, SD 229/41 JTC 3; Alonso de las Alas and Juan Menéndez Marquez, 12–13–1595, SD 229/18 JTC 3; Juan Menéndez Marquez, Alonso de las Alas, and Alonso Sánchez Sáez, 3–12–1608, SD 229/57 JTC 3.

29. Cédula to the royal officials, 8–1–1626, copy enclosed with Nicolás Ponce de León, 12–12–1634, SD 27 ST 1282.

30. *Recop.*, 8:26:6. For a discussion of the bonus fund see Chapter 5, p. 65.

31. Treasury official salaries for the Narváez expedition were set at 130,000 maravedís. By the time of De Soto they were 150,000 (titles to the treasury officials, 12–12–1526, 2–15–1527, 4–20–1537, and 10–5–1537, CT 3309 ST 20).

32. Pedro Redondo Villegas, 4–20–1601, SD 232/13 JTC 4; Juan Menéndez Marquez II, 1–25–1667, SD 229/130 JTC 3.

33. Fr. Alonso del Moral [seen in Council 11–5–1676], summary, SD 235/104 JTC 4; Pedro Redondo Villegas, 4–20–1601, SD 232/13 JTC 4.

34. Ignacio de Leturiondo, [copyist's date, 1707], SD 858/4 pp. 206ff. JTC 6; Arnade, *Florida on Trial,* p. 74; Ex-Gov. Hita Salazar, 5–15–1683, in investigation of the trade goods, 12–7–1680 to 6–28–1683, SD 229/159 JTC 3; Gov. Marques Cabrera, 12–8–1680, Junta de Guerra summary, SD 226/66 JTC 3.

35. Cédula to the royal officials, 11–20–1641, SD 235/38B ST 1341E.

36. Fiscal of the Council, 8–30–1686, comment on Francisco de la Rocha and Juan de Pueyo, 4–1–1684, SD 229/164 JTC 3.

37. Cédula to the royal officials, 6–3–1578, SD 2528 ST 256.

38. Antonio Ponce de León, 2–26–1687, SD 864/6 JTC 6; idem, 1–29–1702, SD 863/43 JTC 6; Arnade, *Siege of St. Augustine,* p. 61; Juan de Pueyo and Juan Benedit Horruytiner, 11–10–1707, SD 847/10 JTC 6.

39. Alonso de Leturiondo, 3–18–1689, SD 847/A1 JTC 6; Ignacio de Leturiondo, 10–29–1694, SD 235/135 JTC 4.

40. Friars in chapter to Gov. Marques Cabrera, 5–10–1681 to 5–30–1681, SD 226 JTC 3; Fernández de Pulgar, *Historia General de la Florida,* Madrid, [after 1640], JTC 7.

41. Arana, pp. 16–26; "Registros," pp. 134–35, 152–53; Gov. Zúñiga y Cerda, 9–30–1702, and Junta action, 8–23–1703, SD 840/58 JTC 5; Gaspar Marques, Chief of San Sebastian and Tocoy, 6–23–1606, SD 232/47 JTC 4; Catalina de Valdés, [1616], SD 232/76 JTC 4; cédula to the royal officials, 10–15–1686, SD 834/415 ST 2517; Alonso de Pastrana, [1616], SD 232/75 JTC 4; Pedro Benedit Horruytiner, 11–10–1657, SD 233/55 JTC 4. See also Chapter 2, pp. 17–18, 22, on dowries, minors' plazas, and salaries to slaves.

42. Pedro Beltrán de Santa Cruz, Havana, 11–20–1655, and comment by the fiscal of the Council, 7–5–1657, SD 233/48 JTC 4; Gov. Hita Salazar, 3–13–1679, SD 226/49 JTC 3; Arana, p. 26.

43. Ignacio de Leturiondo, 10–29–1694, SD 235/135 JTC 4; Francisco Ramírez, Juan de Cueva, and Francisco Menéndez Marquez, 1–4–1621, SD 229/82 JTC 3; Guale chiefs, 10–16–1657, SD 235 JTC 4; Fr. Alonso del Moral, [seen in Council 11–23–1676], summary, SD 235/104 JTC 4.

44. Friars in chapter to Gov. Rebolledo, 5–10–1657, enclosed with their letter of 9–10–1657, SD 235 JTC 4; Antonio Matheos to Gov. Marques Cabrera, San Luis,

5–19–1686, SD 224/102 JTC 2; Florencia visita of 1694–95, EC 157-A/91 JTC 1.

45. Pedro Redondo Villegas, 4–20–1601, SD 232/13 JTC 4; petitions of the Florida soldiers and cédulas, [before 1627] to 8–21–1629, SD 233/5 JTC 4; Francisco Ramírez, Juan de Cueva, and Francisco Menéndez Marquez, enclosed with Gov. Rojas y Borja, 5–30–1627, SD 225 ST 1196; Gov. Rojas y Borja, 1–20–1625, SD 225 JTC 4; Gov. Méndez de Canzo to Gov. Ybarra, 1603, SD 232 JTC 4.

46. Gov. Fernández de Olivera, 10–13–1612, SD 229/74 JTC 3; Gov. Marques Cabrera, 3–20–1686, SD 852 JTC 6; Juan de Pueyo and Juan Benedit Horruytiner, 4–18–1708, SD 847/13 JTC 6; Santos de las Heras, 2–10–1658, SD 229/117 JTC 3.

47. Anon., 11–20–1655, Juan Ruíz Maroto, 11–28–1655, and Gregorio Bravo, 12–5–1655, all in SD 225 JTC 3; cédula to Salvador de Cigarroa, 10–24–1680, SD 834/271 ST 2172.

48. Bartolomé de Argüelles, instructions to the steward, 5–12–1591, SD 229/16 JTC 3; Gillaspie, pp. 51–52; Salvador de Cigarroa, Madrid, 6–25–1659, SD 229/121 JTC 3; anon., 11–20–1655, SD 225 JTC 3; Juan Menéndez Marquez, 9–20–1602, SD 229/49 JTC 3; Salvador de Cigarroa and Francisco de la Rocha, 2–18–1680, SD 229/150 JTC 3.

49. *Recop.,* 8:17:7, 12–3–1630; Alonso Sánchez Sáez, memorial, 1–4–1596, SD 231/72 JTC 4; Juan de Cevadilla, Havana, 5–23–1580, SD 118 ST 423.

50. Bushnell, "Menéndez Marquez Cattle Barony," pp. 422–25; Alonso de Leturiondo, 4–29–1697, SD 235/143 JTC 4; cédula to Gov. Quiroga y Losada, 6–7–1691, SD 835/173 ST 2990; Ex-Gov. Rojas y Borja, 7–27–1630 and n.d., and Miguel Gerónimo Portal y Mauleón's lawyer, n.d., EC 154-B Escribanía.

51. *Recop.,* 8:4:18, 25, 31, 41. An interim ecclesiastical post carried full pay. See cédula to the royal officials, 12–30–1686, SD 834/427 ST 2537.

52. Thomás Menéndez Marquez, 8–27–1697, SD 230/124 ST 3468; Matheo Luis de Florencia, 4–1–1692, SD 230/88 ST 3064; Gov. Quiroga y Losada, 4–18–1692, SD 228/37 ST 3073; cédula to the accountant, 6–16–1698, SD 835/468 ST 3557.

53. Alonso Sánchez Sáez, 5–8–1586, SD 229 JTC 3; cédula to Pedro Redondo Villegas, 11–14–1600, "Registros," p. 328; Bartolomé de Argüelles, 2–20–1600, SD 229/32 JTC 3.

54. Gov. Ybarra to Alonso Sánchez Sáez, 4–9–1605, SD 224 ST 1003, and 5–11–1609, SD 232 ST 1004; Gov. Ybarra, 4–8–1608, SD 224/91 JTC 2; acts against Alonso Sánchez Sáez, 2–4–1609 and 3–17–1609, SD 224/96 and 97 JTC 2; Geiger, pp. 215–18.

55. Hoffman and Lyon, pp. 66–67; Juan López de Avilés, 2–23–1600, SD 229/35 JTC 3.

56. Alonso de las Alas, 5–24–1602, SD 229/47 JTC 3; cédula to Juan Menéndez Marquez, 3–21–1603, "Registros," p. 344.

57. Council proposals for accountant, 4–5–1607, SD 6 ST 949; cédula to the governor and royal officials, 11–7–1610, SD 232 ST 1044; doña María de Quiñones, n.p. [seen in Council 5–11–1622], SD 26 ST 1143.

58. Council proposals for accountant, 5–24–1630, SD 6/43 JTC 2; Nicolás Ponce de León, 7–3–1632, SD 229/91 JTC 3.

59. Nicolás Ponce de León, 11–20–1637, SD 225 JTC 3, and 9–12–1638, SD 233/24 JTC 4; Francisco Menéndez Marquez and Pedro Benedit Horruytiner, 5–17–1646, SD 229/98 JTC 3; King to the Conde de Salvatierra, Viceroy of New

Spain, 8–3–1646, SD 229/95 JTC 3; Pedro Beltrán de Santa Cruz, Havana, 11–20–1655, SD 233/48 JTC 4.

60. Gov. Guerra y Vega to Gov. Francisco Dávila Orejón Gastón, 7–7–1668, SD 233 JTC 4; correspondence re Joseph de Prado, 5–30–1684 to 9–16–1686, SD 226/116 JTC 3; Junta de Guerra reply, n.d., to a letter from Gov. Marques Cabrera, 10–6–1686, SD 848/21 JTC 6. Such leaves with pay were taxed after 1664 according to a schedule set by law (*Recop.*, 8:19:4, *reglas* 14 and 15 of 1664).

61. Juan de Mendoza, declaration, [San Luis?], [1687], in residencia of Deputy Gov. Antonio Matheos, EC 156-E, fols. 17–39, 50–53, ST-Hann; Nicolás Ponce de León II, 8–4–1690, SD 234/113 JTC 4; Martín de Santiago, declaration, in act against Gov. Marques Cabrera, 6–22–1687, SD 234/82 JTC 4.

62. Moore, p. 81; Nicolás Ponce de León, 7–3–1632, SD 229/91 JTC 3. When Gov. Córcoles y Martínez moved to arrest Sergeant Major Ayala y Escobar, he first seized his baton (Gillaspie, pp. 107–9).

63. Juan Moreno y Segovia, affidavit, 11–2–1663, enclosed with Joseph de Prado and Domingo de Leturiondo, 11–4–1663, SD 229/127 JTC 3.

64. Sánchez-Bella, pp. 137, 265–67.

65. *Recop.*, 8:4:10–12; Alonso de las Alas, 1–12–1600, SD 229/29 JTC 3; royal officials, 1–5–1580 [Council summary, 6–4–1580], IG 739 JTC 7; cédulas to the royal officials, 9–30–1580, and the governor and royal officials, 4–26–1583, "Registros," pp. 145, 155; Hoffman, *Defense of the Caribbean*, pp. 161–62.

66. Juan de Cevadilla, Havana, 8–18–1586, SD 229/14 JTC 3; Geiger, pp. 122, 168–69; Alonso de las Alas, 1–12–1600, SD 229/29 JTC 3.

67. Arnade, *Florida on Trial*, pp. 16–17; Geiger, pp. 122–23, 76; Gov. Méndez de Canzo to Gov. Ybarra, 1603, SD 232 JTC 4; Pedro Redondo Villegas, 4–18–1600, SD 231/101 JTC 4; Bartolomé de Argüelles, 10–31–1598, SD 229/25 JTC 3; cédulas to the royal officials of Mexico City and of Florida, 11–5–1598, "Registros," pp. 299–300.

68. Boniface, pp. 70–72; Bartolomé de Argüelles, Juan Menéndez Marquez, and Pedro López de San Julián, 1–23–1602, SD 229/43 JTC 3; cédula to Gov.-elect Ybarra, 2–10–1603, "Registros," pp. 338–39; Cristóbal González and Antón Martín, [seen in Junta de Guerra 1608], SD 232/52 JTC 4; Gov. Ybarra, 1–8–1604, SD 224/74 JTC 2.

69. Francisco Ramírez, Juan de Cueva, and Francisco Menéndez Marquez, 1–4–1621, and answer, 11–10–1621, SD 229/82 JTC 3.

70. Cédula to Gov. Rodríguez de Villegas, 7–17–1631, SD 2591 ST.

71. Cédula to the royal officials of Mexico City, 11–5–1598, "Registros," p. 298; friars' information to the governor of Cuba, 9–16–1602, SD 235/10 JTC 4; Gov. Guerra y Vega, 4–8–1666, SD 225 JTC 3; Nicolás Ponce de León II, Antonio Menéndez Marquez, and Francisco de la Rocha, 10–15–1674, SD 229/138 JTC 3; Gov. Hita Salazar, 10–30–1678, SD 845 JTC 5.

72. Gov. Marques Cabrera, 1–25–1682 and 6–28–1683, SD 234/45 and 55 JTC 4; Int. Gov. Aranda y Avellaneda, 6–22–1687, SD 234/81 JTC 4; Ana Ruíz, 8–16–1685, SD 234/61 JTC 4; Alonso de Leturiondo, 4–18–1687, SD 234/75 JTC 4.

73. Gov. Quiroga y Losada, 6–8–1690, SD 227/109 ST 2911.

74. Ibid., 5–16–1691, SD 228/19 ST 2982; and (as ex-gov.), [Cádiz], [Council summary, 10–19–1697], SD 840/TT1 JTC 5; royal officials, 4–20–1695, SD 230/114

ST 3363; cédula to the royal officials, 4–8–1698, SD 835/412 ST 3515.

75. Arnade, *Siege of St. Augustine*, pp. 57–59; Gov. Zúñiga y Cerda, orders, 11–6–1702, SD 858/B-26 JTC 6; idem, 1–6–1703, SD 840/61 JTC 5.

76. The viceroy of Peru refrained from attending the first day of silver smelting because in his presence the workers had to stand at attention with their hats off (Sánchez-Bella, p. 267).

77. Alonso de Leturiondo, 4–29–1697, SD 235/143 JTC 4.

78. Acclamation of Philip V, 1–7–1702, SD 840/45 JTC 5.

79. Sánchez-Bella, pp. 138, 195–96.

80. Fr. Francisco Gutiérrez de Vega to [Gov. Marques Cabrera], 5–19–1681, SD 226 JTC 3; Juan Lorenzo Castañeda to Gov. Zúñiga y Cerda, La Chua, 2–3–1705, SD 858/4 JTC 6.

81. Gov. Ybarra to Fr. Pedro Bermejo, 7–27–1605, SD 232/102 JTC 4.

82. Francisco de Fuentes to Gov. Marques Cabrera, Sapala, 5–4–1681, SD 226 JTC 3; Francisco de Bielma, declaration, in act against Gov. Marques Cabrera, 6–22–1687, SD 234/82 JTC 4.

83. Juan Menéndez Marquez, 9–20–1602, SD 229/49 JTC 3; cédula to Gov. Menéndez Marquez, 4–19–1583, "Registros," pp. 150–51.

NOTES TO CHAPTER 4

1. Sánchez-Bella, pp. 133–34.

2. Antonio Menéndez Marquez and Francisco de la Rocha to Gov. Marques Cabrera, n.d., in the act on Mayaca and Enacape, [between 3–15–1682 and 9–7–1682], SD 226/95 JTC 3; Fr. Baltasar López, 9–15–1602, in the friars' information on St. Augustine and Florida, 9–16–1602, SD 235/10 JTC 4; Gov. Zúñiga y Cerda, 10–24–1701, SD 840/21 JTC 5.

3. Cédula to the governor, 3–22–1685, SD 852/34 JTC 6; Thomás Menéndez Marquez and Joachin de Florencia, 4–15–1697, SD 230/120 JTC 4; Bartolomé de Argüelles, 10–31–1598, SD 229/25 JTC 3; cédula to Pedro Redondo Villegas, 11–14–1600, "Registros," p. 329.

4. Lázaro Sáez de Mercado, 7–18–1582, SD 231 ST 459; Alonso Sánchez Sáez, 5–8–1586, SD 229/12 JTC 3.

5. Gov. Quiroga y Losada and royal officials, 5–8–1689, SD 234/99 JTC 4; Nicolás Ponce de León, [seen in Council 2–8–1631], summary, SD 27 ST; muster of 5–28–1683, enclosed with Gov. Marques Cabrera, 6–28–1683, SD 229/160 JTC 3.

6. Marginal notation on Francisco Menéndez Marquez and Pedro Benedit Horruytiner, 5–17–1646, SD 229/98 JTC 3.

7. Thomás Menéndez Marquez, 12–12–1688 and 4–12–1696, SD 230/63 and 111 ST 2774 and 3360; royal officials, 4–21–1697, SD 230/124 ST 3427; cédula to the royal officials, 5–10–1698, SD 835/437 ST 3531; cédula to the governor, 4–2–1694, SD 835/314 ST 3252, repeated on 3–14–1698, SD 835/398 ST 3504; Pedro Sánchez Griñán, report, Madrid, 7–7–1756, JTC 7.

8. Lyon, *Enterprise of Florida*, pp. 74, 101; Gov. Marques Cabrera, orders to Antonio Matheos, 2–28–1687, enclosed with report on Espíritu Santo Bay, 5; Robert Allen Matter, "The Spanish Missions of Florida: The Friars Versus the Governors in the 'Golden Age', 1606–1690" (Ph.D. diss., University of Washington, 1972), pp. 84, 108; Gov. Méndez de Canzo to Vicente González, 3–1–1598, in

service record of Hernando de Mestas, SD 24 ST 755; cédula to Bartolomé de Argüelles, 8–18–1593, "Registros," p. 240; Gov. Marques Cabrera, 5–5–1682, summary, SD 839/71 NC 5.

9. He had to be kept there under guard. See Gov. Ybarra, 2–5–1605 and 12–23–1605, SD 232/31 and 37 JTC 4.

10. Cédula to the chief constable, other constables and justices, etc., 4–19–1583, "Registros," p. 152; Gov. Quiroga y Losada and the royal officials, 5–8–1689, SD 234/99 JTC 4; Sánchez-Bella, p. 240.

11. Royal officials, 1–12–1608, SD 224 ST 978; Gov. Ybarra, 2–5–1605, SD 232/31 JTC 4; Juan Menéndez Marquez, Alonso de las Alas, and Alonso Sánchez Sáez, 3–12–1608, SD 229/57 JTC 3; *Recop.*, 8:4:57, 10–11–1630; Nicolás Ponce de León and Francisco Menéndez Marquez, [seen in Council 10–17–1631], summary, SD 27 ST; Gov. Quiroga y Losada and the royal officials, 5–8–1689, SD 234/99 JTC 4; Juan Diez de la Calle, *Memorial y noticias sacras y reales del imperio de las Indias Occidentales,* Madrid, 1646, JTC 10.

12. Gov. Marques Cabrera, 6–28–1683, SD 229/160 JTC 3; Parish Register Marriages; Gov. Quiroga y Losada and the royal officials, 5–8–1689, SD 234/99 JTC 4; Matheo Luis de Florencia and Juan de Pueyo, 3–15–1702, SD 840/41 JTC 5.

13. *Recop.*, 8:4:38.

14. Bartolomé de Argüelles, 3–30–1601, SD 232/7 JTC 4. Laws on public auctions are in *Recop.*, 8:25 and 8:8:37.

15. Lyon, *Enterprise of Florida,* p. 88; cédula to Gov. Menéndez Marquez, 2–9–1580, "Registros," pp. 136–37.

16. Juan de Cevadilla, Havana, 5–12–1580, SD 229/6, *Colonial Records,* 2:290; Bartolomé de Argüelles, 5–12–1591, SD 229/16 JTC 3.

17. Cédula to the royal officials, 9–16–1586, "Registros," pp. 174–75.

18. Cédulas re Petronila de Junco, "Registros," pp. 250, 254–55, 282–83; Bartolomé de Argüelles, 5–12–1591, SD 229/16 JTC 3.

19. Bartolomé de Argüelles, instructions to the steward, 5–12–1591, SD 229/16 JTC 3.

20. Hoffman and Lyon, p. 66; Pedro Redondo Villegas, 4–20–1601, SD 232/13 JTC 4.

21. Juan de Arrazola, Andrés de Sotomayor, and Joseph de Olivera, 5–28–1612, SD 229/68 JTC 3.

22. Cédula to Gov. Méndez de Canzo, 8–12–1598, "Registros," p. 291; Hoffman and Lyon, p. 66.

23. Juan López de Avilés, 2–23–1600, SD 229/35 JTC 3. Argüelles also complained of an extra load, but it seems clear who was doing the work (11–2–1598, SD 229/26 JTC 3).

24. Alonso de las Alas, 1–24–1602, SD 229/45 JTC 3; Gov. Fernández de Olivera, 10–13–1612, SD 225/4 ST 1052; Juan de Arrazola, Andrés de Sotomayor, and Joseph de Olivera, 5–28–1612, with marginal note of 8–12–1613, SD 229/68 JTC 3.

25. Hoffman and Lyon, pp. 66–67; cédula to the royal officials, 12–5–1620, PAT 255 ST 1107.

26. Council re the royal officials, 9–4–1628, SD 27 ST 1214; John J. TePaske, with José and Mari Luz Hernández Palomo, *La Real Hacienda de Nueva España: La Real Caja de México (1576–1816)* (Mexico City: Instituto Nacional de Antropología e

Historia, 1976), p. 8; Juan de Cueva, [seen in Council 5–25–1629], SD 27 ST 1222; Council re accountant for Florida, 5–24–1630, SD 6/43 JTC 2.

27. Bartolomé de Argüelles, 2–20–1600 and 11–2–1598, SD 229/32 and 26 JTC 3.

28. Francisco Menéndez Marquez, [1644–46], SD 225/57 ST 1361.

29. Nicolás Ponce de León, 9–12–1638, SD 233/24 JTC 4.

30. Pedro Sánchez Griñán, report, Madrid, 7–7–1756, JTC 7.

31. Gov. Marques Cabrera to the royal officials, 9–6–1681, in investigation of the trade goods, 12–7–1680 to 6–28–1683, SD 229/159 JTC 3. Auditor Irigoyen was expected to work six hours a day (Sánchez-Bella, p. 277).

32. Juan de Cueva, 1–9–1631, enclosed with Gov. Rodríguez de Villegas, 12–27–1630, SD 225/30 ST 1249; Gov. Treviño Guillamas, 10–7–1614, SD 232/73 JTC 4. The ubiquity of the notary is revealed in *Recop.*, 8:5.

33. Sebastian de Ynclán, 2–24–1600, SD 229/36 JTC 3; Alonso de las Alas, 11–23–1609, SD 229/61 JTC 3; Fr. Francisco Pareja et al., 1–14–1617, SD 235/18 JTC 4; Gov. Treviño Guillamas to the royal officials and notary, 1–27–1617, SD 229/79 JTC 3. Both this notary and the one of rations and munitions sometimes received royal titles, but they were appointed locally. See cédula to Gov. Méndez de Canzo, 11–9–1598, "Registros," pp. 300–306, and Gov. Treviño Guillamas, 10–7–1614, SD 232/73 JTC 4.

34. Hernando de Mestas, 3–12–1603, SD 232/25 JTC 4.

35. Royal officials, n.d., and Council reply, 10–6–1631, summary, SD 27 ST; royal officials, 4–20–1678, SD 229/143 ST 2052; Thomás Menéndez Marquez and Joachin de Florencia, 1–20–1697, SD 228/96 ST 3392; Juan de Solana, 2–6–1697, and Gov. Torres y Ayala, 2–6–1697, SD 228/99 and 100 ST 3396.

36. Francisco de San Buenaventura, Bishop of Tricale, 4–29–1736, SD 863/119 JTC 6.

37. *Recop.*, 8:6:16 and 8:29:27. For typical deficits see Pedro Beltrán de Santa Cruz, Havana, 11–20–1655, SD 233/48 JTC 4.

38. Gov. Quiroga y Losada, 8–16–1689, SD 227/88 ST 2827; Gov. Hita Salazar, 9–6–1677, SD 839/46 JTC 5.

39. Fr. Baltasar López, 9–15–1602, in friars' information on St. Augustine and Florida, 9–16–1602, SD 235/10 JTC 4; Gov. Aranguíz y Cotes, 11–1–1659, SD 852/4 ST 1515; Pueyo visita of 1695, EC 157-A/91 JTC 1.

40. *Recop.*, 8:3:11–15; cédula to the governor, 10–11–1681, SD 834/294 ST 2216.

41. *Recop.*, 8:6:9, 8–26–1579; Francisco Menéndez Marquez and Nicolás Ponce de León, 1–5–1634, and Council reply, 11–13–1635, SD 229/93 JTC 3; Bartolomé de Argüelles, 5–12–1591, SD 229/16 JTC 3.

42. Francisco Menéndez Marquez and Pedro Benedit Horruytiner, 5–17–1646, SD 229/98 JTC 3.

43. Gov. Ybarra to the royal officials, 1–2–1609, SD 232 ST 1004; Gov. Treviño Guillamas, 1–27–1617, SD 229/79 JTC 3; Gov. Marques Cabrera, 5–30–1684, SD 226/116 JTC 3. Crown policy on the choice of situador was reversed more than once. See Juan de Cevadilla, Havana, 1–22–1582, SD 229 ST 449; cédula to the governor, 9–9–1598, SD 2528 ST 256; cédulas to Juan de Posada, 4–21–1592, and the governor, 11–9–1598, "Registros," pp. 204, 308–9.

44. Gov. Salinas, 8–19–1619, summary, SD 26 ST; Gillaspie, passim.

45. Royal officials, 3–6–1580, SD 229/5, *Colonial Records*, 2:278–80; Sán-

chez-Bella, pp. 316–17. The general orders on libranzas are found in *Recop.*, 8:28.

46. Bartolomé de Argüelles, 2–20–1600, SD 229/32 JTC 3; Gov. Treviño Guillamas, 1–27–1617, SD 229/79 JTC 3; Francisco Menéndez Marquez and Nicolás Ponce de León, 1–5–1634, SD 229/93 JTC 3.

47. Gov. Marques Cabrera to the royal officials, 2–20–1687, in report on Espíritu Santo Bay, [2–28–1687], SD 839/112 JTC 5; idem, 5–30–1684, with comment by the fiscal of the Council on 8–23–1686, SD 226/116 JTC 3.

48. Francisco de la Rocha and Salvador de Cigarroa, 5–4–1684, SD 230/18 ST 2379A; Alonso de las Alas, 12–11–1595, SD 229/17 JTC 3; Baltasar del Castillo y Ahedo, Havana, 2–12–1577, SD 125, *Colonial Records*, 1:226.

49. Bartolomé de Argüelles, 10–31–1598, SD 229/25 JTC 3; Gov. Ybarra, 12–23–1605, SD 232/37 JTC 4; Gov. Treviño Guillamas to the royal officials, 1–27–1617, SD 229/79 JTC 3.

50. Sánchez-Bella, p. 313; Fr. Antonio del Espíritu Santo, 4–16–1609, SD 232 ST 1004; cédula to Gov. Fernández de Olivera, 9–14–1610, México 1065 ST 943; Ex-Gov. Quiroga y Losada, [Cádiz], [Council summary, 10–19–1697], SD 840/TT1 JTC 5.

51. *Recop.*, 8:28:1–15; Thomás Menéndez Marquez, 10–3–1686, SD 230/32 ST 2511.

52. Gov. Marques Cabrera, 10–18–1686, with his letter to the bishop of Cuba, 10–29–1686, SD 234/69 JTC 4.

NOTES TO CHAPTER 5

1. Sánchez-Bella, pp. 255–56. The general laws on *"situaciones"* are in *Recop.*, 8:27.

2. Hoffman, *Defense of the Caribbean*, pp. 127, 139, 145–46; cédulas to the royal officials of Tierra Firme and Vera Cruz, both dated 2–18–1574, "Registros," pp. 61–64.

3. Hoffman, "Florida Defense Costs," p. 419; cédula to the royal officials of Mexico City, 4–21–1592, "Registros," p. 202. In an effort to relieve specie and provisioning problems, the crown in 1702 ordered the bishop of Puebla de los Angeles to pay the situado out of the sales taxes of his city (Gillaspie, pp. 75–76).

4. Cédula to the royal officials of Tierra Firme, 11–15–1571, "Registros," pp. 19–20.

5. Council, 10–21–1579, IG 739 JTC 7; royal officials, 3–6–1580, SD 229/5, *Colonial Records*, 2:268–76. A description of the prior system is found in Nicolás de Aguirre, report, 11–30–1578, PAT 255 JTC 1 (transcribed and translated in *Colonial Records*, 2:202–9).

6. Pedro Redondo Villegas, 4–20–1601, SD 232/13 JTC 4; Fr. Juan Moreno, 4–18–1673, SD 235/95 JTC 4; Arnade, *Florida on Trial*, p. 83; Alonso de las Alas, 3–12–1608, SD 229/57 JTC 3.

7. Friars in chapter, 10–16–1612, SD 232/61 JTC 4; Gov. Treviño Guillamas, 12–19–1617, SD 225 ST 1056; cédula to the royal officials, with copy to the royal officials of Mexico City, 8–21–1646, SD 235/46 JTC 4; cédula to the viceroy of New Spain, 2–7–1677, SD 834/176 ST 2004. For the history of the number of friars versus the number of soldiers in the authorized strength, see Matter, pp. 171–205. His

appendix on pp. 417–18 gives the estimated numbers of each at selected times from 1565 to 1763. Arana (pp. 16–30) gives a detailed analysis of authorized versus effective strengths from 1671 to 1702.

8. Gov. Zúñiga y Cerda, 10–15–1701, SD 840/20 JTC 5.

9. Cédula to Gov.-elect Ybarra, 5–19–1603, "Registros," pp. 346–47; cédula to the royal officials, 1–1–1635, SD 233/19 ST 1291A.

10. Cédula to the governor and royal officials, 9–13–1678, SD 834/216 ST 2069; Gov. Hita Salazar, 11–10–1678, SD 226/38 ST 2075.

11. Junta de Guerra, 3–8–1687, SD 833 JTC 4; cédula to the royal officials, 12–30–1693, SD 835/296 ST 3217.

12. Cédula to Gov.-elect Martínez de Avendaño, 6–18–1595, SD 2528 ST 256; Juan Menéndez Marquez, Juan López de Avilés, and Bartolomé de Argüelles, 9–13–1600, SD 229/41 JTC 3; list of cédulas and licenses given to Gov.-elect Fernández de Olivera, made on 5–12–1613 for Gov. Treviño Guillamas, summary, SD 225 JTC 3; cédula to the royal officials of New Spain, 9–9–1598, SD 2528 ST 256.

13. Cédula to the royal officials, 9–29–1593, SD 2528 ST 256; friars in chapter, 10–16–1612, SD 232/61 JTC 4; Juan Menéndez Marquez, 3–14–1608, SD 229/58 JTC 3; Carita Doggett Corse, *The Key to the Golden Islands* (Chapel Hill: University of North Carolina Press, 1931), pp. 57–58.

14. Francisco Menéndez Marquez, Juan de Cueva, and Francisco Ramírez, 1–30–1627, SD 229/87 JTC 3; Joseph de Prado, 12–30–1654, SD 229/115 JTC 3.

15. Francisco Menéndez Marquez and Pedro Benedit Horruytiner, 3–18–1647, SD 229 JTC 3; cédula to the governor, 8–1–1698, SD 835/470 ST 3566.

16. Junta de Guerra, 9–18–1703, filed with Duke of Albuquerque, Viceroy of New Spain, 4–10–1703, SD 840/A26-63 JTC 5; Gov. Rojas y Borja, 11–6–1628, SD 233/9 JTC 4; cédula to Gov. Rojas y Borja, 1–22–1629, SD 65 ST 1217; cédula [to Gov. Torres y Ayala], 11–7–1693, SD 839/127 JTC 5.

17. Cédula to the royal officials of Mexico City, 6–18–1635, summary, SD 225 JTC 3.

18. Gov. Fernández de Olivera, 10–13–1612, SD 229/74 JTC 3; Francisco de la Rocha and Salvador de Cigarroa, 9–3–1681, enclosed with investigation of the trade goods, 12–7–1680 to 6–28–1683, SD 229/159 JTC 3. For building fund misapplications during the eighteenth century see John J. TePaske, *The Governorship of Spanish Florida, 1700–1763* (Durham, N.C.: Duke University Press, 1964), pp. 91–97.

19. Cédula to Gov. Ybarra, 6–9–1603, "Registros," pp. 349–50; Gillaspie, p. 15; Francisco de la Rocha and Juan de Pueyo, 1–16–1684, SD 229/163 JTC 3; Fr. Francisco Martínez, memorial, [seen in Council 6–15–1658], summary, SD 235 JTC 4.

20. Juan Menéndez Marquez, Juan López de Avilés, and Bartolomé de Argüelles, 9–13–1600, SD 229/41 JTC 3; cédulas to the royal officials of Mexico City, 9–29–1602 and 8–30–1603, "Registros," pp. 334, 356–57.

21. Cédulas to Gov. Ybarra, 6–9–1603 and 7–25–1603, "Registros," pp. 349–50, 352–53, Juan Menéndez Marquez, 4–21–1603, SD 232/27 JTC 4; cédula to the royal officials, 8–1–1626, enclosed with Nicolás Ponce de León, 12–12–1634, SD 27 ST.

22. Cédula to the governor, 2–21–1590, "Registros," pp. 186–87; Santos de las Heras, 2–10–1658, and reply, 4–7–1660, SD 229/117 JTC 3; Junta de Guerra, 2–6–1680, in reply to Gov. Hita Salazar, 11–4–1678, SD 229/148 JTC 3.

23. Cédula to the governor, 12–19–1686, SD 834/424 and 426 ST 2535; cédulas to the royal officials, 6–5–1687; the governor, 6–5–1687; and the viceroy of New Spain, 5–16–1698, SD 835/39, 40, and 440, ST 2610, 2611, and 3538.

24. Diego de Velasco, 8–31–1575, PAT 259, *Colonial Records,* 1:140; cédula to the royal officials of Mexico City, 9–18–1604, "Registros," p. 363; Bartolomé de Argüelles, 5–12–1591, SD 229/16 JTC 3; Juan Menéndez Marquez, Havana, 6–1600, sent from St. Augustine, 4–13–1601, SD 232/11 JTC 4. Ingots were worth two reales less per mark than coined silver (cédula to the royal officials of Vera Cruz, 2–9–1580, SD 2528 ST 256).

25. Pedro Beltrán de Santa Cruz, Havana, 11–20–1655, SD 233/48 JTC 4; [Manuel Solana to Gov. Zúñiga y Cerda], San Luis, [before 5–14–1703], in Boyd, Smith, and Griffin, eds., *Here They Once Stood,* pp. 46–48.

26. Gov. Joseph de Córdova Ponce de León, Havana, 10–6–1683, SD 234/55 JTC 4; Pedro Beltrán de Santa Cruz, Havana, 11–20–1655, SD 233/48 JTC 4.

27. Summary of proceedings against two counterfeiters, in Pueyo visita of 1695, EC 157-A/91 JTC 1; Amy Bushnell, "'That Demonic Game': The Campaign to Stop Indian *Pelota* Playing in Spanish Florida, 1675–1684," *The Americas* 35 (July 1978):6; Gov. Quiroga y Losada, 8–16–1689, SD 227/89 ST 2828; Gov. Zúñiga y Cerda, 10–15–1701, SD 840/20 JTC 5.

28. Council to the House of Trade, 3–27–1612, IG 1970 JTC 7; Juan de Arrazola, Andrés de Sotomayor, and Joseph de Olivera, 10–8–1612, SD 229/70 JTC 3; Sánchez-Bella, p. 228.

29. Nicolás Ponce de León, 9–25–1642, SD 229/95 JTC 3; Juan de Instueta, 2–5–1646, SD 233/34 ST 1370; Gov. Guerra y Vega, 4–8–1666, SD 225 JTC 3; Gillaspie, p. 17.

30. Juan Jiménez, 6–1–1627, SD 229 ST; Salvador de Cigarroa and Francisco de la Rocha, 7–20–1678, SD 229/145 ST 2063; Juan Fernández de Florencia, 1–21–1676, SD 234/15 ST 1962.

31. Joseph de Prado and Juan Menéndez Marquez, 6–30–1668, SD 229/134 JTC 3; Nicolás Ponce de León II, 3–24–1675, SD 848/18 JTC 6.

32. Cédula to the royal officials, 6–18–1595, SD 225/48 ST 1316; Gov. Salinas, 5–15–1621, SD 225 ST 1132; Council re Alonso de Argüelles, 3–23–1627, SD 233 ST.

33. Gov. Horruytiner, 11–20–1637, SD 225/47 ST 1315; Martín de Cueva, 1–25–1637, SD 225/43 ST 1308.

34. Cédula to the governor and royal officials, 7–16–1638, SD 2603/26 ST 1322; Fr. Alonso del Moral, Madrid, 9–24–1676, re cédula of 3–29–1568, SD 235/103 ST 1980; Christóval de Viso to Francisco de Altamira y Angulo, [Spain], 7–14–1682, SD 235/117 JTC 4.

35. Nicolás Ponce de León, 9–20–1651, SD 233/45 JTC 4; Pedro Beltrán de Santa Cruz, 11–28–1645, SD 229/102 JTC 3; Francisco Menéndez Marquez and Pedro Benedit Horruytiner, 5–17–1646, SD 229/98 JTC 3; anon., 11–20–1655, SD 225 JTC 3.

36. Juan de Cevadilla, Havana, 5–23–1580, SD 118, *Colonial Records,* 2:312; Juan de Cevadilla and Lázaro Sáez de Mercado, 3–8–1581, SD 229 ST 442; Alonso Sánchez Sáez, memorial, 1–4–1596, SD 231/72 JTC 4; Juan Menéndez Marquez and Alonso de las Alas, 11–26–1609, SD 229/62 JTC 3; Santos de las Heras to the Lord Secretary, Mexico City, 3–15–1654, SD 229/113 JTC 3.

37. Pedro Menéndez Marquez, Santa Elena, 10–21–1577, SD 231/17, *Colonial*

Records, 1:274; Juan Menéndez Marquez, Havana, 6–1600, sent from St. Augustine, 4–13–1601, SD 232/11 JTC 4.

38. Pedro Beltrán de Santa Cruz, Havana, 11–28–1645, SD 229/102 JTC 3, and 11–20–1655, SD 233/48 JTC 4.

39. Alonso de Leturiondo, 3–18–1689, SD 847/A1 JTC 6.

40. Gov. Menéndez Marquez, Santa Elena, 10–21–1577, SD 231/17, *Colonial Records,* 1:274; idem to Treasurer Martín de Quirós, 4–8–1578, PAT 261/5, ibid., 2:40; Gillaspie, p. 21. The exchange cost from gold to silver at Lima was 12 percent in 1557 (Sánchez-Bella, p. 255).

41. Santos de las Heras to the Lord Secretary, Mexico City, 3–15–1654, SD 229/113 JTC 3; Juan Menéndez Marquez, Havana, 6–1600, and St. Augustine, 4–13–1601, SD 232/11 JTC 4; cédulas to Pedro Redondo Villegas, 11–14–1600, and the royal officials of Vera Cruz, 9–29–1593, "Registros," pp. 328–29, 245–46; Bartolomé de Argüelles, report on the situadores, 1585–1598, 5–15–1602, SD 229/46 JTC 3.

42. Gillaspie (pp. 46–47, 50, 78, 91–95) records the following accidents to the ships of Procurador Juan de Ayala y Escobar:

1694 150-ton ship with the 1693 situado is captured
1695 Sloop loses mast on way from St. Augustine to Havana
1703 Frigate with cargo of pelts is sunk in Vigo harbor
1705 74-ton ship is driven onto a reef off Cuba
1708 Sloop is captured between Havana and New Spain

43. Francisco de la Rocha and Francisco de Cigarroa, 5–21–1686, EC 156-D/15 JTC 1; Pilot Gaspar Pérez de Mancilla, 1–20–1682, SD 234/44 JTC 4; Gov. Salinas, 1–30–1623, summary, SD 225 JTC 3; Pedro Beltrán de Santa Cruz, Havana, 11–20–1655, SD 233/48 JTC 4; cédula to Gov. Torres y Ayala, 6–5–1698, SD 835/435 ST 3548.

44. Antonio de Herrera to Gov. Salinas, 12–14–1619, and Gov. Salinas to the royal officials, 1–7–1620, SD 229 ST 1118; Council re Antonio de Herrera, 2–17–1623, SD 26 ST 1155; Gov. Salinas, 7–18–1623, SD 232 ST 1134; Gov.-elect Rojas y Borja to Antonio de Herrera, Madrid, 1–22–1624, SD 225 ST 1165.

45. Francisco Menéndez Marquez, 2–8–1648, SD 229/109 JTC 3; Bartolomé de Argüelles, 10–31–1598, SD 229/25 JTC 3; Francisco Menéndez Marquez, Juan de Cueva, and Francisco Ramírez, 1–30–1627, SD 229/87 JTC 3; [Alonso de Cáceres], report, [Havana], [after 12–12–1574], PAT 19/33 JTC 1; Gillaspie, p. 54.

46. Junta de Guerra, 4–1–1659, summary, SD 225 JTC 3; Francisco de San Buenaventura, Bishop of Tricale, 4–29–1736, SD 863/121 JTC 6.

47. Council re Florida soldiers, 10–12–1604, SD 232 ST 866. Juan de Cevadilla and Lázaro Sáez de Mercado summarized the surcharges that were the practice when they arrived, 3–6–1580, SD 229/5, *Colonial Records,* 2:270.

48. Cédulas to the royal officials, 9–10–1626, CT 5092/3 ST 875; to the Council, 2–25–1617, SD 2529 ST 1090; and to the governor and royal officials, 12–18–1677, SD 815/199 ST 2042.

49. Arnade, *Florida on Trial,* p. 54; Alonso de Leturiondo, 3–18–1689, SD 847/A1 JTC 6; cédula to the royal officials of Vera Cruz, 2–9–1580, SD 2528 ST 256.

50. Pedro Redondo Villegas, 4–20–1601, SD 232/13 JTC 4; Juan Menéndez Marquez, 4–21–1603, SD 232/27 JTC 4; cédula to the royal officials, 9–18–1604, "Registros," p. 362; Pilot Andrés González, 1628, SD 233 ST; Oliver Dunn, "Trouble at Sea: The Return Voyage of the Fleet of New Spain and Honduras in

1622," *Terrae Incognitae* 11 (1979):38–39. Gaspar Fernández Perete may have found the mermas enough to live on. He drew out none of his salary as steward, but let it accumulate in the treasury (Bartolomé de Argüelles, 5–15–1602, SD 229/46 JTC 3).

51. Ex-Gov. Hita Salazar, [seen in Council 2–8–1684], SD 839/84 JTC 5.

52. Gillaspie, pp. 92–94; Arana, pp. 92–93. A similar exploitation of soldiers is reported by Max L. Moorhead, in *The Presidio. Bastion of the Spanish Borderlands* (Norman: University of Oklahoma Press, 1975), pp. 14, 25–26, 34–35.

NOTES TO CHAPTER 6

1. Sánchez-Bella, pp. 56–59.

2. To compare the tax exemptions in the Menéndez contract with those promised to four earlier adelantados of Florida, see Lyon, *Enterprise of Florida*, appendix 2 ("A Comparison of Provisions of Various Sixteenth-Century Asientos"), pp. 220–23.

3. C. H. Haring, *The Spanish Empire in America* (New York: Harcourt Brace and World, 1947), p. 266.

4. Sánchez-Bella, pp. 221–22; friars in chapter, to Gov. Marques Cabrera, 5–19–1681, SD 226 JTC 3.

5. Gov. Quiroga y Losada, 4–1–1688, SD 839/118 JTC 5; "Agreement with Pedro Menéndez de Avilés," in Lyon, *Enterprise of Florida*, pp. 213–19.

6. Bartolomé de Argüelles, 3–30–1601, SD 232/7 JTC 4; Francisco de la Rocha and Francisco de Cigarroa, 7–10–1685, SD 227 NC 6; Juan Menéndez Marquez, 9–20–1602, SD 229/49 JTC 3.

7. Gov. Horruytiner with Francisco Menéndez Marquez and Nicolás Ponce de León, 5–14–1636, SD 235/31 JTC 4; Bishop of Cuba, [Spain], 6–4–1622, SD 150 ST 1145; Archbishop of Havana, Havana, 11–25–1635, SD 235/32 ST 1295A; Santos de las Heras and Joseph de Prado, 8–21–1653, with enclosures of 10–27–1626, [after 1655], and 7–15–1656, SD 229/111 JTC 3.

8. Francisco Menéndez Marquez and Pedro Benedit Horruytiner, 5–17–1646, SD 229/98 JTC 3.

9. Nicolás Ponce de León, 12–12–1634, SD 27 ST.

10. Act on an abbacy, 9–30–1645 to 10–5–1645, SD 229/123 JTC 3; crown to the audiencia of Santo Domingo, 9–13–1656, summarizing a letter from Gov. Rebolledo, 10–24–1655, SD 229/118 JTC 3; Gov. Juan de Salamanca, Havana, 11–1–1658, SD 229/119 JTC 3.

11. Cédula to the royal officials, received 9–13–1656, and answer from Santos de las Heras and Domingo de Leturiondo, 5–31–1658, SD 229/118 JTC 3; Francisco de la Rocha and Francisco de Cigarroa, 7–10–1685, SD 227 NC 6. For two articles on Spanish ranching see Charles W. Arnade, "Cattle Raising in Spanish Florida, 1513–1763," *Agricultural History* 35 (July 1961):116–24, and Bushnell, "Menéndez Marquez Cattle Barony."

12. Nicolás Ponce de León II, Antonio Menéndez Marquez, and Francisco de la Rocha, 10–15–1674, SD 229/138 JTC 3.

13. Salvador de Cigarroa and Francisco de la Rocha, 2–18–1680, SD 229/150 JTC 3; Thomás Menéndez Marquez and Joachin de Florencia, 12–29–1693, SD 847/A2 JTC 6.

14. Juan de Pueyo and Joachin de Florencia, 9–13–1699, SD 230/141 ST 3639, answering cédula of 10–2–1697; idem, 9–16–1699, answering cédula of 7–1–1697, SD 230/143 ST; Alonso de Leturiondo, 4–29–1697, SD 235/143 JTC 4; Diego de Evelina y Compostela, Bishop of Cuba, to Gov. Torres y Ayala, n.p., 5–30–1697, with Gov. Torres y Ayala, 7–2–1697, SD 235/145 JTC 4.

15. Haring, p. 267.

16. Moore, pp. 258–59.

17. Francisco Menéndez Marquez and Pedro Benedit Horruytiner, 4–24–1647, SD 229/106 ST 1383; Sebastian Pérez de la Cerda, 7–16–1681, SD 235/111 ST 2207; cédula to Gov. Marques Cabrera, 11–27–1683, SD 834/377 ST 2352.

18. Gov. Cendoya, 3–24–1672, summary, SD 226 JTC 3; cédula to the governor, 2–6–1696, SD 835/342 ST 3334; Antonio Ponce de León, affidavit, 2–26–1687, SD 864/6 JTC 6.

19. Royal officials, 4–25–1696, SD 228/78 ST 3366; Alonso de Leturiondo, 8–23–1697, SD 235/149 ST 3458; Council re bulls of the crusade, 4–26–1698, SD 835/454 ST 3524.

20. Lyon, *Enterprise of Florida,* pp. 51, 216.

21. Francisco de la Rocha and Francisco de Cigarroa, 3–20–1685, SD 227 NC 6.

22. Lorenzo Horruytiner, 5–6–1685, SD 227/12 NC 6; Florencia visita of 1694–95, EC 157-A/91 JTC 1.

23. Gov. Hita Salazar, 10–30–1678, SD 845 JTC 5; Francisco de la Rocha and Francisco de Cigarroa, 7–10–1685, SD 227 NC 6. Four years later the proprietors of Carolina introduced what seems to have been a similar form of land tenure, with cash quitrents (Bolton and Marshall, p. 210).

24. Gov. Hita Salazar, 10–30–1678, SD 845 JTC 5. Two petitions, those of Marcos Delgado, [between 12–10–1694 and 12–13–1694], in the Florencia visita of 1694–95, EC 157-A/4 JTC 1, and of Lorenzo Horruytiner, 5–6–1685, SD 227/12 NC 6, suggest that the measurement was radial.

25. Francisco de la Rocha and Salvador de Cigarroa, 3–2–1680, SD 229/152 JTC 3.

26. Fiscal of the Council, Madrid, 10–3–1680, comment on Francisco de la Rocha and Salvador de Cigarroa, 3–2–1680, SD 229/152 JTC 3; Francisco de la Rocha and Francisco de Cigarroa, 10–6–1685, SD 227 NC 6.

27. Council, 10–13–1687, cited by Gov. Marques Cabrera, 4–28–1685, SD 227/13 NC 6; Council, 10–6–1690, comments on three ranchers, 8–28–1689, SD 234/104 JTC 4.

28. [Charles II] to Gov. Quiroga y Losada, 8–31–1688, SD 235/119 JTC 4.

29. Gov. Ybarra, report on foreigners, 8–1–1607, SD 224 JTC 2; Gov. Cendoya, 3–24–1672, summary, SD 226 JTC 3.

30. Int. Gov. Nicolás Ponce de León, 9–20–1651, with comment by the fiscal, 8–26–1653, and cédula to Gov. Rebolledo, 8–15–1653, SD 233/45 JTC 4; contract for sale of the Salazar Vallecilla estate, 10–16–1651, SD 233 JTC 4.

31. Joseph de Prado, 12–30–1654, SD 229/115 JTC 3; Santos de las Heras and Domingo de Leturiondo, 10–8–1657, SD 233/50 JTC 4; Gov. Rebolledo, 10–18–1657, SD 233 JTC 4; Gov. Moral Sánchez, 9–8–1735, SD 844/41 JTC 5.

32. Royal officials, 1–5–1580, summarized with Council comments 6–4–1580,

IG 739 JTC 7; Bartolomé de Argüelles, 5–12–1591, SD 229/16 JTC 3; Int. Gov. Nicolás Ponce de León II, n.d., with Junta de Guerra reply of 11–29–1674, SD 226 JTC 3.

33. Cédulas to the governors of Florida, 4–19–1583, 8–11–1593, and 2–10–1603, "Registros," pp. 153, 235–36, 337–38.

34. Gov. Hita Salazar, 10–30–1678, SD 845 JTC 5; Alonso Solana, report on the blacksmiths, 5–20–1683, in investigation of the trade goods, 12–7–1680 to 6–28–1683, SD 229/159 JTC 3.

35. Arnade, *Florida on Trial,* p. 85; Agustín and Juan, natives of San Juan del Puerto, [el Morro, Havana], 7–2–1636, SD 27/28 JTC 2; Francisco Menéndez Marquez and Pedro Benedit Horruytiner, 7–27–1647, SD 235 JTC 4; Juan Menéndez Marquez II, 1–25–1667, SD 229/130 JTC 3.

36. Bartolomé de Argüelles, 8–3–1598, SD 229/24 JTC 3; Ex-Gov. Quiroga y Losada, [Cádiz], [Council summary, 10–19–1697], SD 840/TT1 JTC 5.

37. See Chapter 3, pp. 32–34, on the sale of offices.

38. Juan de Cueva, report on offices, 1–9–1631, in Gov. Rodríguez Villegas, 12–27–1630, SD 225/30 ST 1249.

39. Cédula to Gov. Torres y Ayala, 1–24–1696, SD 835/356 ST 3323. See also Chapter 4, pp. 58–59.

40. Council, answer, 5–30–1628, to Eugenio de Espinosa, n.d., SD 2591 ST. The general laws on the half-annate are in *Recop.,* 8:19. Their application to a captaincy general similar to Florida's is described by Marc Simmons in *Spanish Government in New Mexico* (Albuquerque: University of New Mexico Press, 1968), p. 58.

41. Gov. Horruytiner, 1633 [after July], SD 233 ST.

42. Cédula to the governor and royal officials, 12–14–1672, SD 2529/32 ST 1772; Pedro Beltrán de Santa Cruz, Havana, 11–20–1655, SD 233/48 JTC 4.

43. Junta de Guerra comment, 12–10–1680, on ex-Gov. Hita Salazar, n.d., SD 234/38 JTC 4; cédula to the royal officials, 2–26–1684, SD 834/387 ST 2367; Joachin de Florencia and Thomás Menéndez Marquez, 4–2–1696, SD 230/106 ST 3353.

44. Francisco Menéndez Marquez II and Salvador García Villegas, 4–16–1735, with Gov. Moral Sánchez, 4–20–1735, SD 2541 JTC 7; cédula to the royal officials of Santo Domingo, 6–18–1660, SD 2654 ST 1536; *Recop.,* 8:19:4, *regla* 81 of 1664.

45. Santos de las Heras and Joseph de Prado, 8–21–1653, SD 229/111 JTC 3. See also Chapter 5, pp. 67–68.

46. Lyon, *Enterprise of Florida,* pp. vii, 217; [Alonso de Cáceres], report, [Havana], [after 12–12–1574], PAT 19/33 JTC 1; Juan Diez de la Calle, *Memorial y noticias,* Madrid, 1646, JTC 10.

47. Cédula to the governor, 8–29–1584, IG 606 ST 498; Gov. Ybarra, 12–26–1605, SD 224 ST 918.

48. Eugenio de Espinosa, n.d., and Junta de Guerra, 4–1–1659, SD 225 JTC 3. This privilege he held in common with the sergeant majors of Havana and Panama (idem, Junta de Guerra, 9–18–1631, and reply, 9–7–1634, summary, SD 133 ST).

49. *Recop.,* 8:23:18, 12–28–1638; Moore, p. 259; Joseph de Prado and Domingo de Leturiondo, 11–4–1663, SD 229/127 JTC 3.

50. Three ranchers, 8–28–1689, SD 234/104 JTC 4.

51. Arnade, *Florida on Trial,* p. 18; Alonso Menéndez, declaration, in act on St. Augustine, San Juan de Ulúa, 5–30–1601, SD 235/9 JTC 4.

52. Gillaspie, p. 48; Pedro Beltrán de Santa Cruz, Havana, 11–20–1655, SD 233/48 JTC 4; Arnade, *Florida on Trial,* p. 79.

53. Juan Menéndez Marquez, Juan López de Avilés, and Bartolomé de Argüelles, 9–13–1600, SD 229/41 JTC 3; cédula to Gov. Méndez de Canzo, 11–9–1598, "Registros," pp. 300–306; Bartolomé de Argüelles, 10–31–1598, SD 229/25 JTC 3.

54. The laws on almorifazgos are in *Recop.,* 8:15.

55. "Agreement with Pedro Menéndez de Avilés," in Lyon, *Enterprise of Florida,* p. 217.

56. Gillaspie, p. 21; cédulas to the royal officials, 9–30–1580, and to the governor and royal officials, 4–26–1583, "Registros," pp. 144–45, 155.

57. Bartolomé de Argüelles, 5–15–1602, SD 229/46 JTC 3; cédula to the royal officials, 11–5–1598, SD 2528 ST 256; Bartolomé de Argüelles, Juan Menéndez Marquez, and Alonso de las Alas, 4–20–1603, SD 229/52 JTC 3.

58. Cédula to the royal officials of Vera Cruz, 9–29–1593, "Registros," pp. 245–46.

59. Bartolomé de Argüelles, 10–31–1598, SD 229/25 JTC 3.

60. Juan Menéndez Marquez, Juan López de Avilés, and Bartolomé de Argüelles, 9–13–1600, SD 229/41 JTC 3.

61. Bartolomé de Argüelles, Juan Menéndez Marquez, and Pedro López de San Julián, 1–23–1602, SD 229/43 JTC 3; *Recop.,* 8:15:8–10.

62. Cédula to the royal officials, 9–18–1604, "Registros," p. 362.

63. *Recop.,* 8:15:7, 8–11–1606; Gov. Salinas to the royal officials, and replies by Francisco Ramírez, Juan de Cueva, and Francisco Menéndez Marquez, 9–8–1621, SD 233 ST 1181; Captains Andrés de las Alas and Alonso Pastrana to the royal officials, 6–12–1623, and Gov. Salinas to same, 6–19–1623, SD 233 ST 1181; cédulas to the royal officials, 9–10–1626, and to the president and Council of the Exchequer, 8–14–1646, CT 5092 vol. 3, ST 875.

64. Bartolomé de Argüelles, Juan Menéndez Marquez, and Pedro López de San Julián, 1–23–1602, SD 229/43 JTC 3; Gov. Ybarra, 2–5–1605, SD 232/31 JTC 4.

65. Gov. Ybarra, 4–8–1608, SD 224/91 JTC 2; Geiger, pp. 207, 212–18; Sánchez-Bella, p. 242.

66. Cédula to the House of Trade, 1–23–1566, CT 5012 ST 111.

67. Francisco Ramírez, Francisco Menéndez Marquez, and Juan de Cueva, 6–2–1627, with comment by the fiscal of the Council, 1–12–1628, SD 229/88 JTC 3.

68. Gov. Marques Cabrera, 10–8–1683, SD 226/111 JTC 3; royal officials, 4–1–1684, SD 230/5 ST 2377; idem, 3–22–1686, SD 852/40 ST 2473.

69. *Recop.,* 8:17:11, [effective 8–31–1657]; Sánchez-Bella, p. 188; Moore, p. 164.

70. Francisco Menéndez Marquez, 2–8–1648, SD 229/109 JTC 3.

71. Pedro Beltrán de Santa Cruz, Havana, 11–20–1655, SD 233/48 JTC 4.

72. Gillaspie, pp. 21–23; Gov. Salinas, 8–19–1619, and Council reply, n.d., summary, SD 26 ST; Francisco de Madrigal to the House of Trade, Madrid, 2–9–1673, CT 5044 ST 1785.

73. Gillaspie, pp. 55–57.

74. Nicolás Ponce de León and Francisco Menéndez Marquez, 12–24–1632, SD 27 ST 1264; friars in chapter, 9–10–1657, SD 235 JTC 4; Bushnell, "Menéndez Marquez Cattle Barony," pp. 417, 424; Gov. Joseph de Córdova Ponce de León, Havana, 10–6–1683, SD 234/55 JTC 4.

75. *Recop.,* 8:13:17 and 24, 8:13:11, 3–21–1621.

76. The laws of treasure taxes are in *Recop.,* 8:10 and 8:12.

77. "Agreement with Pedro Menéndez de Avilés," in Lyon, *Enterprise of Florida*, p. 217; Arnade, *Florida on Trial*, pp. 30–42.

78. John Tate Lanning, *The Spanish Missions of Georgia* (Chapel Hill: University of North Carolina Press, 1935), p. 25; Gov. Rojas y Borja, 6–30–1628, SD 225 ST 1210.

79. Gov. Moral Sánchez, 9–8–1735, SD 844/41 JTC 5.

80. Pedro Flores de la Coba, n.p., [ca. 1610], SD 25 ST 1016.

81. On the medicinal and commercial importance of Florida plants see P. F. X. de Charlevoix, S.J., *History and General Description of New France* (1744), trans. John Gilmary Shea (1870), 6 vols. (Chicago: Loyola University Press, 1962), 1:140–43.

82. Some of these little-known activities of the French have been described by Mary Ross in three articles in the *Georgia Historical Quarterly*: "French Intrusions and Indian Uprisings in Georgia and South Carolina (1577–1580)," 7 (September 1923):251–81; "The Restoration of the Spanish Missions in Georgia, 1598–1606," 10 (September 1926):171–99; and "The French on the Savannah, 1605," 8 (September 1924):167–94. Her work is cited and added to by Paul Quattlebaum in *The Land Called Chicora: The Carolinas Under Spanish Rule, with French Intrusions, 1520–1670* (Gainesville: University of Florida Press, 1956).

83. Bartolomé de Argüelles, Juan Menéndez Marquez, and Alonso de las Alas, 4–20–1603, SD 229/52 JTC 3.

84. Anon., 11–20–1655, SD 225 JTC 3; Juan de la Rosa, [San Luis], 12–24–1677, fol. 584 in Leturiondo visita of 1677–78, EC 156-A/87-90 JTC 1; [Pedro Menéndez Marquez], fragment of a voyage description, [1573], no AGI number, *Colonial Records*, 1:330.

85. *Jonathan Dickinson's Journal*, p. 43; Joseph de Prado and Domingo de Leturiondo, 9–3–1661, SD 229/124 JTC 3.

86. *Recop.*, 8:10:50, 7–27–1594; Juan Menéndez Marquez, Alonso de las Alas, and Alonso Sánchez Sáez, 3–12–1608, SD 229/57 JTC 3; anon., 11–20–1655, SD 225 JTC 3.

87. Gov. Ybarra to Fr. Pedro Bermejo, 7–27–1605, SD 232 JTC 4; Fr. Francisco Pareja et al., 1–17–1617, SD 235 JTC 4; Joseph de Prado and Domingo de Leturiondo, 9–3–1661, SD 229/124 JTC 3.

88. Gov. Rojas y Borja, 6–30–1628, SD 225 JTC 3.

89. Cédula re bartering in Florida, 4–21–1592, "Registros," pp. 202–3; Gov. Ybarra, n.d., with Council reply, 11–21–1605, IG 1425 JTC 7; *Recop.*, 8:12:8.

90. Cédula to Gerónimo de Rojas Avellaneda, 4–22–1577, and letter from Gov. Juan Bautista de Rojas, Havana, 7–6–1578, SD 118 JTC 2; Alonso de Cáceres, sentence of Pedro Menéndez Marquez, Havana, 2–20–1574, PAT 177, *Colonial Records*, 1:341; Eugene Lyon, "The Captives of Florida," *Florida Historical Quarterly* 50 (July 1971):20.

91. Arnade, *Siege of St. Augustine*, pp. 39–40; idem, *Florida on Trial*, pp. 7, 83–84. Drake took thirteen or fourteen large bronze guns from the captured fort (Chatelain, pp. 48–49).

92. Gov. Salinas, 1–30–1623, SD 225 JTC 3; the royal officials, 1–28–1628, SD 27 ST 1199; Gov. Rojas y Borja, 1–20–1625, SD 225 JTC 4.

93. Enrique Primo de Rivera, 11–26–1690, SD 234/115 JTC 4; Joseph Rodríguez de Santa María and Antonio de Valladar Velasco, Havana, 9–4–1677, SD

848/6 ST 2017; Gov. Guerra y Vega, 9–25–1667, summary, SD 225 JTC 3; Joseph de Prado and Juan Menéndez Marquez II, 6–30–1668, SD 229/134 JTC 3; Gov. Marques Cabrera, 6–28–1683, SD 226/104 JTC 3.

94. Cédula to Pedro Redondo Villegas, 11–14–1600, "Registros," p. 327; Chatelain, pp. 48–49. The acting officials in 1586 were Alonso Sánchez Sáez, Juan de Junco, and Bartolomé de Argüelles. Their report on the raid is in 6–17–1586, SD 229/13 JTC 3.

95. Lyon, "Captives of Florida," p. 20.

96. Gov. Horruytiner, 7–6–1637, SD 225/46 ST 1312.

97. Gov. Zúñiga y Cerda to the council of Guale chiefs, Santa María, 2–7–1701, SD 858/4–179 JTC 6; *Jonathan Dickinson's Journal,* p. 43.

98. Geiger, pp. 57–58, 76.

99. Lyon, *Enterprise of Florida,* pp. 53, 131–35.

100. Gov. Ybarra, 5–10–1605, 1–4–1606, and 5–16–1607, SD 224/76, 80, and 81, JTC 2; Juan Rodríguez de Cartaya, [Spain], 1–1606, SD 24 ST 925; Juan de las Cabezas Altamirano, Bishop of Cuba, 9–4–1606, SD 150 ST 939.

101. Juan Menéndez Marquez and Alonso de las Alas, 11–26–1609, SD 229/62 JTC 3.

102. Council of war, 11–3–1694, and Gov. Torres y Ayala, 3–11–1695, SD 839/130 JTC 5.

103. Gov. Marques Cabrera, 9–8–1686, with cédula of 9–2–1687, SD 839/130 JTC 5.

104. Juan Diez de la Calle, *Memorial y noticias,* Madrid, 1646, JTC 10. Gov. Rodríguez Villegas' statement is cited in Boniface, pp. 81–82.

105. Florencia visita of 1694–95, EC 157-A/91 JTC 1; *Francisco Pareja's "Confessionario,"* p. 67; Francisco de la Rocha and Salvador de Cigarroa, 3–2–1680, SD 229/152 JTC 3.

106. Alonso de las Alas and Juan Menéndez Marquez, 12–13–1595, SD 229/18 JTC 3; Gaspar Marquez, Chief of San Sebastian and Tocoy, 6–23–1606, SD 232/47 JTC 4.

107. Cédula to the royal officials of Yucatán, 3–5–1571, SD 2528 ST; papers of Captain Thomás Bernaldo de Quirós, 1–26–1580, SD 125 ST 414; Eugene Lyon, "More Light on the Indians of the Ais Coast," typescript (1967), P.K. Yonge Library of Florida History, p. 4.

108. Alonso de las Alas and Juan Menéndez Marquez, 12–13–1595, SD 229/18 JTC 3.

109. Alonso Sánchez Sáez, 1–6–1596, SD 231/72 JTC 4; Fr. Francisco Pareja et al., 1–14–1617, SD 235/18 JTC 4; Alonso de las Alas, 12–11–1595, SD 229/17 JTC 3; Arnade, *Florida on Trial,* p. 57.

110. Bartolomé de Argüelles, 8–3–1598, SD 229/24 JTC 3; Geiger, pp. 77–78; Arnade, *Florida on Trial,* pp. 72, 74.

111. Juan de las Cabezas Altamirano, Bishop of Cuba, 9–4–1606, SD 150 ST 939.

112. Fr. Francisco Pareja, 1–17–1617, SD 235 JTC 4; Agustín and Juan, natives of San Juan del Puerto, [el Morro, Havana], 7–2–1636, SD 27/28 JTC 2.

113. Antonio Menéndez Marquez and Francisco de la Rocha, n.d., in act on Mayaca and Enacape, 3–15–1682 to 9–7–1682, SD 226/95 JTC 3; *Recop.,* 8:9:4, 7–21–1570; council of Guale chiefs, Santa María, 2–7–1701, SD 858/4–179 JTC 6.

114. For the variety of Indian services and those exempt from them, see Florencia visita of 1694–95, EC 157-A/91 JTC 1.

115. Cédula to the governor, 10–15–1680, SD 834/269 ST 2170.

116. Thomás Menéndez Marquez and Joachin de Florencia, 7–1–1697, SD 839/136 JTC 5.

117. Juan de Pueyo, 9–10–1699, SD 230/139 ST 3636; Governor [either Torres y Ayala or Zúñiga y Cerda], 9–16–1699, SD 228/150 ST 3642; Nicolás Esteban de Carmenatis to Secretary Sierralta, 10–12–1699, SD 234/142 ST 3659; cédula to Gov. Zúñiga y Cerda, 8–14–1700, SD 836/16 ST 3724.

118. Joachin de Florencia and Juan de Pueyo, 9–16–1699, SD 230/143 ST 3645.

NOTES TO CHAPTER 7

1. Affidavit of recording a cédula, 6–23–1630, EC 154-B Escribanía.

2. Sobrecédula on the eclipse, 5–20–1580, IG 427 JTC 7.

3. See cédula to "the royal officials of the island of Florida and its province," 12–2–1613, SD 2603 ST 1075; Pedro Beltrán de Santa Cruz, Havana, 5–25–1657, SD 233/49 JTC 4.

4. Joseph de Prado and Domingo de Leturiondo, 9–7–1663, SD 229/126 JTC 3; Lorenzo Horruytiner, 5–6–1685, SD 227/12 NC 6.

5. Juan Menéndez Marquez, 3–14–1608, SD 229/58 JTC 3; Francisco Menéndez Marquez and Pedro Benedit Horruytiner, 5–17–1646, SD 229/98 JTC 3.

6. Haring, p. 105; royal officials, 10–6–1685, SD 230/29 ST 2445.

7. Gannon, pp. 46–48, 61–67.

8. Gov. Ybarra, 5–10–1605, 1–4–1606, and 5–16–1607, SD 224/76, 80, and 81 JTC 2; Juan de las Cabezas Altamirano, Bishop of Cuba, 9–4–1606, SD 150 ST 939.

9. Gov. Marques Cabrera to Fr. Pedro de Luna, 3–20–1685, and 4–14–1685 reply, SD 864/2 JTC 6; [Alonso de Leturiondo], 6–13–1690, SD 228/9 ST 2926; idem, 6–14–1690, SD 235/127 JTC 4.

10. Geiger, pp. 236–37.

11. Fr. Alonso del Moral, [seen in Council 11–23–1676], SD 235/104 JTC 4. Conflicts arising between governors and friars have been studied by Geiger and Matter. Both see them as administrative rather than economic.

12. Gov. Treviño Guillamas, 10–12–1617, SD 232/77 JTC 4.

13. Ibid.

14. Arana, pp. 66–72; Council proposals for governor, 3–1632, SD 6/46 ST 1259.

15. Anon., 11–20–1655, SD 225 JTC 3; Arana, pp. 72–75.

16. Bushnell, "Menéndez Marquez Cattle Barony"; Guillermo Lohmann Villena, *Los americanos en las órdenes nobiliarias (1529–1900)*, 2 vols. (Madrid: Consejo Superior de Investigaciones Científicas, Instituto Gonzalo Fernández de Oviedo, 1947), 1:268; Ex-Gov. Marques Cabrera, 9–22–1688, EC 156-C/47 JTC 1; service record of Francisco Menéndez Marquez II, compiled by Luis Arana.

17. Junta de Guerra, [1685], comment on a letter from Antonio Menéndez Marquez and Francisco de la Rocha, 5–25–1683, SD 229/155 JTC 3. Gov. Benavides complained that Francisco II meddled in everything, including the military (Gillaspie, p. 126).

18. Nicolás Ponce de León, 7–3–1632, SD 229/91 JTC 3; Juan de Cueva, 1–9–1631, enclosed with Gov. Rodríguez de Villegas, 12–27–1630, SD 225/30 ST 1249.

19. Francisco de Salazar, 6–9–1593, SD 231 ST 672.
20. Thomás Menéndez Marquez, 10–7–1686, SD 230/35 ST 2516; cédula to Thomás Menéndez Marquez, 9–22–1687, SD 835/48 and 49 ST 2636 and 2637.
21. Hoffman and Lyon, p. 63; Nicolás de Aguirre, report, 11–30–1578, PAT 255 JTC 1.
22. Royal officials, 9–23–1611, SD 229 ST 1027.
23. Nicolás de Aguirre, report, 11–30–1578, PAT 255 JTC 1; Gov. Marques Cabrera, 11–4–1686, SD 227/38 ST 2524; Boniface, pp. 168, 173, 183; friars in chapter, 9–10–1657, SD 235 JTC 4.
24. Fr. Juan Gómez de Palma, [ca. 1640], British Museum MS 13976, fol. 87 or 89, JTC 7; Juan Menéndez Marquez, 9–20–1602, SD 229/49 JTC 3; Bartolomé de Argüelles, instructions to the steward, 5–12–1591, SD 229/16 JTC 3; Nicolás Ponce de León, 9–12–1638, SD 233/24 JTC 4.
25. *Recop.*, 8:3:2, 2–18–1567; cédulas re the royal officials, 6–10–1580, and to Gov. Menéndez Marquez, 4–19–1583, "Registros," pp. 143–44, 152.
26. *Recop.*, 8:3:1, 6–11–1621, and 8:3:20, 4–28–1617; acclamation of Philip V, 1–7–1702, SD 840/45 JTC 5; Nicolás Ponce de León, 7–3–1632, SD 229/91 JTC 3.
27. Gov. Menéndez Marquez, 1–23–1581, reply to Domingo González, n.d., SD 14 ST 486; Nicolás Ponce de León, Mexico City, 9–25–1642, and cédula in response, 8–4–1643, SD 229/95 JTC 3.
28. Baltasar del Castillo y Ahedo, Havana, 2–12–1577, SD 125, *Colonial Records,* 1:232; Alonso Sánchez Sáez, memorial, 1–4–1596, SD 231/72 JTC 4; Hoffman and Lyon, p. 67.
29. Lyon, *Enterprise of Florida,* pp. 115–17; general cabildo, Santa Elena, 2–27–1576, SD 231/12, *Colonial Records,* 1:146–56; Bolton and Marshall, p. 20.
30. Hoffman and Lyon, p. 64; TePaske, *Governorship of Spanish Florida, 1700–1763,* pp. 26–27; Arana, p. 8. Chatelain (p. 28) says that the form of cabildo continued, but without vitality.
31. Acclamation of Philip V, 1–7–1702, SD 840/45 JTC 5; Gov. Marques Cabrera, 6–14–1681, SD 226 JTC 3.
32. Haring, pp. 151–52; Bartolomé de Argüelles, 11–2–1598, SD 229/26 JTC 3, and títulos of regidor to Juan de Posada (4–17–1592, "Registros," pp. 198–99) and to the treasury officials accompanying Narváez and De Soto (2–15–1527, 5–4–1537, and 10–5–1537, CT 3309 ST 20 and 34). Parry (p. 42) says that council memberships in the Indies became generally venal in 1591, but Council re Baltasar del Castillo y Ahedo (4–26–1580, IG 739, *Colonial Records,* 2:284–86) shows that those in Havana had been given a money value earlier.
33. Acclamation of Philip V, 1–7–1702, SD 840/45 JTC 5; Alonso de Leturiondo, 4–29–1697, SD 235/143 JTC 4.
34. Cédula to the royal officials, 6–18–1595, "Registros," p. 260; friars in chapter, 12–5–1693, with comments by the fiscal of the Council, 11–27–1695, SD 235/134 JTC 4.
35. Ignacio de Leturiondo, 10–29–1694, SD 235/135 JTC 4.
36. For an exposition of the term "ecumene" and its application to Spanish Florida, see Boniface, pp. 52–54, 59.
37. Gov. Marques Cabrera to the royal officials, 2–20–1687, in report on Espíritu Santo Bay, [2–28–1687], SD 839/112 JTC 5.

38. Act on moving the Guale villages, 8–26–1684, SD 226/118 JTC 3. The governor was later criticized because the junta had not included any Guale friars (act against Ex-Gov. Marques Cabrera, Havana, 8–4–1688, SD 864/8 JTC 6).

39. Cédula to Gov. Salazar Vallecilla, 5–4–1643, summary, SD 225 JTC 3; Gov. Ybarra, 11–8–1604, SD 232 ST 1004, and 12–19–1604, SD 224 ST 859. For the treasurer's side of the dispute, see Juan Menéndez Marquez, 6–14–1608, SD 232 ST 1004.

40. Francisco Menéndez Marquez and Pedro Benedit Horruytiner, 5–17–1646, SD 229/98 JTC 3.

41. Gov. Horruytiner, in residencia of Gov. Rodríguez de Villegas, [1633–35], no AGI number, ST; fiscal of the Council, comments of 4–5–1647 on Francisco Menéndez Marquez and Pedro Benedit Horruytiner, 5–17–1646, SD 229/98 JTC 3.

42. Cédula to Gov. Salinas, 8–14–1621, SD 27 ST 1135; cédula to Nicolás Ponce de León II, 10–2–1663, SD 834/25 ST 1590; Joseph de Prado and Juan Menéndez Marquez, 6–30–1668, SD 229/134 JTC 3.

43. Junta de Guerra comment, 5–16–1684, on Gov. Marques Cabrera, 6–28–1683, SD 226/107 JTC 3.

44. Cédula to the governor of Havana, 9–23–1698, SD 835/480 ST 3378; TePaske, *Governorship of Spanish Florida, 1700–1763,* pp. 126–27.

45. Junta de Guerra, 7–14–1660, SD 839 JTC 5; Juan Menéndez Marquez and Joseph de Prado, 9–22–1667, SD 847/4 JTC 6.

46. Arnade, *Florida on Trial,* pp. 60–69; Gov. Ybarra, 7–27–1605, SD 232 JTC 4.

47. Gov. Marques Cabrera, 1–25–1682, SD 226/81 JTC 3; Fr. Juan de Paiva, *pelota* manuscript, 9–23–1676, in Leturiondo visita of 1677–78, EC 156-A/88, fols. 568–83 JTC 1.

48. Gov. Quiroga y Losada, 12–20–1687, SD 839/114 JTC 5; Alonso de las Alas, 12–11–1595, SD 229/17 JTC 3.

49. Cédula to the royal officials, 9–29–1593, "Registros," p. 246; Francisco Menéndez Marquez, Juan de Cueva, and Francisco Ramírez, 1–30–1627, SD 229/87 JTC 3; investigation of the trade goods, 12–12–1680 to 6–28–1683, SD 229/159 JTC 3; Joseph de Prado, 12–30–1654, SD 229/115 JTC 3.

50. Haring, pp. 55–56, 121; Bartolomé de Argüelles, 3–18–1599, SD 229/27 JTC 3; fiscal of the Council, 4–11–1668, comments on Juan Menéndez Marquez II, 1–25–1667, SD 229/131 and 130 JTC 3.

51. Gov. Guerra y Vega, 9–18–1667, and Joseph de Prado and Juan Menéndez Marquez II, 9–22–1667, SD 229/132 JTC 3; Parish Register Marriages and Births.

52. Fr. Juan Luengo, n.p., 11–30–1676, attached to and answering a memorial by Fr. Alonso del Moral, summarized 11–5–1676, SD 235/104 JTC 4.

53. Gov. Marques Cabrera, 1–28–1682, fiscal of the Council, 9–11–1682, and Council answer, 9–23–1682, SD 226/84 JTC 3; Gov. Marques Cabrera, 3–5–1681, SD 226/76 JTC 3, and 3–28–1685, SD 227/16 ST 2406.

54. Act on the Indian complaints, 10–30–1681 to 6–28–1683, SD 226/105 JTC 3; act on moving the Guale villages, 8–26–1684, SD 226/118 JTC 3; Antonio Ponce de León, Havana, 1–29–1702, SD 863/43 JTC 6; Gov. Zúñiga y Cerda, 11–15–1701, SD 840/26 JTC 5; Florencia visita of 1694–95, EC 157-A, fols. 172–89 ST-Hann. Except for these 18 folios dealing with a murder case, the Florencia visita is also found in EC 157-A/91 JTC 1.

55. Moore, passim.

56. Francisco Ramírez, Juan de Cueva, and Francisco Menéndez Marquez, 1–4–1621, SD 229/82 JTC 3.

57. Alonso de Cáceres, sentence against Pedro Menéndez Marquez, Havana, 2–20–1574, PAT 177, *Colonial Records,* 1:342; three ranchers, 8–28–1689, SD 234/104 JTC 4; Florencia visita of 1694–95, EC 157-A/91 JTC 1; Moore, pp. 86, 94.

58. Ex-Gov. Rojas y Borja, 7–27–1630, and Miguel Gerónimo Portal y Mauleón's lawyer, [1630], EC 154-B Escribanía.

59. Sánchez-Bella, p. 200; Bartolomé de Argüelles, 8–3–1598, SD 229/24 JTC 3; Juan Núñez de los Rios, 1–19–1600, SD 231/97 JTC 4.

60. Simmons, p. 201.

61. Ibid.

62. Cristóbal González and Antón Martín, [seen in Junta de Guerra 1608], SD 232/52 JTC 4; Gov. Méndez de Canzo to Gov. Ybarra, 1603, SD 232 JTC 4.

63. Council reply of 10–21–1680 to Gov. Hita Salazar, 3–6–1680, SD 226/58 JTC 3; [Charles II] to Gov. Quiroga y Losada, 8–31–1688, SD 235/119 JTC 4; Haring, p. 158. At the request of the parish priest the allowance was increased to 100 pesos to cover cannon salutes (Alonso de Leturiondo, 8–7–1697, SD 235/146 JTC 4).

64. Francisco Ramírez, Francisco Menéndez Marquez, and Juan de Cueva, 6–2–1627, SD 229/88 JTC 3.

65. Gov. Hita Salazar, 10–30–1678, SD 845 JTC 5.

66. Cédula to the governor, 3–6–1598, IG 2869/4 ST 649; cédula to the royal officials, 11–5–1598, SD 2528 ST 256; Santos de las Heras, 2–10–1658, SD 229/117 JTC 3.

67. Joseph de Prado and Domingo de Leturiondo, 1–19–1664, SD 229/127 JTC 3; cédula to the House of Trade, 2–14–1566, CT 5012 ST 111.

68. Repeat cédula to the House of Trade, 3–20–1584, IG 2869/2 ST 485.

69. Cédula to Gov. Menéndez Marquez, 4–19–1583, "Registros," pp. 153–54.

70. See Lázaro Martínez de Avendaño, 9–29–1596, SD 2528 ST 256.

71. Bartolomé de Argüelles, 10–31–1598, SD 229/25 JTC 3; Francisco López, declaration, in act against Alonso Sánchez Sáez, 3–17–1609, SD 224/96 and 97 JTC 2. For a typical estate inventory see the Francisco Menéndez Marquez II probate papers of 7–3–1743, SD 847/73½ ST.

72. Moore, pp. 22, 29–31, 98; Fr. Francisco Alonso de Jesús, n.d., with report of the treasury council on 3–2–1630, SD 235/25 JTC 4; Fr. Juan Gómez de Palma, n.p., [ca. 1640], British Museum MS 13976, fol. 87 or 89, JTC 7; Salvador de Cigarroa, Madrid, 6–25–1659, SD 229/121 JTC 3.

73. Ex-Gov. Guerra y Vega, Madrid, 3–28–1673, SD 226 JTC 3; Gillaspie, passim; Bushnell, "Patricio de Hinachuba," pp. 4–5.

74. Royal officials, 10–12–1580, SD 229 ST 434.

75. Gov. Marques Cabrera, 3–5–1681, SD 226/76, and 6–14–1681, SD 226 JTC 3.

76. Hoffman and Lyon, pp. 64–65; Gov. Marques Cabrera, 5–30–1684, SD 226/116 JTC 3.

77. Friars in chapter to Gov. Marques Cabrera, 5–19–1681, SD 226 JTC 3. The governor's claims to innovative reforms were not always reliable. See Bushnell, "That Demonic Game," pp. 17–18.

78. Gov. Treviño Guillamas to the royal officials, 1–27–1617, SD 229/79 JTC 3.

79. Juan Núñez de los Rios, 1–19–1600, SD 231/97 JTC 4; Bartolomé de Argüelles, 2–20–1600, SD 229/32 JTC 3.

80. Juan Menéndez Marquez, 4–13–1601, SD 232/11 JTC 4; Bartolomé de Argüelles, Francisco Ramírez, Francisco Menéndez Marquez, and Juan de Cueva, 6–2–1627, with reply by the fiscal of the Council, 1–12–1628, SD 229/88 JTC 3.

81. Christóval de Viso to Secretary of the Council, Madrid, 6–27–1682, SD 226/89 JTC 3; TePaske, *Governorship of Spanish Florida, 1700–1763,* pp. 39–40; Francisco Menéndez Marquez, Juan de Cueva, and Francisco Ramírez, 1–30–1627, SD 229/87 JTC 3.

82. Anon., 11–20–1655, SD 225 JTC 3; Ex-Gov. Hita Salazar, 7–2–1683, EC 156-F JTC 1.

83. Pedro Redondo Villegas, 4–18–1600, SD 231/101 JTC 4.

NOTES TO CHAPTER 8

1. Bartolomé de Argüelles and Juan Menéndez Marquez, 1–23–1602, SD 229/44 JTC 3; Eugene Lyon, "Material Relating to Spanish Florida from the *Contaduría* Records in the Archivo General de Indias," typescript (1968), P. K. Yonge Library of Florida History, p. 4.

2. Bartolomé de Argüelles, 1–22–1596, SD 231/73 JTC 4, and 4–20–1600, SD 229/38 JTC 3; Pedro Redondo Villegas, 4–20–1601, SD 232/13 JTC 4; [Alonso de Cáceres], report, [Havana], [after 12–12–1574], PAT 19/33 JTC 1.

3. Hoffman and Lyon, p. 59; Francisco Ramírez, Juan de Cueva, and Francisco Menéndez Marquez, enclosed with Gov. Rojas y Borja, 5–30–1627, SD 225 ST 1196.

4. Hoffman, *Defense of the Caribbean,* p. 254.

5. Juan Menéndez Marquez, Havana, 6–1600, and St. Augustine, 4–13–1601, SD 232/11 JTC 4; cédula to the royal officials of Mexico City, 6–18–1635, summary, SD 225 JTC 3.

6. Manuel Luengo Muñoz, "Sumaria noción de las monedas de Castilla e Indias en el siglo XVI," *Anuario de Estudios Americanos* 7 (1950):345, 353; Enrique Primo de Rivera, 11–26–1690, SD 234/115 JTC 4; Gillaspie, p. 88.

7. The clearest exposition I have found of the forms of currency used in the Indies is in the methodological appendix of Paul Hoffman's *Defense of the Caribbean,* pp. 254–60. Unfortunately for my purposes, his conversion figures extend only to 1585.

8. Hoffman, "Florida Defense Costs," p. 402.

9. Nicolás de Aguirre, 11–30–1578, PAT 255 JTC 1; Bartolomé de Argüelles and Juan Menéndez Marquez, 1–23–1602, SD 229/44 JTC 3; Sánchez-Bella, p. 264; Hoffman and Lyon, pp. 57–58. Instructions on books to be kept are in *Recop.,* 8:7.

10. From Simancas the account copies were moved in 1784 to the new Archive of the Indies in Seville, where in 1924 many of the sixteenth-century Florida records were damaged and disarranged because of a fire (Hoffman, *Defense of the Caribbean,* pp. 238, 244–45). For a photograph of a typical page with the auditor's marginal comments, see Hoffman and Lyon, p. 60.

11. Hoffman, *Defense of the Caribbean,* pp. 241–42.

12. Gannon, p. 4; cédula to the governors of Florida, 6–19–1586, "Registros," pp. 173–74; Diego Sans de San Martín for Juan de Cevadilla, n.p., 1585, SD 229 ST 513; Sánchez-Bella, pp. 269–71; Hoffman, *Defense of the Caribbean*, pp. 240–41.

13. Hoffman, "Florida Defense Costs," pp. 402–5; Andrés de Eguino, Florida audit and visita, Havana and other places, 8–9–1569 to 9–9–1570, PAT 257 ST 248.

14. Lyon, *Enterprise of Florida*, pp. 191–92; Hoffman, *Defense of the Caribbean*, p. 146; cédula to the royal officials of Santo Domingo, 2–18–1573, IG 524 ST 322.

15. Alonso de Cáceres, sentence of Pedro Menéndez Marquez, Havana, 2–20–1574, PAT 177, *Colonial Records*, 1:338–49; Francisco Manrique de Rojas, declaration, in act against Pedro Menéndez Marquez, Havana, 6–31–1574 [sic], SD 124, *Colonial Records*, 1:102–8.

16. [Alonso de Cáceres], report, [Havana], [after 12–12–1574], PAT 19/33 JTC 1.

17. Hoffman, "Defense of the Indies," pp. 271–73.

18. Cédula to the royal officials, 6–3–1578, SD 2528 ST 256; Council re Pedro Menéndez Marquez, Madrid, 2–15–1578, IG 739, *Colonial Records*, 2:34; Pedro Menéndez Marquez, Havana, 7–1–1574, SD 124, *Colonial Records*, 1:112; idem, 6–15–1578, SD 231/20, *Colonial Records*, 2:88.

19. Hoffman and Lyon, p. 65; cédula to Baltasar del Castillo y Ahedo, 12–31–1575, SD 2528 ST; Council re Baltasar del Castillo y Ahedo, 10–4–1574, IG 738, *Colonial Records*, 1: 332. He eventually took the assignment at a salary of 275,000 maravedís (Baltasar del Castillo y Ahedo, Havana, 2–12–1577, SD 125, *Colonial Records*, 1:232).

20. Doña Mayor de Arango, 12–1577, IG 1387 ST; act on the Indian uprising, La Yaguana, Española, 1–19–1577, SD 224/10, *Colonial Records*, 1:196; Bartolomé Martínez, Havana, 2–17–1577, SD 125, *Colonial Records*, 1:242–44; Baltasar del Castillo y Ahedo, Havana, 12–28–1578, SD 118, *Colonial Records*, 2:216.

21. Baltasar del Castillo y Ahedo, Havana, 1–18–1577, SD 125 ST 345; idem, 2–12–1577, SD 125, *Colonial Records*, 1:202–32; idem, 12–10–1577, SD 125, *Colonial Records*, 2:20; Council re Indian uprising, 3–20–1577, IG 739, *Colonial Records*, 1:248–50; Pedro Menéndez Marquez, Santa Elena, 10–21–1577, SD 231/17, *Colonial Records*, 1:262–76; cédula re Baltasar del Castillo y Ahedo, 10–13–1578, SD 2528 ST 256.

22. Hoffman, "Florida Defense Costs," p. 408; TePaske, *Real Hacienda de Nueva España*, p. 9; [Juan de Cevadilla and Lázaro Sáez de Mercado], 3–6–1580, SD 229/5, *Colonial Records*, 2:264–80; Juan de Cevadilla, 5–12–1580, SD 229/6, *Colonial Records*, 2:290; idem, 1–22–1582, SD 229 ST 449; "Registros," pp. 143–55.

23. Cédulas to Gov. Menéndez Marquez, 11–22–1585, and Int. Gov. Gutierre de Miranda, 5–6–1590, "Registros," pp. 163–64, 190–91.

24. Bartolomé de Argüelles, 11–2–1598, SD 229/26 JTC 3; cédula to Gov. Menéndez Marquez, 3–31–1583, "Registros," p. 149; Alonso de Cáceres, sentence of Pedro Menéndez Marquez, Havana, 2–20–1574, PAT 177, *Colonial Records*, 1:338–49; Lic. Montoya de la Serna to Juan de Ovando, President of the Council, Monte Real y Bayona, 11–30–1572, PAT 257/4-2C, *Colonial Records*, 1:14–28.

25. Cédula to Gov. Méndez de Canzo, 10–22–1599, "Registros," pp. 314–15; Gov. Ybarra, 5–10–1605, SD 224 JTC 2.

26. Diego Sans de San Martín for Juan de Cevadilla, n.p., 1585, SD 229 ST 513;

cédulas to Pedro Menéndez de Avilés, 2–23–1573, and to the governors of Florida, 6–19–1586, "Registros," pp. 27–31, 173–74.

27. Bartolomé de Argüelles, 11–2–1598 and 5–15–1602, SD 229/26 and 46 JTC 3; cédulas to the royal officials, 5–22–1596, and re Petronila de Junco, 6–13–1596, "Registros," pp. 279–80, 282–83.

28. Cédula to Pedro Redondo Villegas, 11–5–1598, "Registros," pp. 295–98.

29. Ibid.; Bartolomé de Argüelles and Juan Menéndez Marquez, 1–23–1602, SD 229/44 JTC 3; Gov. Méndez de Canzo, 1–2–1602, SD 224 ST 832.

30. Cédula to the royal officials, 10–28–1598, "Registros," p. 294; Juan Menéndez Marquez, Juan López de Avilés, and Bartolomé de Argüelles, 9–13–1600, SD 229/41 JTC 3; Pedro Redondo Villegas, 4–20–1601, SD 232/13 JTC 4; Bartolomé de Argüelles, 5–15–1602, SD 229/46 JTC 3. On the surplus see Chapter 5, pp. 67–68.

31. Cédula to Pedro Redondo Villegas, 11–14–1600, "Registros," pp. 326–28.

32. Alonso de las Alas, 2–23–1600, SD 229/34 JTC 3; cédula to Diego Ruíz Osorio, [receptor of the] Council, 11–24–1598, "Registros," pp. 312–13; Juan Menéndez Marquez, 9–20–1602, SD 229/49 JTC 3; Hernando de Mestas, 3–12–1603, SD 232/25 JTC 4.

33. Cédula to Gov. Ybarra, 7–25–1603, "Registros," pp. 351–52; Hernando de Mestas, 3–12–1603, SD 232/25 JTC 4.

34. Arnade, *Florida on Trial*, pp. 80–81, 85, 90; Cámara of New Spain, Madrid, 5–6–1608, SD 6 ST 985.

35. Hoffman and Lyon, pp. 66–68; cédulas to Bartolomé de Argüelles, 5–26–1603 and 1–31–1604, and Juan Menéndez Marquez, 5–26–1603, "Registros," pp. 347–48, 357–58; Council, 1–21–1615, SD 6/32 ST 1083; Francisco Menéndez Marquez, [seen in Council 1–9–1627], SD 229/86 JTC 3.

36. The 1605 Ordinances of the Tribunals of Accounts are found in *Recop.*, 8:1.

37. Juan Menéndez Marquez, Alonso de las Alas, and Alonso Sánchez Sáez, 3–12–1608, SD 229/57 JTC 3.

38. Gannon, pp. 87–88; cédula re bartering in Florida, 4–21–1592, "Registros," pp. 202–3; Thomás Menéndez Marquez and Joachin de Florencia to Gov. Torres y Ayala, 4–15–1697, SD 228/113 NC 9. For the ordinary Florida exports to Havana, see Juan de Pueyo and Juan Benedit Horruytiner, 11–10–1707, SD 847/11 JTC 6, and Bushnell, "Menéndez Marquez Cattle Barony," pp. 423–24.

39. Alonso de las Alas and Juan Menéndez Marquez, 12–13–1595, SD 229/18 JTC 3 (also in SD 231/69 JTC 4); Gillaspie, pp. 17–18.

40. [Alonso de Cáceres], report, [Havana], [after 12–12–1574], PAT 19/33 JTC 1.

41. Nicolás Ponce de León, [seen in Council 2–8–1631], summary, SD 27 ST.

42. Petition of the Menéndez Marquez heirs, Madrid, [before 6–30–1630], SD 6/42 JTC 2. For what it was worth, the six of them at length received a joint grant of 400 ducats from surpluses of Florida or an encomienda in Peru. Their grandmother and their mother had both had similar grants that never materialized. (See Council, 6–30–1630, and addendum, 9–18–1631, SD 6/44 and 42 JTC 2; Bartolomé de Argüelles, 3–18–1599, SD 229/27 JTC 3).

43. Pedro Beltrán de Santa Cruz, Havana, 11–20–1655, SD 233/48 JTC 4; act on St. Augustine, San Juan de Ulúa, 5–30–1601, SD 235/9 JTC 4.

44. Pedro Beltrán de Santa Cruz, Havana, 11–28–1645, SD 229/102 JTC 3, and 5–25–1657, SD 233/49 JTC 4.
45. Nicolás Ponce de León, 11–20–1637, SD 225 JTC 3, and 9–12–1638, SD 233/24 JTC 4.
46. Fiscal of the Council, [between 9–17–1667 and 10–21–1667], comments on Gov. Guerra y Vega, 8–27–1666, SD 225/100 ST.
47. Francisco Menéndez Marquez and Pedro Benedit Horruytiner, 5–17–1646, SD 229/98 JTC 3.
48. Ibid., with marginal comment.
49. Ibid.
50. *Recop.*, 8:6:17, 6–9–1644.
51. Pedro Beltrán de Santa Cruz, Havana, 11–28–1645, with marginal comment by the fiscal of the Council, 3–3–1646, SD 229/102 JTC 3; idem, 11–20–1655, SD 233/48 JTC 4.
52. Pedro Beltrán de Santa Cruz, Havana, 11–20–1655, SD 233/48 JTC 4.
53. Ibid.; Salvador de Cigarroa, Madrid, 6–25–1659, SD 229/121 JTC 3. For a discussion of Francisco's and his son Thomás's ranching enterprises see Bushnell, "Menéndez Marquez Cattle Barony."
54. Pedro Beltrán de Santa Cruz, Havana, 11–20–1655, with comment by the fiscal of the Council, 7–5–1657, SD 233/48 JTC 4.
55. Idem, 5–25–1657, SD 233/49 JTC 4.
56. Pedro Benedit Horruytiner, 11–10–1657, SD 233/55 JTC 4; Salvador de Cigarroa, Madrid, 6–25–1659, SD 229/121 JTC 3; Gov. Guerra y Vega, 8–27–1666, with comments by the fiscal of the Council, [between 9–17–1667 and 10–21–1667], SD 225/100 ST.
57. Joseph de Prado and Domingo de Leturiondo, 11–24–1660, with marginal comment of 11–23–1661, SD 229/122 JTC 3; idem, 9–7–1663, SD 229/122 and 126 JTC 3; Juan Menéndez Marquez and Lorenzo Joseph de León, 9–9–1666, SD 229/129 JTC 3; fiscal of the Council, [between 9–17–1667 and 10–21–1667], comments on Gov. Guerra y Vega, 8–27–1666, SD 225/100 ST.
58. *Recop.*, 8:6:6, [1665–75]; royal officials, 3–7–1672, SD 229/135 ST 1752; Gov. Hita Salazar, 11–15–1680, SD 226/64 JTC 3.
59. Gov. Marques Cabrera, 6–14–1681, SD 226. The book was published in 1674 according to the Connor transcript (JTC 3); ten years earlier, according to Woodbury Lowery, Reel 9.
60. Gov. Marques Cabrera, 11–16–1686, 9–24–1686, 3–20–1686, in SD 839/110, 107, 103, ST 2530, 2502, and 2469; idem, 1–1–1687, SD 227/41 ST 2556.
61. Idem to Pedro de Aranda y Avellaneda, 4–11–1687, EC 156-C/15 JTC 1; Gov. Torres y Ayala, 4–15–1697, SD 228/108 ST 3406.
62. Gov. Quiroga y Losada, 8–16–1689, SD 227/77 ST 2816; Acclamation of Philip V, 1–7–1702, SD 840/45 JTC 5.
63. Thomás Menéndez Marquez, 4–12–1696, SD 230/111 ST 3360, referring to a cédula of 12–14–1693; Gov. Quiroga y Losada, 12–12–1691, SD 228/27 ST 3043A; idem, as ex-gov., [Cádiz], [Council summary, 10–19–1697], SD 840/TT1 JTC 5; *Recop.*, 8:6:16.
64. Ex-Gov. Quiroga y Losada, [Cádiz], [Council summary, 10–19–1697], SD 840/TT1 JTC 5; idem, 12–10–1698, summary, SD 840/4T-12 ST 3590; Pedro Díaz de Florencia, Havana, 11–26–1700, SD 143/1 ST 3772.
65. Gov. Quiroga y Losada, 6–8–1690, SD 227/110 ST 2912; Alonso de Leturiondo, 4–29–1697, SD 235/143 JTC 4.

Bibliography

PRIMARY SOURCES

The originals used in the Collections of Documents and in the Published Documents sections are located in the following repositories:

Archivo General de Indias, Seville (AGI)
  Patronato (PAT): Legajos 19, 179, 252, 255, 257, 261
  Contratación (CT): Legajos 3309, 5092
  Justicia (JUS): Legajo 750
  Santo Domingo (SD): Legajos 6, 14, 24–27, 118, 124–25, 127, 129, 133, 143, 150,
      168, 224–35, 815, 833–36, 839–40, 842, 844–45, 847–48, 851–53, 858, 863–64,
      2528–29, 2591, 2603, 2654
  México: Legajo 1065
  Indiferente General (IG): Legajos 427, 524, 606, 738–40, 1373, 1387, 1963, 2869
  Escribanía de Cámara (EC): Legajos 154, 156–57
Archivo de Valencia de Don Juan, Madrid
  Consejo de las Indias: Envío 25-H
British Museum, London
  MS 13976, folio 87 or 89
Cathedral Parish Records, St. Augustine
  Deaths, 1623–38
  Marriages, 1594–1713
  Baptisms, 1594–1693
  Confirmations, 1606

Collections of Documents

With microfilm reel numbers used at the P. K. Yonge Library (PKY) of Florida
  History, University of Florida, Gainesville.

Cathedral Parish Records, Parish of St. Augustine. Photostats and transcript. St. Augustine Historical Society. PKY 284, Reels A–G.

Jeannette Thurber Connor Papers (JTC). Transcripts and photostats. Library of Congress, Washington, D.C. PKY 142, Reels D–L, and 143, Reels A–I.

"Letters of Pedro Menéndez de Avilés, and Other Documents Relative to His Career, 1555–1574." Translated by Edward W. Lawson. 2 vols. Typescript, 1955. P. K. Yonge Library, University of Florida, Gainesville.

Woodbury Lowery Collection. Transcripts of unpublished manuscripts, 1551–1680, relating to Florida. Library of Congress, Washington, D.C. PKY 141, Reels A–I.

Eugene Lyon. Summaries and transcripts from the Archivo de Valencia de Don Juan. Vero Beach, Fla.

"Registros: Reales órdenes y nombramientos dirigidos a autoridades y particulares de la Florida. Años 1570 a 1604." Typescript, 1907. P. K. Yonge Library, University of Florida, Gainesville.

Buckingham Smith Collection. Transcripts. New York Public Library. PKY 141, Reels J–L.

Spain, Archivo General de Indias, Servicio de Microfilms. Escribanía de Cámara, PKY 26, Reel A; 27, Reels A–T.

Spanish Records of the North Carolina Historical Commission (NC). Photostats, transcripts, and translations. North Carolina Historical Commission, Raleigh. PKY 10, Reels A–W; 11, Reel X.

John B. Stetson Collection (ST). Photostats. P. K. Yonge Library, University of Florida, Gainesville. PKY 144-A, Reels 1–6; 144-B, Reels 1–62. Several individuals have made transcripts and translations of documents in the Stetson Collection. I have been favored to see and use valuable material of this kind prepared by Luis R. Arana, Charles Arnade, Julian Granberry, Eugene Lyon, and John H. Hann. Dr. Hann's summaries and translations were sponsored by the Division of Archives, History, and Records Management of the Florida Department of State, Tallahassee.

Published Documents

Boyd, Mark F., Hale G. Smith, and John W. Griffin, eds. *Here They Once Stood: The Tragic End of the Apalachee Missions.* Gainesville: University of Florida Press, 1951.

Connor, Jeannette Thurber, trans. and ed. *Colonial Records of Spanish Florida.* 2 vols. Deland: Florida State Historical Society, 1925, 1930.

Díaz Vara Calderón, Gabriel. *A 17th Century Letter of Gabriel Díaz Vara Calderón, Bishop of Cuba, Describing the Indians and Indian Missions of Florida.* Translated by Lucy L. Wenhold. Smithsonian Miscellaneous Collections, vol. 95, no. 16. Washington: Smithsonian Institution, 1936.

Dickinson, Jonathan. *Jonathan Dickinson's Journal or, God's Protecting Providence. . . .* Edited by Evangeline Walker Andrews and Charles McLean Andrews. Stuart, Fla.: Valentine Books, 1975.

Pareja, Francisco. *Francisco Pareja's 1613 "Confessionario": A Documentary Source for*

Timucuan Ethnography. Edited by Jerald T. Milanich and William C. Sturtevant. Translated by Emilio F. Moran. Tallahassee: Florida Department of State, 1972.
Recopilación de leyes de los Reynos de las Indias [1681]. Facsimile ed. 4 vols. Madrid: Ediciones Cultura Hispánica, 1973.

SECONDARY SOURCES

Books Cited

Arnade, Charles W. *Florida on Trial, 1593–1602.* Coral Gables: University of Miami Press, 1959.
———. *The Siege of St. Augustine in 1702.* Gainesville: University of Florida Press, 1959.
Bolton, Herbert E. *The Spanish Borderlands: A Chronicle of Old Florida and the Southwest.* New Haven: Yale University Press, 1921.
Bolton, Herbert Eugene, and Thomas Maitland Marshall. *The Colonization of North America, 1492–1783.* New York: Macmillan, 1920.
Charlevoix, P. F. X. de, S.J. *History and General Description of New France* [1744]. 6 vols. Translated by John Gilmary Shea [1870]. Chicago: Loyola University Press, 1962.
Chatelain, Verne E. *The Defenses of Spanish Florida, 1565 to 1763.* Washington: Carnegie Institution, 1941.
Corse, Carita Doggett. *The Key to the Golden Islands.* Chapel Hill: University of North Carolina Press, 1931.
Gannon, Michael V. *The Cross in the Sand: The Early Catholic Church in Florida, 1513–1870.* Gainesville: University of Florida Press, 1965.
Geiger, Maynard, O.F.M. *The Franciscan Conquest of Florida (1573–1618).* Washington: Catholic University of America, 1937.
Haring, C. H. *The Spanish Empire in America.* New York: Harcourt, Brace and World, 1947.
Hoffman, Paul E. *The Spanish Crown and the Defense of the Caribbean, 1535–1585: Precedent, Patrimonialism, and Royal Parsimony.* Baton Rouge: Louisiana State University Press, 1980.
Lanning, John Tate. *The Spanish Missions of Georgia.* Chapel Hill: University of North Carolina Press, 1935.
Lohmann Villena, Guillermo. *Los americanos en las órdenes nobiliarias (1529–1900).* 2 vols. Madrid: Consejo Superior de Investigaciones Científicas, Instituto Gonzalo Fernández de Ovideo, 1947.
Lyon, Eugene. *The Enterprise of Florida: Pedro Menéndez de Avilés and the Spanish Conquest of 1565–1568.* Gainesville: University Presses of Florida, 1976.
Milanich, Jerald, and Samuel Proctor, eds. *Tacachale: Essays on the Indians of Florida and Southeastern Georgia during the Historic Period.* Gainesville: University Presses of Florida, 1978.
Moore, John Preston. *The Cabildo in Peru Under the Hapsburgs: A Study in the Origins and Powers of the Town Council in the Viceroyalty of Peru, 1530–1700.* Durham, N.C.: Duke University Press, 1954.

Moorhead, Max L. *The Presidio. Bastion of the Spanish Borderlands.* Norman: University of Oklahoma Press, 1975.

Parry, John H. *The Sale of Public Office in the Spanish Indies Under the Hapsburgs.* Ibero-Americana no. 37. Berkeley: University of California Press, 1953.

Peña y de la Cámara, José María de la, comp. *A List of Spanish Residencias in the Archives of the Indies, 1516–1775.* Washington, D.C.: Library of Congress, Reference Dept., 1955.

Quattlebaum, Paul. *The Land Called Chicora: The Carolinas Under Spanish Rule, with French Intrusions, 1520–1670.* Gainesville: University of Florida Press, 1956.

Sánchez-Bella, Ismael. *La organización financiera de las Indias (Siglo XVI).* Seville: Escuela de Estudios Hispano-Americanos, 1968.

Sauer, Carl Ortwin. *Sixteenth Century North America: The Land and the People as Seen by the Europeans.* Berkeley: University of California Press, 1971.

Simmons, Marc. *Spanish Government in New Mexico.* Albuquerque: University of New Mexico Press, 1968.

TePaske, John J. *The Governorship of Spanish Florida, 1700–1763.* Durham, N.C.: Duke University Press, 1964.

TePaske, John J., with José and Mari Luz Hernández Palomo. *La Real Hacienda de Nueva España: La Real Caja de México (1576–1816).* Mexico: Instituto Nacional de Antropología e Historia, 1976.

Vicens Vives, Jaime, with Jorge Nadal Oller. *An Economic History of Spain.* Translated by Frances M. López-Morillas. Princeton, N.J.: Princeton University Press, 1969.

Zubillaga, Félix, S.J. *La Florida: La misión jesuítica (1566–1572) y la colonización española.* Rome: Institutum Historicum S.I., 1941.

Articles Cited

Arnade, Charles W. "The Avero Story: An Early Saint Augustine Family with Many Daughters and Many Houses." *Florida Historical Quarterly* 40 (July 1961):1–34.

———. "Cattle Raising in Spanish Florida, 1513–1763." *Agricultural History* 35 (July 1961):116–24.

Bushnell, Amy. "Patricio de Hinachuba: Defender of the Word of God, the Crown of the King, and the Little Children of Ivitachuco." *American Indian Culture and Research Journal* 3 (July 1979):1–21.

———. "The Menéndez Marquez Cattle Barony at La Chua and the Determinants of Economic Expansion in Seventeenth-Century Florida." *Florida Historical Quarterly* 56 (April 1978):407–31.

———. "'That Demonic Game': The Campaign to Stop Indian *Pelota* Playing in Spanish Florida, 1675–1684." *The Americas* 35 (July 1978):1–19.

Dunn, Oliver. "Trouble at Sea: The Return Voyage of the Fleet of New Spain and Honduras in 1622." *Terrae Incognitae* 11 (1979):29–41.

Hoffman, Paul E. "A Study of Florida Defense Costs, 1565–1585: A Quantification of Florida History." *Florida Historical Quarterly* 51 (April 1973):402–22.

Hoffman, Paul E., and Eugene Lyon. "Accounts of the *Real Hacienda,* Florida, 1565 to 1602." *Florida Historical Quarterly* 48 (July 1969):57–69.

Luengo Muñoz, Manuel. "Sumaria noción de las monedas de Castilla e Indias en el siglo XVI." *Anuario de estudios Americanos* 7 (1950):325–66.

Lyon, Eugene. "The Captives of Florida." *Florida Historical Quarterly* 50 (July 1971):1–24.

———. "St. Augustine 1580: The Living Community." *El Escribano* 14 (1977): 20–33.

Phelan, John Leddy. "Authority and Flexibility in the Spanish Imperial Bureaucracy." *Administrative Science Quarterly* 5 (June 1960):47–65.

Ross, Mary. "French Intrusions and Indian Uprisings in Georgia and South Carolina (1577–1580)." *Georgia Historical Quarterly* 7 (September 1923): 251–81.

———. "The French on the Savannah, 1605." *Georgia Historical Quarterly* 8 (September 1924):167–94.

———. "The Restoration of the Spanish Missions in Georgia, 1598–1606." *Georgia Historical Quarterly* 10 (September 1926):171–99.

Unpublished Works Cited

Arana, Luis R. "The Spanish Infantry: The Queen of Battles in Florida, 1671–1702." Master's thesis, University of Florida, 1960.

Boniface, Brian George. "A Historical Geography of Spanish Florida, circa 1700." Master's thesis, University of Georgia, 1971.

Gillaspie, William R. "Juan de Ayala y Escobar, *Procurador* and Entrepreneur: A Case Study of the Provisioning of Florida, 1683–1716." Ph.D. dissertation, University of Florida, 1961.

Hoffman, Paul E. "The Defense of the Indies, 1535–1574. A Study in the Modernization of the Spanish State." Ph.D. dissertation, University of Florida, 1969.

———. "Table for Converting the *Legajo* Numbers in the John B. Stetson, Jr., Collection of Documents Relating to the History of Spanish Florida." Typescript, 1968. P. K. Yonge Library, University of Florida, Gainesville.

Lyon, Eugene. "Material Relating to Spanish Florida from the *Contaduría* Records in the Archivo General de Indias." Typescript, 1968. P. K. Yonge Library, University of Florida, Gainesville.

———. "More Light on the Indians of the Ais Coast." Typescript, 1967. P. K. Yonge Library, University of Florida, Gainesville.

Matter, Robert Allen. "The Spanish Missions of Florida: The Friars Versus the Governors in the 'Golden Age,' 1606–1690." Ph.D. dissertation, University of Washington, 1972.

Seaberg, Lillian M. "The Zetrouer Site: Indian and Spaniard in Central Florida." Master's thesis, University of Florida, 1955.

Index

Acclamation ceremony, viii, 31, 48, 54, 135
Accountant: duties of, 1, 50–54, 61, 73, 105, 109; assistants of, 50–54; royal, 143–48
Accounts, to render and take, 72, 119–25 passim, 132, 135–36
Agramont, Sanche de, 95, 104
Ais Indians, 8, 12, 22, 93, 96
Alcabala, 91, 99–100, 169n3
Almorifazgo, 38, 46, 72, 86–91, 99, 130. See also Trade; Customs
Altamirano, Juan de las Cabezas, 27, 78
Amber, 8, 68, 91–94, 128
Anastasia Island, 26, 47, 83
Apalache Indians: trade with, 11, 28, 68, 82, 91; uprising of, 13, 19, 27–28, 82
Apalache Province, 11, 13–14, 17, 78, 82, 90–91, 99, 105, 110
Apalachicolo Indians, 8, 12
Appeals: civil, criminal, 7, 102, 134; fiscal, 56, 102, 120–36 passim
Aranda y Avellaneda, Pedro de, 47, 108, 142
Arango, Mayor de, 122–23
Aranguíz y Cotes, Alonso de, 102, 110, 134, 142
Archiniega, Sancho de, 3, 89, 114
Argüelles, Antonio de, 19, 32–33
Argüelles, Bartolomé de: accountant, 43, 55–57, 62, 127, 144–45; informant, 86–87, 113, 118, 127; governor, 109, 125, 141; treasurer, 144
Arrazola, Juan de; accountant, 31, 145; governor, 109, 142
Artillery and munitions, 10, 28, 69, 96, 122.

See also Government houses; Steward
"Asturian Dynasty," 5
Audiencias, 7, 45. See also Santo Domingo; Mexico City
Auditors: royal, 7, 31, 42, 66, 120, 125–36; internal, 51, 53; lieutenant, 51–53, 134–35; governors as, 115–16, 123–25, 134–35; clerks of, 126, 132–34; abuses by, 133–34.
Audits, 7, 42, 102, 119–36. See also Appeals
Avendaño, Domingo Martínez de, 61, 109, 114, 125, 141
Ayala y Escobar, Juan de, 61, 90, 115, 153n34

Bishops: comments by, 6, 9, 59, 79, 102–3, 155–56n4; and revenues of office, 33, 76–79, 84, 169n3; secular duties of, 45, 102–3, 134. See also Altamirano; Calderón
Blacks, free, 20, 82. See also Slaves
Bond, 35–36, 42, 55, 59, 60, 71, 108, 119, 125–27, 134
Bonuses, 52, 53, 55, 65, 74, 104
Books: burned by Drake, 5, 125, 137; of Resolutions, 50, 59, 107, 120; of Cédulas, 50, 101; of Accounts, 56, 118–21, 124, 132, 135; of the Coffer, 59, 120; of Libranzas, 61; nontaxable, 89
Booty, 1, 91–92, 96–97
Bourbons, Spanish, viii, 31, 48, 54, 58, 135
Bribes, 33, 70–73 passim, 93, 117, 133–34

192

Index

193

Cabildo: St. Augustine, 12, 49, 101, 107–17; in general, 107, 112–14. *See also* Excise taxes; Fees; Regidores

Cáceres, Alonso de, 121–22, 128

Calderón, Gabriel Díaz Vara, 29, 79

Campeche, 22, 26, 86, 110

Cape Canaveral, 10, 93

Carlos Indians, 8, 12

Cassina, 11, 26, 98–99

Castillo de San Marcos, 15, 23, 25, 47, 64, 68, 81, 85, 113, 114

Cattle: ranches, 11, 13, 15, 18, 37, 77–81, 85, 114, 133 (*see also* La Chua); family cows, 20, 113; oxen, 28, 81

Celaya, Gerónimo de, 48, 110

Cendoya, Manuel de, 91, 117, 142, 147

Certificates for wages, 25, 54, 68–71 passim, 79. *See also* Situado

Cevadilla, Gil de, 55, 125, 126, 143–44

Cevadilla, Juan de, 5, 30, 36, 42, 55, 88, 123, 126–27, 143–44

Charles Town, 9, 28, 67, 96–97

Cigarroa, Salvador de, 61, 115, 133, 147–48

Class distinctions, 7, 15–29, 79–80, 85

Clergy, regular. *See* Franciscans

Clergy, secular: parish priest, 22, 25, 39, 40, 155–56n4 (*see also* Alonso de Leturiondo); services, 22–26 passim, 28, 29, 41, 67, 114; sacristan, 25, 39; assistants, 25, 39, 65, 66; stipends, 38–39, 71, 76, 79, 80, 99; chaplain, 39, 40; organist, 40, 66; in general, 40, 80; suffragan to bishop, 102–3

Clerks: chief, 51–52; assistant (half-annate), 51–52, 83–84, 129; auditors', 126, 132–34

Cloth, 16, 26–27, 71, 96

Clothing, 16–17, 19, 24, 26–27, 40, 66, 96, 135

Coffer: keys to, 1, 36, 45, 60, 61; guarding of, 1, 57; contents of, 1, 73, 114, 134; as vault, 17, 59; inventory of, 36, 59, 124; deficits in, 90, 114–15, 119; *See also* Auditors; Audits; Drake; Goods of the deceased; Searles

Compadrazgo, 20–22, 31. *See also* Kinship network

Confiscations, 38, 42, 53–54, 89, 94, 113

Confraternities, 16, 41, 73, 112

Contraband. *See* Trade; Confiscations; Smuggling

Convicts, 11, 23, 27–28, 53, 74, 82–83, 98–99, 106

Corsairs: Spanish, 2, 96–97; threat of, 10, 62, 72, 94–95, 161n79; undeclared war of, 12; attacks by, 12, 37, 56, 85, 126–27 (*see also* Agramont; Drake; Heyn;

Searles); captives of, 37, 89; captured, 95–96, 102

Council of the Indies: creation of, 2; nominations by, 33–35, 43, 109, officials of, 43, 69–70, 82; actions of, 73, 80, 82, 102, 111. *See also* Appeals

Credit and interest, 10, 32, 59, 69–73 passim, 83

Creditors and moneylenders, 10, 17, 25, 70–73 passim, 128, 133

Cruzada, 40, 79–80, 99

Cuban: poachers, 91, 94, 95, 128; governorship, 96, 121–23; interdependence with Florida, 128. *See also* Franciscans; Bishops, Havana

Cueva, Juan de, 31, 57, 62, 83, 145–46

Cueva, Martín de, 44, 146

Cumberland Island, 121

Currency: shortage of, substitutes for, 10, 25, 57, 68–73 passim, 96; units of, 42, 118–19

Customs, 51–54, 88. *See also* government houses

Defender of the Indians, 40, 111

De Soto, Francisco, 111

De Soto, Hernando, 37, 92, 180n32

De Soto, Lucas, 53

Dickinson, Jonathan, 93, 96

Diez de la Calle, Juan, 97

Donations, 15, 46, 99, 114

Dowries, 17–18, 43

Drake, Francis, 4–5, 46, 57, 94–95, 125, 137

Dutch: trade, 8, 89, 95; War of 1621–48, 12. *See also* Heyn

Eguino, Andrés de, 121, 143

Elections, 32, 82, 104, 105, 107, 132

Embezzlement and fraud, 56, 59, 71, 132–33, 139

Encomienda, 7–8, 37–38

English: trade, 8–9, 95, 96–97; settlements, 12 (*see also* Jamaica; Charles Town); in Anglo-Spanish War of 1585–1603, 12, 118; in Queen Anne's War, 14 (*See also* Moore). See also Drake; Searles

Epidemics, 13, 82, 98, 104

Espinosa, Eugenio de, 18, 44, 45, 84, 109, 142

Excise taxes, 113–14

Expense allowances, 34, 42, 46, 52, 60, 70–71, 126, 134

Factor-overseer: origins of, 1–2; duties of, 1–2, 54–57, 73, 119, 129; office eliminated, 31, 46, 57, 60, 115, 129, 131,

146; royal, 143–46
Famines, 12, 16, 25, 42, 61, 79
Federico, Felipe, 89
Fees, 16, 42, 112–13
Fernández de Avila, Juan, 31, 148
Fernández de Olivera, Juan, 56, 62, 109, 142
Fernández de Perete, Gaspar, 55, 125, 143–44, 173n50
Fines: threat of, 35, 58, 62, 94, 116; revenue of, 38, 69, 112–13
Fisheries, 84, 91
Fleet of the Indies, 10, 40, 122, 126, 128–31 passim
Florencia, Claudio de, 19
Florencia, Diego de, 34, 161n71
Florencia, Juana Caterina, 17
Florencia, Matheo Luis, 34, 42, 146–48
Florencia family, 6, 14, 34, 135, 145–48
Flores de Quiñones, Alvaro, 119
Florida administrative status: as part or counterpart of armada, 2, 5, 24, 31, 63–64, 121, 126, 137–38; as proprietorship or patrimonial estate, 3–4, 38, 123; autonomy of, 6–7; as captaincy general, 6–7, 83–84, 103, 108, 110, 175n40; as royal colony, 38, 123; in Windward Isles, 99, 101–2, 130, 134. *See also* Audits; Appeals
Florida boundaries and frontiers, 2, 4, 12, 151n3. *See also* Pánuco; Indian wars
Florida economy and products, 7–14, 25, 76–79, 82. *See also* Amber; Cassina; Cattle; Maize; Medicinal herbs; Indian trade, Trade; Ship-of-permission
Florida settlement. *See* Santa Elena; San Mateo; St. Augustine; San Luis
Florida treasury. *See* St. Augustine treasury
Floridians, Spanish, 6, 41, 135–36, 139. See also Florencia family; Menéndez Marquez family; Kinship network
Fort Caroline, 2, 95, 137
Franciscan: missions, 5, 50, 51, 111, 128; commissary general, 6, 18, 23, 111; agriculture, 11, 24, 59, 82, 99; controversies, 11, 48, 82, 89, 99, 110, 116; seminary, 18; friars, 18, 23, 53 (*see also* Celaya; Moral); stipends, benefices, 18, 24, 32–33, 39, 74; Custody or Province of Santa Elena, 18, 103; syndic, 24, 40, 42, 64, 89; finances, 24, 70, 99; chapter meeting, 29, 115; exactions, 40, 76, 98–99; guardian, 48, 106; subsidy, supplies, 64, 87, 106, 132
Freight: income of, 67, 85–86, 132; expense of, 10, 70, 85
French: relations with Indians, 4, 8, 92–93,

123, 137–38; corsairs, 4, 126 (*see also* Hugenot Crisis; Fort Caroline); relations with Spanish, 6, 89, 116; captives, 95–96

García, Juan, 15, 113, 141, 145
Garrison, St. Augustine: strength of, 4, 41, 52, 63–65, 71, 74, 115, 120; treasury officials' duties with, 5, 7, 50–52, 103–6, 123, 129; service records, 105, 120; detachments, 99, 105–6, 110. *See also* Soldiers; officers; Plazas; Reformados
Goods of the deceased, 114–15, 120
Government houses: residences, 19, 45–47, 112; warehouse, arsenal, customs house, counting house, treasury, guardhouse, 20, 28, 45–47, 50, 56–57, 62, 86–88, 105, 112; in general, 45–47, 83, 107
Governors: limited powers of, 7, 101–17; lieutenant, interim, 43–44, 84–85, 105, 108–10, 141–42; royal, 141–42. See also Residencias; Office; governors by name
Guale Indians: uprising of, 8, 21, 93, 98, 138; trade with, 25, 59; as allies, 96–97
Guale Province, 11–13, 96–99, 108–9
Guerra y de la Vega, Francisco de la, 111, 142

Habsburgs, Spanish: (Emperor) Charles V, 120; Philip II, 2–4, 46, 64, 66, 95–96, 114, 121, 137; Philip III, 127; Philip IV, 32; (Queen Regent) Mariana. 134; Charles II, 113
Half-annate, 41, 52, 83–84, 99, 129, 132
Havana: garrison and fort, 5, 82–83, 98, 104, 122, 175n48; and Gulf Coast, 11, 14, 24, 82, 91, 128; and clerical connection with Florida, 18, 40, 106; supplying Florida, 25, 60, 72, 86, 89, 104, 121–22, 128, 131; treasury of, 33 (*see also* Auditors; Tribunals); situador stopover, 42, 70–72; nearest Spanish town, 108, 121; governorship of, 109–10, 135–36
Herrera, Antonio de, 73, 146–47
Heyn, Piet, 67, 83, 92, 128
Hidalgos, 3, 7, 15–29, 34
Hita Salazar, Pable de, 15, 41, 47, 59, 74, 81, 113, 114, 117, 134, 142
Hita Salazar family, 135
Horruytiner, Luis de, 61, 70, 83, 130, 142
Horruytiner, Pedro Benedit I: treasury official, 35–36, 115, 130–32, 146–47; governor, 41, 82, 104, 142
Horruytiner, Pedro Benedit II, 134, 147
Horruytiner family, 135
Horses and mules, 11, 28–29, 81, 113, 133
House of Trade, 2, 35, 63, 65, 69, 70, 114

Housing, 19–20, 58, 83. *See also* Government houses
Huguenot Crisis of 1565–68, 2–3, 12, 137
Hurricanes and storms, 46, 47, 55–56, 79, 85, 95. *See also* Shipwrecks

Indian allies, 12, 29, 92, 96–97
Indian allowance, 9, 28, 66, 74, 99, 111
Indian exemptions, 8, 21, 29, 76, 80. *See also* Defender of the Indians
Indian labor, 2, 11, 13, 53, 97. *See also* Convicts; Slaves; Repartimiento
Indian nobility: and connections with Spanish, 17, 20–21, 155n60; women chiefs, 17, 97, 98; raising horses, 28; privileges of, 37, 40, 45, 99 (*see also* Indian allowance); granting land, 81, 99; as agents of Spanish, 96, 99, 110–11, 160n63 (*see also* Repartimiento); in contact with crown, 115
Indian trade: with Spanish, 1, 8–9, 11, 37, 59, 71, 91–94, 105, 138; with foreigners, 8–9, 93, 95 (*see also* French); with poachers, 94, 95, 128
Indian wars and uprisings: Potano, 4; Cusabo, 4, 92; Chacato, Chichimeco, Chisca, Pocoy, Tasquique, Tocobaga, 12; Creek, 14; Surruque, 21, 138. *See also* Ais; Jeaga; Carlos; Apalache; Guale; Timucua
Inquisition, 8, 16, 89, 96, 98, 102–3

Jamaica, 12, 67, 78
Jeaga Indians, 8, 12
Judges of the exchequer, 7, 37, 41–42, 45, 94, 106–7, 112–13, 123
Junco, Juan de I, 54, 121, 125, 143–44
Junco, Juan de II, 126
Junco, Petronila de, 36, 125
Junco, Rodrigo de: factor, 36, 54–55, 125, 143–44; governor, 141, 144
Junta, 108, 109
Junta de Guerra, 6, 33–34, 44, 104

Kings. See Bourbons, Habsburgs
Kinship network, 30, 31, 36, 58–59

Labor. *See* Convicts; Indian labor; Slaves; Repartimiento; Soldiers
La Chua ranch, 21, 37, 91
Land: grants, 8, 34, 37, 80–81, 113; taxes, 19, 80–81, 113; titles, 81, 102
La Rocha, Francisco de, 61, 147–48
Las Alas, Alonso de: factor, 43, 45, 56–57, 98, 125, 127, 144–45; steward, 56, 143; in armada, 56–57; governor, 109, 141

Las Alas, Esteban de, 3–4, 121, 122, 141, 143
Las Heras, Santos de, 31, 67, 70, 133, 147
Laudonnière, René de, 2
Laws, 5–6, 36–38, 94, 101–2, 107, 138–39. *See also Recopilación*; Ordinances; Treasuries in the Indies; Indian exemptions
Leturiondo, Alonso de, 27, 28, 29, 71, 79, 182n63
Leturiondo, Domingo de, 111, 115, 147–48
Libranzas, 25, 61, 62, 68, 69, 71, 82, 116–17, 133, 134
Londono de Otalora, Diego, 122, 143–44
López de Avilés, Juan, 56, 143–45

Maize, 11–12, 20, 41, 76–79, 97–99, 113
Marques Cabrera, Juan: comments by, 7, 33, 44, 60; governor, 45, 47, 62, 80, 85, 89, 91, 102, 105, 111, 117, 134, 142, 148; author, 134
Martínez de Avendaño, Domingo. *See* Avendaño
Medical care, 23–24, 39, 41, 76
Medicinal herbs, 23, 91–93. *See also* Sassafras
Méndez de Canzo, Gonzalo, 15, 46, 48, 61, 64, 86, 87, 94, 98, 110–11, 114, 124, 125–27, 141
Menéndez armada: creation of, 3; subsidy to, 4, 63, 121; and Florida treasury, 5, 24, 31, 56, 63, 121, 122, 126, 137–38, 143
Menéndez clan, vii, 2–5, 53, 63, 121–23, 128, 137, 138
Menéndez contract, 2, 4, 37, 76–96 passim, 125, 161n2
Menéndez de Avilés, Pedro I: seaman, 2 (*see also* Menéndez armada): governor, 2–4, 54, 107, 121–23, 141; household of, 17–18, 31; finances of, 137
Menéndez de Avilés, Pedro II, 4, 122–23, 141, 143, 161n2
Menéndez Marquez, Antonio, 33–34, 104, 147–48
Menéndez Marquez, Catalina, 17, 33
Menéndez Marquez, Francisco I: governor, 13, 27–28, 90, 104, 142; treasurer, 22, 31–32, 35–36, 57, 90, 104, 129–33, 145–47
Menéndez Marquez, Francisco II, 20, 22–23, 104
Menéndez Marquez, Juan I: treasurer, 18, 21, 22, 27, 33, 43, 48–49, 62, 66, 68, 70, 76, 95, 104, 114, 127, 144–46; governor, 31–32, 109, 125, 127, 141–42, 145–46
Menéndez Marquez, Juan II, 22, 28, 33, 104, 111, 147
Menéndez Marquez, Pedro: governor, 3, 4,

94, 115, 121–22, 123–24, 141, 143; seaman, 3, 31, 39, 40, 64, 65, 93, 97, 104, 122–23; accountant, 3, 104, 124, 143
Menéndez Marquez, Thomás, 20, 21, 22, 33–34, 37, 52, 90, 91, 105, 148. *See also* La Chua
Menéndez Marquez family, vii, viii, 17, 18, 22, 31–33, 57, 104, 133, 135, 143–48, 154n47, 185n42
Menéndez y Posada, Alonso, 129, 132, 146–47
Mermas, 74
Mestas, Hernando de, 58, 126–27
Mexico City: audiencia, 6–7, 44, 117, 120, 126, 134, 135; treasury, 9, 62, 63–71 passim, 75, 128; metropolis, 42, 44, 60, 71–72, 102, 129–33 passim; tribunal of accounts, 127–28
Miranda, Gutierre de, 34, 62, 124, 141, 153n18
Miranda, Hernando de: factor, 3–4, 143; governor, 4, 141
Mixed-bloods, 16, 17, 20, 22, 53, 75
Monopolies: playing cards, 84; stamped paper, 84–85; slaughterhouse, 85. *See also* fisheries; Offices, royal; Half-annate
Moore, James, 14, 19–20, 40, 47, 66–67
Moral, Alonso del, 103
Moral Sánchez, Francisco de, 92

Narváez, Pánfilo de, 120, 180n32
New Laws of 1542–43, 37, 120
Nombre de Dios, 97
Notary; rations and munitions, 32, 51, 52, 55, 105, 168n33; on special assignment, 40, 52, 123, 125, 133, 135; public and governmental, 45, 52, 58–59, 61, 73, 83, 101, 105, 107, 112, 116

Officers, 7, 15, 22, 39–46 passim, 84, 99, 105, 114. *See also* reformados
Offices, royal: patronage of, 3, 30, 34, 42, 50–51, 59, 104, 111, 139; salaries of, 4, 25, 35–49, 52–58, 65–74 passim, 76, 86, 87–88, 99, 126; perquisites of, 16, 26, 34, 41–49 passim, 60, 105; transfers, retainers, *futuras* to, 18, 31–34, 42, 145–48; proprietorship of, 30–49, 52, 58; titles to, 31, 35–36, 137; sale of, 32–34, 58, 83, 112, 139; terms and tenure of, 35, 57, 116; suspensions of, 35–43 and 50–62 passim, 89–90; multiple, 39–40, 53–54; leaves of absence from, 43–44, 50–51, 143–48; vacancies in, 57, 65, 67, 76, 84, 129
Olivera, Joseph de: governor, 109, 142;

treasurer, 109, 145
Ordinances: of Populating, 37; of Town Planning, 46; of Audiencias, 120; of Audits, 120, 124; of Tribunals of Accounts, 185n36
Overseer of barter and trade, 1–2. *See also* Factor-overseer

Pánuco, 120, 125, 151n3
Pastrana, Alonso, 23, 142, 146
Peltry, 8, 9, 61, 87–97 passim
Pensacola, 64, 110
Pilots, 39, 58, 74, 85–86, 105
Pirates. *See* Corsairs
Plazas: as dowry, 18, 40; minor's, 18, 40, 81; as honoraria, 40; as salary supplement, 40, 111; retirement, 40–41; soldier's, 40–41, 64; vacant, 40–41, 67–68 (*see also* surpluses): widow's, 41; friar's, 64; disability, 67–68. *See also* Garrison
Ponce de León, Antonio, 40, 45
Ponce de León, Nicolás I: accountant, 31, 36, 43–44, 52, 57, 78, 90, 106, 129, 130, 146–47; governor, 43–44, 45, 82, 109, 142, 147
Ponce de León, Nicolás II, 18, 45, 84, 109, 117, 142
Population, 12–14, 17, 50, 98–99, 110–11, 139
Portal y Mauleón, Miguel, 29, 146
Portuguese, 14, 21, 81, 89, 94, 116
Posada, Juan de: treasurer, 5, 33, 34, 55, 144; governor, 5, 141; factor, 143
Prado, Joseph de, 31, 44, 147–48
Prices: rising, 12, 23–25, 39, 71, 128; clothing and jewelry, 16–27 passim; land, 19; houses, 19–20; slaves, 21, 23; labor, 23, 25; medical care, 23–24; imported food and wine, 24–26; religious services, 25–26; weapons, 28; livestock, 28, 79
Primo de Rivera, Enrique, 105
Prison, 35, 58, 62, 113, 125–35 passim, 144–45, 148
Procurador, 51, 52, 60–61, 65, 104, 115, 133
Protocol, 27, 47–48, 108
Provinces, 11, 13–14, 58, 96, 103, 110–11. *See also* Guale, Timucua, Apalache
Puebla de los Angeles, 71–72, 169n3
Pueyo, Juan de, 53, 148, 159n56

Quintos, 38, 91–97, 100
Quiroga y Losada, Diego de, 27, 47, 90, 104, 135, 142
Quirós, Thomás Bernaldo de, 97, 141

Ramírez, Francisco, 31, 33, 57, 62, 145–46

Rations, 24, 38–41 passim, 52, 59, 64, 76, 79, 82, 88, 105

Rebolledo, Diego de, 78, 93–94, 117, 133, 142

Recopilación, 6, 83, 102, 113

Redondo Villegas, Pedro, 5, 67, 87–88, 95, 117, 118, 125–27, 138

Reformados, 37, 103–4, 108

Regidores, 7, 19, 35–49 passim, 83, 107–17, 123–24. See also Cabildo

Repartimiento, 11–13, 16–25, and 37–46 passim, 97–99, 106, 110–11, 138

Residencias, 35, 116, 117, 121–22, 135

Ribault, Jean, 94

Rodríguez de Villegas, Andrés, 97, 109, 142, 146

Rojas y Borja, Luis de, 32, 66, 73, 89, 92, 98, 113

Ruíz Mejía, Juan, 131, 146

Sáez de Mercado, Lázaro, 5, 30, 31, 42, 123, 143–44

St. Augustine: founding of, viii, 2; harbor, 10, 46, 53, 62, 71, 72, 85; layout of, 20, 46–47, 138; various locations of, 45–46, 138; citizens of, 74; foreign residents in, 14, 21, 81, 89, 94, 116. See also Cabildo; Drake; Garrison; Moore; Searles; St. Augustine treasury

St. Augustine treasury: 7, 31, 35, 118–36, 137–40; revenues, 63–74, 75–100. See also Almorifazgo; Confiscations; Cruzada; Donations; Fines; Freight; Half-annate; Monopolies; Quintos; Tithes; Tribute

Salamototo, 83

Salazar, Francisco de, 104, 141

Salazar Vallecilla, Benito Ruíz de, 32, 66, 78, 81–82, 89–90, 109, 132, 142

Salinas, Juan de, 46, 57, 73, 95, 109, 142

Salvage, 8, 46, 91–96 passim, 100, 128

Sánchez Sáez, Alonso, 42–43, 62, 89, 115, 144–45

San Juan del Puerto, 98–99, 155n57

San Juan de Ulúa, 10, 70, 71, 72, 88

San Luis de Apalache, 11, 17, 99, 110

San Luis Potosí, 57

San Marcos, 90

San Martín (Suwannee–Santa Fe), 37, 91, 128

San Mateo, 4, 107

San Pedro, 59, 87, 98, 109

Santa Cruz, Pedro Beltrán de, 68, 70, 84, 115, 130–34

Santa Elena: abandoned, 4, 5, 55, 67, 80, 106, 110, 137; northernmost settlement, 13, 93; Custody or Province, 18, 103;

land grants in, 80; cabildo, 107

Santa María, 98, 99

Santo Domingo, 6–7, 35, 63, 89, 121, 133

Sassafras, 8, 71, 87, 91, 92–93

Savannah River, 8, 92–93, 138

Searles, Robert, 44, 84

Servants, 21, 23–25, 34, 41, 53

Shipmasters, 2, 51, 58, 85–86, 104, 119, 123, 132, 135

Ship-of-permission, 9, 61, 71, 86, 90, 115

Ships, 32, 53, 85, 86, 96

Shipwrecks, 5, 8, 30, 55, 67, 72, 94–95. See also Salvage; Hurricanes and storms

Situado: dependence on, vii, 99–100; beginnings of, 3–4, 63–64, 121; amount of, 9, 64, 71, 119; impounding of, 10, 72, 130; in arrears, 11–12, 67–79 passim, 128; funds, 43, 64–68; servicing, surcharges, 69–74 passim (see also situador); importance of, 129–39. See also Mexico City, Vera Cruz, Tierra Firme, Puebla de los Angeles

Situador, 25, 34, 42–44, 51–60 passim, 64–74 passim, 106, 119–35 passim, 143–48. See also Expense allowance; bribes

Slave: raids, 9, 12–13, 14; occupations, 16, 22–23, 41, 81; prices, 21, 23; runaways, 22, 67; as part of estate, 22–23, 54, 58, 81, 114; maintenance, 23–25; armed, 28, 29; licenses, 34

Slaves, race: Indian, 7–8, 9, 12–13, 14, 21–22; Moorish, 21; black, 21–23; Spanish, 91

Slaves, royal: uses of, 5, 82–83, 99; rationing of, 11, 76, 82, 106; numbers of, 22, 82, 122; managing of, 39, 82; accounting for, 51, 56, 62, 82, 130

Smuggling, 89, 94, 124. See also confiscations; Trade

Soldiers, 9, 25, 35–46 passim, 53, 74, 105, 121, 123

Steward of provisions and munitions: duties of, 30–31, 54–56, 73, 74, 105, 130; patronage of, 51, 54, 129–31; combined with treasurer, 57, 129–31; appointees, 143–47

Surpluses, 38, 67–73 passim, 84, 126, 134. See also offices; situado

Tierra Firme, 63–64

Timucua Indians, 13

Timucua Province, 11, 13, 78, 81–82, 105

Tithes, 38, 46, 54, 76–79, 99, 130

Torres y Ayala, Laureano, 27, 62, 99, 135, 142

Trade, contraband: with foreigners, 10, 89, 116 (*see also* Portuguese; French; Dutch); with Spain, 10, 90. *See also* Smuggling; Confiscations
Trade, restricted: 8–10, 24–26, 71–72, 90–91. *See also* Havana; San Martín; Apalache
Tradespeople, 27, 41, 69, 73, 175n34
Travel time and licenses, 30–35 passim, 87
Treasurer: precious metals, 1, 2, 7, 9, 34, 68–73 passim, 95–96, 114, 118, 123, 134; pearls, 17, 84, 91, 92; diamonds, 92, 127; buried, 95–96. *See also* Amber
Treasurer: duties of, 1, 16, 57–58, 73, 119; royal, 143–46. *See also* Treasurer-steward
Treasurer-steward, 57, 73, 129–31; royal, 146–48
Treasuries in the Indies, 1–2, 30–49, 63, 75–91 passim, 106, 120, 123, 138. *See also* St. Augustine treasury; and other cities by name
Treasury council, 51, 58–62, 107, 116
Treasury officials: antecedents of, 1; substitutes, interim, 31, 42–43, 52, 90–91, 143–48; collegiality of, 36, 51–62 passim, 105, 115, 129, 130–31. *See also* Accountant; Clerks; Factor; Offices; Garrison; Judges; Regidores; Treasurer

Treviño Guillamas, Juan de, 19, 61, 103, 142
Tribunals of Accounts, 7, 127–28, 134, 136
Tribute: to Spanish, 2, 37, 38, 50, 54, 83, 97–99, 100, 138; to Indians, 37, 99. *See also* Indian allowance

Vázquez de Espinosa, Antonio, 74
Vega Castro y Pardo, Damián de, 90, 142
Velasco, Diego de, 4, 21, 141
Vera Cruz, 60, 64–74 passim, 86, 87, 88, 131–32
Viceroy, 7, 44, 45, 69, 90, 99, 133, 136
Visita, visitador, 14, 27, 31, 109, 111, 119, 121–23, 134, 155n59, 159n56

Wars. *See* corsairs; English; French; Dutch; Indian wars and uprisings
Weapons: control, 9, 28–29, 34, 51, 94; expenses, 27–28; ownership, 27–28, 41
Wheat farm, 78, 81–82
Windward Isles, 99, 101–2, 130, 134

Ybarra, Pedro de, 46, 48, 62, 64, 65, 66, 84, 89, 94, 96, 109, 110, 124, 142
Yucatán, 5, 97

Zúñiga y Cerda, Joseph de, 96, 142